Visual Media Processing Using MATLAB Beginner's Guide

Learn a range of techniques from enhancing and adding artistic effects to your photographs, to editing and processing your videos, all using MATLAB

George Siogkas

[PACKT]

PUBLISHING

BIRMINGHAM - MUMBAI

Visual Media Processing Using MATLAB Beginner's Guide

First published: September 2013

Production Reference: 1170913

Published by Packt Publishing Ltd.
Livery Place
35 Livery Street
Birmingham B3 2PB, UK.

ISBN 978-1-84969-720-0

www.packtpub.com

Cover Image by George Siogkas (siogkas@gmail.com)

Credits

Author
George Siogkas

Reviewers
R. Surya Murali
Ashish Uthama
Alexander Wright

Acquisition Editor
Joanne Fitzpatrick

Lead Technical Editor
Anila Vincent

Technical Editors
Chandni Maishery
Iram Malik
Manal Pednekar

Project Coordinator
Navu Dhillon

Proofreader
Elinor Perry-Smith

Indexers
Hemangini Bari
Monica Ajmera Mehta

Graphics
Ronak Dhruv

Production Coordinator
Kirtee Shingan

Cover Work
Kirtee Shingan

About the Author

George Siogkas is currently the Associate Dean of the Department of Engineering and Informatics at New York College, Greece, where he has been teaching as a senior lecturer for the past four years. He also has more than ten years of research experience in the academia. His keen passion for MATLAB programming, especially in the areas of image and video processing, was developed while working towards a PhD in the field of computer vision for intelligent transportation systems.

Dr. Siogkas received his PhD in Electrical and Computer Engineering from the University of Patras, Greece in 2013.

For more information about the author, visit his webpage, at `http://www.cvrlab.com/gsiogkas`.

I would like to first and foremost thank my beautiful wife, Maro, who put up with my exhausting writing schedule for both this book and my PhD thesis, while staying focused enough to organize our wedding. I would also like to thank my parents and my brother for their continuous support, especially during this past year. Without the encouragement from all of them, this project would never even have got started in the first place.

I would also like to thank everyone at Packt Publishing who got involved in this book, especially Joanne Fitzpatrick, Hardik Patel, Navu Dhillon, and Anila Vincent. They played a very important role in helping me understand the rationale behind such a writing project and provided invaluable feedback throughout the writing process. Also, a special thanks goes to the reviewers, R. Surya Murali, Ashish Uthama, and Alexander Wright, who provided very useful and insightful comments and suggestions for improving the quality of the book. Without them all, this book would never have reached its publishing stage.

About the Reviewers

R. Surya Murali received his PhD in Chemical Engineering from Osmania University. He has seven years of research experience on Membrane technology for gas and liquid separations. He has worked as a senior research fellow and junior research fellow at the Indian Institute of Chemical Technology. He also has experience in the installation, operation, and maintenance of membrane separation systems at laboratory and pilot plant levels. He has developed expertise in the synthesis, modification, and characterization of various types of membranes for different membrane processes. He has also gained knowledge in developing simulation programs in Microsoft Excel, C, and MATLAB.

> I am thankful to my family and friends for their constant support and encouragement.

Ashish Uthama is a developer in the Image Processing Toolbox team at Mathworks, makers of MATLAB. He has a Bachelor's degree in Electronics and Communication from PESIT, Bangalore, India, and a Master's degree in Applied Science from UBC, Vancouver, Canada.

Alexander Wright is a computer vision programmer specializing in histopathological image analysis for the automated diagnosis of cancer patients. He has been using MATLAB and C++ in this domain since 2006 in collaboration with the School of Computing and the Section of Pathology, Anatomy and Tumour Biology, at the University of Leeds. Alex has co-authored many research articles that base their research on his image analysis algorithms, and is interested in the standardization of automated histology image analysis for routine clinical application. In his spare time, Alex enjoys performing image manipulation in MATLAB and Adobe Photoshop for web design projects, and playing his bass guitar at unnecessarily loud volumes.

www.PacktPub.com

Support files, eBooks, discount offers and more

You might want to visit www.PacktPub.com for support files and downloads related to your book.

Did you know that Packt offers eBook versions of every book published, with PDF and ePub files available? You can upgrade to the eBook version at www.PacktPub.com and as a print book customer, you are entitled to a discount on the eBook copy. Get in touch with us at service@packtpub.com for more details.

At www.PacktPub.com, you can also read a collection of free technical articles, sign up for a range of free newsletters and receive exclusive discounts and offers on Packt books and eBooks.

http://PacktLib.PacktPub.com

Do you need instant solutions to your IT questions? PacktLib is Packt's online digital book library. Here, you can access, read and search across Packt's entire library of books.

Why Subscribe?

- Fully searchable across every book published by Packt
- Copy and paste, print and bookmark content
- On demand and accessible via web browser

Free Access for Packt account holders

If you have an account with Packt at www.PacktPub.com, you can use this to access PacktLib today and view nine entirely free books. Simply use your login credentials for immediate access.

Table of Contents

Preface

Digital visual media has, undoubtedly, become a vital part of our everyday lives. Analog means of storing and processing information have gradually faded and are nowadays used either by aficionados of analog media, or for very specialized applications. Capturing and storing image or video information have rapidly become common, fast, and cheap processes, since almost everyone can have access to a digital electronic device that can be used for these aims, whether it is a photographic or video camera, or even a mobile phone. The outburst of visual media-capturing devices has led to an increase of amateur photographers and weekend filmmakers, who often have a problem deciding what software to use to process their stored images or videos. The rule of thumb is that free software solutions often have limited functionalities or are very complicated, while commercial solutions tend to be very expensive and sometimes do not provide all the functionalities that a user would hope for.

This book presents a rather uncommon alternative solution that might not be considered by users who only need an image, or a video editing software, but could certainly appeal to users who are also students, scientists, or just have easy access to the multifunctional, high level programming environment, called MATLAB.

What this book covers

Chapter 1, *Basic Image Manipulations,* introduces you to the environment of MATLAB and takes you on a tour to its basic tools and functionalities. Then, image importing and displaying in MATLAB is discussed, followed by a demonstration of the MATLAB GUI for image manipulation. Basic image transformations are covered, such as rotating/flipping, resizing, and cropping an image. Finally, different ways of writing an image are presented. The chapter includes hands-on examples that tie most of the processes covered, together.

Chapter 2, *Working with Pixels in Grayscale Images,* is based on examples of pixel-based processing of an image. Several classic processes for image enhancement are discussed, such as thresholding, local, or global contrast enhancement. The methods presented use several techniques that gently introduce you to the secrets of MATLAB programming. A practical example in image enhancement concludes this chapter.

Chapter 3, *Morphological Operations and Object Analysis,* introduces the basic methods of morphological image analysis. In it, you will learn of ways to perform binarization of a grayscale image using the thresholding methods. Edge detection and other morphological operators are presented and explained, so that you learn how to select and manipulate particular image regions that interest you the most. You will also learn the techniques that automatically detect corners, circles, and lines in an image. Several hands-on examples will vividly demonstrate all these techniques.

Chapter 4, *Working with Color Images,* extends previous methods to color images. Some of the processes mentioned for grayscale are now revisited for color image processing. Different color spaces and their advantages are explained with examples on color enhancement in MATLAB. You will learn how illumination and color can be separated and processed independently. The technique for color isolation is explained through a practical example and finally, some of the methods mentioned previously are used to teach you how to develop a popular application: red eye correction in your photographs.

Chapter 5, *2-Dimensional Image Filtering,* dives into some more complex issues for image filtering, such as deblurring and sharpening of images. You will get to work on more sophisticated techniques for image denoising. Some more interesting and fun examples will let you start enjoying your experience more deeply. We will work on ways to apply some of the filter locally, to enhance or blur specific image regions.

Chapter 6, *Mixing Images for Science or Art,* will wake up the artist, or the scientist in you. You will learn the techniques that mix channels of multispectral images for scientific visualization. Then, we will present fun, hands-on examples for blending, or stitching images, to produce artistic results. We will also work on ways to create artistic HDR (High Dynamic Range) images in MATLAB. Finally, we will present a simple way to create panoramic images.

Chapter 7, *Adding Motion – From Static Images to Digital Videos,* introduces you to video processing by building on the previous knowledge you have acquired. The fact, that videos can be generated by static images, will help you to better comprehend basic ideas. So, after covering the basics of video frame processing in MATLAB and demonstrating how we can load and play back videos, we will show how to create a video from static images. The construction of a time-lapse video is the basic hands-on example we will be working on in this chapter.

Chapter 8, *Acquiring and Processing Videos,* demonstrates the functionalities of the image acquisition tool for MATLAB. You will be given step-by-step examples on ways to shoot video with your camera and use your computer as a Digital Video Recorder, using the special GUI tool contained in MATLAB. Video compression and basic color video processing techniques are also demonstrated in this chapter, accompanied by a discussion on performance issues.

Chapter 9, *Spatiotemporal Video Processing,* introduces you to command line manipulation and processing of videos. After covering basic video frames manipulations in MATLAB, you will learn how to deinterlace videos, using intra-frame, inter-frame, or mixed techniques. Furthermore, spatiotemporal video filtering is presented, with hands-on examples to help you get the idea.

Chapter 10, From Beginner to Expert – Handling Motion and 3-D, introduces you to methods of motion detection in videos. Building on basic knowledge, we will get to the point of creating a simple surveillance system in MATLAB. You will also be taught the basics of estimating motion using popular optical flow algorithms, included in one of the toolboxes of MATLAB. You will also be introduced to feature-based image registration for motion compensation. The working example for this will be video stabilization. Finally, we will introduce an example of three-dimensional video and cover a very basic and fun example of turning a regular video to a 3-D one.

What you need for this book

In order to practice what you read in this book, you should have access to a computer with an installed version of MATLAB. The screenshots you will see in this book are all taken from MATLAB Version R2012b, which was the most recent one at the time of writing this book. However, since MATLAB is also a programming language, you will not need to worry about any differences in the way R2012b looks compared to earlier versions. The great majority of the things we will cover in this book will be 100 percent compatible with most previous versions. In the rare cases, when we use a brand new functionality, we will also provide alternative solutions for previous versions.

The most important thing to make sure of, however, is that you have to find an installed version of MATLAB that includes at least the two basic toolboxes for image and video processing: **Image Processing Toolbox** and **Image Acquisition Toolbox**. An extra toolbox, named **Computer Vision Toolbox**, will also be used for a very small part of video processing. Toolboxes are collections of ready-made functions for special purposes. For those of you with a little familiarity with programming, they could be thought of as libraries. The more toolboxes included in your installation of MATLAB, the more functionalities the environment will provide for you. Most of our code in this book will be based on basic MATLAB functions included in all installations and the two toolboxes that were mentioned previously.

Who this book is for

This guide to visual media processing using MATLAB will be very useful to a beginner programmer who has little or no knowledge of the environment, but would like to use it as an alternative, or possibly, substitute solution to common image and video editors. The only thing that you will need to have before starting this book is a basic prior knowledge of image and video processing to grasp the material covered more easily. Also, some basic programming experience could come in handy, but is not necessary, since most parts of the book start from scratch.

Conventions

In this book, you will find several headings appearing frequently.

To give clear instructions of how to complete a procedure or task, we use:

Time for action – heading

1. Action 1
2. Action 2
3. Action 3

Instructions often need some extra explanation so that they make sense, so they are followed with:

What just happened?

This heading explains the working of tasks or instructions that you have just completed.

You will also find some other learning aids in the book, including:

Pop quiz – heading

These are short multiple-choice questions intended to help you test your own understanding.

Have a go hero – heading

These practical challenges give you ideas for experimenting with what you have learned.

You will also find a number of styles of text that distinguish between different kinds of information. Here are some examples of these styles, and an explanation of their meaning.

Code words in text are shown as follows: "Adapthisteq performs global histogram equalization."

A block of code is set as follows:

```
function [output] = CroppedContrastEnhancement(input,method)

% Function that performs area-based image contrast enhancement with
% methodsincorporated in MATLAB toolboxes
% Inputs:
%           input - Input image
%           method - Enhancement method (1: histeq, 2: imadjust,
```

```
%                                    3: adapthisteq)
% Output:
%             output - Output image (with enhanced contrast)
```

When we wish to draw your attention to a particular part of a code block, the relevant lines or items are set in bold:

```
img = imread('my_image.bmp'); % Read image
subplot (1,2,1) % Open a figure for 2 images
imshow(img) % Show original image
title ('Original image') % Add title
threshold = 150; % Set threshold level
img(img > threshold) = 255; % Set pixels above 150 to 255
img(img <= threshold) = 0; % Set pixels below 150 to 0
img = logical(img); % Convert img to binary
subplot (1,2,2) % Make second image spot active
imshow(img) % Show thresholded image
title ('Thresholded image') % Add title
```

New terms and **important words** are shown in bold. Words that you see on the screen, in menus or dialog boxes for example, appear in the text like this: "You should start with the first and easiest step, which is loading and displaying our photograph into the **Workspace** window.".

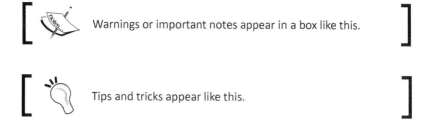

Warnings or important notes appear in a box like this.

Tips and tricks appear like this.

Reader feedback

Feedback from our readers is always welcome. Let us know what you think about this book—what you liked or may have disliked. Reader feedback is important for us to develop titles that you really get the most out of.

To send us general feedback, simply send an e-mail to feedback@packtpub.com, and mention the book title through the subject of your message.

If there is a topic that you have expertise in and you are interested in either writing or contributing to a book, see our author guide on www.packtpub.com/authors.

Customer support

Now that you are the proud owner of a Packt book, we have a number of things to help you to get the most from your purchase.

Downloading the example code

You can download the example code files for all Packt books you have purchased from your account at http://www.packtpub.com. If you purchased this book elsewhere, you can visit http://www.packtpub.com/support and register to have the files e-mailed directly to you.

Errata

Although we have taken every care to ensure the accuracy of our content, mistakes do happen. If you find a mistake in one of our books—maybe a mistake in the text or the code—we would be grateful if you would report this to us. By doing so, you can save other readers from frustration and help us improve subsequent versions of this book. If you find any errata, please report them by visiting http://www.packtpub.com/submit-errata, selecting your book, clicking on the **errata submission form** link, and entering the details of your errata. Once your errata are verified, your submission will be accepted and the errata will be uploaded to our website, or added to any list of existing errata, under the Errata section of that title.

Piracy

Piracy of copyright material on the Internet is an ongoing problem across all media. At Packt, we take the protection of our copyright and licenses very seriously. If you come across any illegal copies of our works, in any form, on the Internet, please provide us with the location address or website name immediately so that we can pursue a remedy.

Please contact us at copyright@packtpub.com with a link to the suspected pirated material.

We appreciate your help in protecting our authors, and our ability to bring you valuable content.

Questions

You can contact us at questions@packtpub.com if you are having a problem with any aspect of the book, and we will do our best to address it.

1
Basic Image Manipulations

Since it was first released, MATLAB has been associated with technical computing and scientific programming. Due to its high uptake in academia and its large and active community, it has grown to become a versatile and multifunctional tool, providing solutions in a vast diversity of fields. Its usage in image and video processing for scientific applications has been popular for a while, but more recent versions have included processing tools that are more user-friendly and aimed at a broader spectrum of users. The usefulness of MATLAB for image processing is rather self-explanatory, since it is a programming environment specialized for matrix manipulation and images are nothing more than matrices.

In this chapter, you will be introduced to the very basics of image manipulation using MATLAB. Prior experience in using MATLAB is not required, since we will be covering everything from scratch. Some basic understanding of programming would be beneficial.

More specifically, in this chapter we will cover:

- ♦ The basic details of the MATLAB environment and especially those that will be used extensively in this book
- ♦ The various ways of loading, displaying, and saving an image using MATLAB
- ♦ The most basic image manipulations that can be handled by MATLAB, that is, rotation, cropping, and resizing

So, let's get started.

Getting acquainted with the MATLAB environment

In order to be able to start working with MATLAB, you should install it on your system. Since the installation is a very straightforward process, we will not cover it here. The only thing you have to be certain of, is that your installation includes the **Image Processing** and **Image Acquisition** toolboxes, which are necessary for the purposes of this book. A few examples towards the end will also need the **Computer Vision System Toolbox** in order to work. The version of MATLAB we will be using is 2012b, the latest available version at the time of writing this book.

> The functions and processes covered in this book have also been tested in MATLAB 2013a during the revision process, and work without any problems.

The first thing we see when opening MATLAB 2012b is a window comprising other windows and a ribbon with various toolbars. The ribbon has grouped sets of many processes that can be helpful for a beginner, but may prove distracting when the user has acquired more experience. This is why, besides giving a few details in this chapter, we will be avoiding extensive use of the ribbon, limiting it to the most time-saving and relevant processes to digital media processing. The subwindows residing in the environment of MATLAB will be our basic tools in this book, along with the MATLAB editor, which is the basic core tool for writing your own scripts and functions.

Default subwindows of the environment

The pre-set windows you will face when first using the application will be:

- The **Command Window**
- The **Workspace** window
- The **Command History** window
- The **Current Folder** window
- The **Details** window

Downloading the example code

You can download the example code files for all Packt books you have purchased from your account at http://www.packtpub.com. If you purchased this book elsewhere, you can visit http://www.packtpub.com/support and register to have the files e-mailed directly to you.

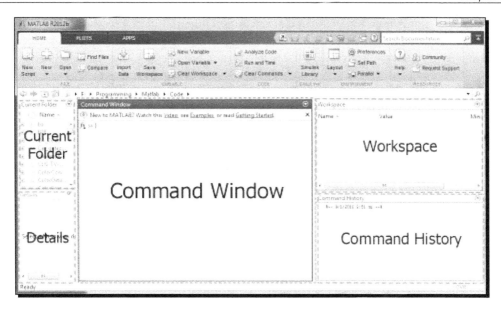

It is worth noting that the environment of MATLAB 2012b has been altered significantly compared to previous versions, mainly because of the inclusion of a ribbon menu resembling the one used in Microsoft Office 2007 onward. However, since most of the processes described in this book are based on using the command line, users of previous versions will not have problems following the examples.

The Command Window

Most of the MATLAB usage time will probably be spent on typing commands in the command line. The command line resides in the **Command Window** and starts with the symbol **fx** which is clickable and contains a list of all installed functions organized by toolbox. Following this symbol, there is the prompt symbol, **>>**, followed by a blinking cursor at the place where you can enter commands. All codes that must be written in the command line will be preceded by the prompt symbol in this book.

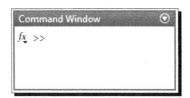

The available commands are all the inherent MATLAB functions, most of which help you manipulate matrices (hence the name: MATrixLABoratory). In this book, we will mainly be using functions for image manipulation, included in the Image Processing and Image Acquisition toolboxes.

The Current Folder window

The **Current Folder** window is basically a file manager, resembling Windows Explorer. You can navigate your way through the folders in your computer, in order to find files you would like to use in your work, for example, an image you would like to load. By default, MATLAB can access the contents of the current folder and a number of folders that have been included in its path. During installation, all the folders containing the installed toolboxes have been added to MATLAB's path; hence the functions and files contained in them can be accessed no matter what the current folder is.

The Details window

The **Details** window is also informative, displaying information about the file you have selected in the current folder window. The details are displayed only when the selected file is recognized by MATLAB.

The Workspace window

The **Workspace** window is used for a constant view of all variables that are present, providing information about their names, types, plus minimum and maximum values, where this is applicable.

The ribbon

The ribbon contains a collection of basic MATLAB processes and resides in the top part of the environment window. It is based on the latest Graphical User Interface trends, like the ones used in Microsoft Office software products since the 2007 version. It has three main tabs:

- HOME
- PLOTS
- APPS

These three tabs are briefly described in the following sections.

The HOME tab

The **HOME** tab contains the most basic and generic processes used in MATLAB. In this book, we will only need some of them.

As we can see in the previous image, there are six main groups of processes present on the **HOME** tab; **FILE**, **VARIABLE**, **CODE**, **SIMULINK**, **ENVIRONMENT**, and **RESOURCES**.

From these six groups, we will certainly need the **FILE** group processes to create or open MATLAB files. The **VARIABLE** group is a new addition in MATLAB 2012b, providing an intuitive, yet unnecessary way for variable creation. The group named **CODE** is useful for code analysis, the **SIMULINK** group is used for a tool that is not covered in this book, the **ENVIRONMENT** group is a way to tweak the setting of the MATLAB environment, and finally, **RESOURCES** are processes for getting online and offline help.

The PLOTS tab

The **PLOTS** tab is a tool that helps you plot variables. Besides traditional plotting capabilities (for example, creating a graph from x and y coordinates), it can also be used as an alternative way to show images stored in variables or even to play videos stored in variables.

The APPS tab

The **APPS** tab is also a rather new addition and provides a quick way to access basic MATLAB tools by clicking on their icons, rather than writing their name in the command line. We can use it to quickly access the **Image Acquisition** or the Image Viewer tools, which are useful for digital media processing.

The editor

A very important tool in MATLAB, besides the default ones you see when first opening the environment, is the editor. The editor can be invoked in various ways, depending on what you want to accomplish. The three basic ways are:

♦ Click on the **New Script** icon on the **HOME** tab

♦ Click on the **New** icon on the **HOME** tab and then click on either one of the first four choices: **Script**, **Function**, **Example**, or **Class**

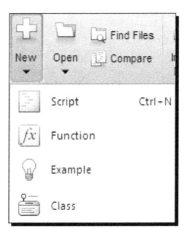

♦ Click on the **Open** icon on the **HOME** tab and then either search for a file in your computer with a .m extension (MATLAB code) by clicking on **Open...**, or selecting a file from the **RECENT FILES** list

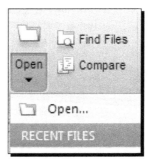

The EDITOR window

Once you have invoked the editor using any of the ways mentioned previously, a new window will pop up. In this window, you can write, alter, and save your code using a powerful code editor. We will not go into detail here, since to fully comprehend the functionalities of this tool, we first have to learn how to write code in MATLAB.

Importing and displaying an image

Now that we have seen most of the menus and windows we will be using, let's start with the very basics of image processing. MATLAB is a computing language that works with matrices. Consequently, in order for us to work with images, they have to be imported as matrix variables in MATLAB. There are several ways to accomplish this. Here, we will see the most practical ones.

Importing and displaying an image using the command line

The most generic—compatible with almost all versions of the software that include the Image Processing Toolbox—way to import an image in MATLAB is through the command line.

In the command line, you can type commands that invoke the functions that have been installed with MATLAB. Functions can be thought of as black boxes, which can be fed with appropriate inputs and provide appropriate outputs.

The MATLAB function that can be used to import images is `imread`. The easiest way to use it is to type it into the command line, passing the path to an image as the input string. This will import the image into a variable in the MATLAB workspace. The name of the variable is defined by you, by assigning a name to the output. Once you have done this, you can then display your image by using `imshow`. This function is designed to display a matrix variable as an image. Let's see now how you can import and display your first image using the command line.

Time for action – importing and displaying an image

Let's assume that you have an image called `my_image.bmp`, which you want to import and then display in MATLAB. The steps you should follow are these:

1. Ensure that your current folder (its contents are shown in the **Current Folder** window) contains the image. If not, either copy it there or select the folder that contains it.

2. Click in the **Command Window** area to be able to write something in the command line. Once you see a blinking cursor in the command line, you are ready to type.

3. Type the following commands in the command line:

```
>> img = imread('my_image.bmp');
>> imshow(img)
```

4. A window displaying the selected image must now be open. You can maximize, minimize, or adjust its size according to your liking.

What just happened?

The steps you followed in the previous section used two predefined MATLAB functions, one for opening an image (imread) and one for displaying it (imshow). Step 1 is a prerequisite for imread to find the file. An alternative to navigating to the folder containing the image would be to include the full path to the filename given as input. If, for example, the folder containing the image was C:\images\ ,then the first command would be:

```
>> img = imread('C:\images\my_image.bmp');
```

Either way, imread stores the image in the variable img which is a matrix of size equal to that of the image.

 The image used in the previous example, as well as all images and videos used throughout this book, can be found at the author's website. Its URL is http://www.cvrlab.com/gsiogkas/.

Importing and displaying an image using imtool

Using the command line is not the only way to open and display images. MATLAB also provides a basic image processing tool, called imtool. This tool can be invoked by typing its name in the command line, or by clicking on its icon on the ribbon in the **APPS** tab. If you select to invoke imtool, a new window which includes basic image manipulation choices, opens. To open an image in imtool, we must click on **File** and then **Open...** to browse through the folders and load the image of our choice. Let's work with the same image as before, namely, my_image.bmp. Once the image is open in imtool, we can see and access most available functionalities of the tool on its toolbar. Starting from left to right, the icons appearing in the toolbar can be used to:

- ◆ Navigate the image using a smaller, overview window
- ◆ Inspect pixel values in a neighborhood of your choice
- ◆ Display image information
- ◆ Adjust image contrast
- ◆ Get Help.
- ◆ Crop the image
- ◆ Measure distances
- ◆ Zoom in/out

- Drag image to pan
- Adjust contrast/brightness via mouse motion
- Change the scale of the displayed image 100%

Time for action – using imtool to extract useful information

Now that we know what the `imtool` can do, let's use it to get some more information about our image. Suppose that we want to know the color, depth, and size of our image, the values of the pixels around an area we want to inspect, and the distances (in pixels) of some pairs of points on the image, we will have to take the following steps:

1. Click on the third icon from the left, ⓘ, that displays information about the image. You will see that the new window that appears contains a lot of information about the image, including its width, height, and bit depth.

2. To make your task easier, you should first zoom in using the magnifying glass with the plus symbol (^Q). Let's zoom in on the area containing the moving track (top of the image).

3. Then, click on and place the blue crosshair that appears on the image on the track. You will now be able to see the values of the pixels in the small area selected by your crosshair. If you enlarge the selected area by dragging its sides, the values will not be visible, but you will still be able to inspect details in the image.

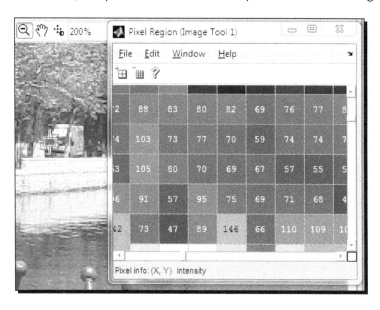

4. Now let's measure the dimensions of the track that we have zoomed in on. Zoom in as much as you like to see the details and then click on .

5. To measure the length between two points, you should left-click on the first point and keeping the left mouse button clicked, move the cursor to the second point and release the mouse button. This will draw a line between the two points you selected and place a label on it, displaying its length in pixels. Let's repeat this process to measure the dimensions of the truck.

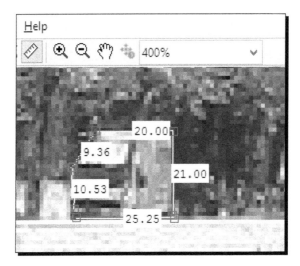

6. Now that you have measured the distances you needed, you might want to save the resulting image with the overlaid distance measurements. Click on **File** and then **Print to Figure**, in order to display your processed image in a new window and then navigate to **File** | **Save As** to get a chance to select the name and type of the image you want to save.

What just happened?

The process described previously is generally useful for people who work with image enhancement and analysis. In image processing, you will often need to inspect an image in terms of color values or measured in terms of distance, and so on. The analysis of the image regions should be easily extractable so that the results can be passed on to others. These functionalities are covered by imtool. In our example, we used the image information icon, which gave us an idea on what values to expect (8 bit depth means values from 0 to 255) and what the image dimensions are. Then, we located and inspected the region of our choice using the zoom in/out and the pixel values inspection tools. When we decided on the actual part of the image we wanted to measure, we used the distance measurement tool to see the dimensions of the selected object on screen. Finally, we exported our enhanced results to a new image of our chosen format, using the **Print to Figure** functionality.

Applying geometric transformations

By now you have already mastered how to open an image and display it as it is using the **Command Window**. Now, it is time to learn how to apply basic geometric transformations to an image and display them along with the original. Geometric transformations are probably the most common functionalities of every image editor, no matter how basic it is. They do not generally alter the content of an image, but actually change the grid of pixels so that processes, such as image rotation or mirroring are achieved. Cropping and resizing of images are also two basic geometric transformations. In this section, we will see how all these transformations can be achieved in MATLAB.

Performing image rotation

For image rotation, you can use the function `imrotate`. Again, you will be working in the **Command Window**, where you will have to type the functions to perform the transformations. Only this time, we will use a few more lines of code, to display the results in a single window.

Time for action – rotating an image and displaying the result

Let's start rotating and displaying the image. Assuming you have solved the problem of the image being in a visible path, you should follow these steps:

1. Open the image. Let's use the previous one:

   ```
   >> img = imread('my_image.bmp');
   ```

2. Now, rotate the image using `imrotate`. Let's try rotating the image by 90, 180, and 270 degrees, storing each result in a different variable:

   ```
   >> img90 = imrotate(img,90);
   >> img180 = imrotate(img,180);
   >> img270 = imrotate(img,270);
   ```

3. Hopefully, you have typed all commands correctly, so now you should be able to see four different matrices in the **Workspace** window, each one containing a rotated version of the original image. Now let's try to display all the images in the same window. In the **Command Window**, type:

   ```
   >> figure
   >> subplot(2,2,1)
   >> imshow(img)
   >> title('Original Image')
   >> subplot(2,2,2)
   >> imshow(img90)
   >> title('Image Rotated 90 degrees')
   ```

```
>> subplot(2,2,3)
>> imshow(img180)
>> title('Image Rotated 180 degrees')
>> subplot(2,2,4)
>> imshow(img270)
>> title('Image Rotated 270 degrees')
```

You should now be able to see a window displaying the original (not rotated or rotated by 0 degrees) image and its three aforementioned rotated versions, like the following screenshot:

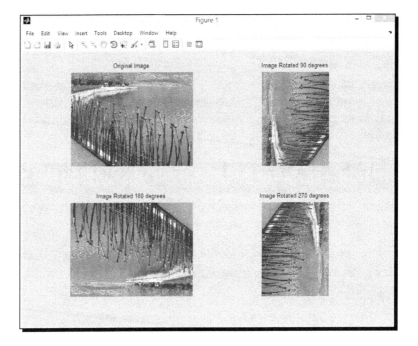

What just happened?

The process you just performed can be split into two parts; the first part is the image rotation process, which took place in step 2, producing three rotated versions of your original image. The function imrotate can take two inputs, an image and an angle by which the image will be rotated. The angle need not necessarily be a multiple of 90. It could be any arbitrary angle, between -360 and 360 degrees. Also note that the rotation is performed in a counter-clockwise fashion. If you wish to perform clockwise rotation, you should use a negative angle as a second input to imrotate.

The second part of the process described previously, is for displaying the produced images. The subplot command splits the window that opens into m rows and n columns and then activates the subwindow that resides in the r-th position. Following this notation, the subplot function should be called as subplot(m,n,r). In our example, we used two rows and two columns; hence the first two inputs were equal to two. The third input was changed each time, so that the images displayed after each subplot (using imshow) would be placed in a different subwindow. Another thing worth noting is that the subwindows in a subplot are numbered in a column-wise fashion (that is, 1 is for the first row-first column, 2 is for the first row-second column, and so on). Finally, for clarity of the displayed information, we have added a title over each displayed image, using the title function, with the message we want entered as a string input.

If you want to display your images in different windows, you should replace each subplot(m,n,r) command with figure. This way, you would end up with four open windows for the example illustrated previously.

Performing image mirroring

In order to perform image mirroring, we will use one of the following functions: fliplr, flipud, and flipdim. If you want to mirror a grayscale image, the first two functions can be used. The first one, fliplr, is used to mirror an image about its vertical axis. This means that the columns of the image will be interchanged, so that the first column becomes the last and vice versa. Accordingly, flipud can be used to mirror an image about the horizontal axis. These two functions only work when the input matrix is 2-dimensional (that is, a grayscale image). When we have to deal with color images, we need to use flipdim because it can also accept a second input declaring the dimension that will be flipped.

Time for action – mirroring an image and displaying the result

Now let's try to perform image mirroring in both dimensions using the first two functions described previously. Again, we will use the same grayscale image as before. If you have started from scratch repeat step 1 from the previous example. Then, take the following steps:

1. Use fliplr and flipud in the **Command Window** to perform left-right and up-down flipping of your image:

```
>> img_lr = fliplr(img);
>> img_ud = flipud(img);
```

2. Now, display the original image and the mirrored versions in different windows, using:

```
>> figure, imshow(img)
>> figure, imshow(img_lr)
>> figure, imshow(img_ud)
```

Now you should see three different windows displaying the original image and its two mirrored versions. Each window that appears will be placed on top of the previous one, so you should drag-and-drop them next to each other in order to get a result as follows:

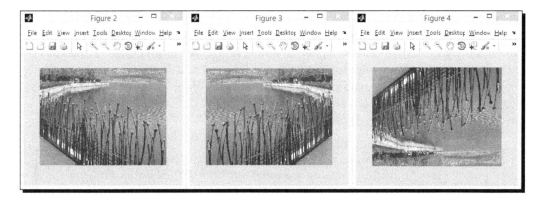

What just happened?

The process you just followed is mostly self-explanatory. You have used the same grayscale image as before, stored in the matrix variable img, and then used the flipping functions of MATLAB to perform mirroring about the two axes. Then, at step 2, you executed the command to show the images in different windows. Notice that you can write more than one command in the same line, provided that they are separated either by a comma (in which case, any result generated by the command will be printed in the **Command Window**) or a semicolon (nothing will be printed in the **Command Window**).

Have a go hero – using flipdim and comparing the results

Now let's try to use the alternative function, which can also be used for color images. How would you use flipdim to produce the same results as in the previous example and then display all results in one window with respective titles?

This is actually a simple process, involving some of the steps described previously. Assuming you still have img_lr and img_ud in your **Workspace** window from the previous process, you should first perform image flipping using the flipdim command.

The result you will get is a window containing the left-right flipped images on the first line and the up-down flipped images on the second line. If you have done everything correctly, the two images in the first row should be identical and so should remove the two images in the second row.

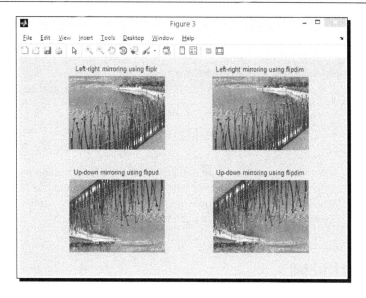

Resizing an image

A very common functionality of any self-respecting image editor is that of image resizing. MATLAB is no different, since it provides the user with resizing capabilities, using popular algorithms. More specifically, MATLAB's Image Processing Toolbox incorporates the `imresize` function, which accepts at least two inputs. The first input is the matrix variable containing the image you want to resize and the second input is either a scaling factor (by which the original image size will be multiplied) or a matrix with two elements; a number of rows and a number of columns for the resized image. As an example, let's assume we have a grayscale image of 240 rows and 320 columns stored in the matrix A. If we wanted to resize it to half its original size, that is 120 rows and 160 columns and assign the result to matrix B, then we would have the following two equivalent ways of accomplishing that through the command line:

```
>> B = imresize(A,0.5);
>> B = imresize(A,[120 160]);
```

 Note that the default resizing algorithm prior to MATLAB Version R2007a was different. So, if you want to replicate results generated with earlier versions, you should use the function `imresize_old`.

The result in both cases would be exactly the same, but there is also a third method of acquiring it. Let's suppose that we want to resize image A, so that it fits vertically into a predefined space, which we know consists of 120 pixels. In that case, we wouldn't need to know its exact number of columns and instead of the commands we used previously, we could use:

```
>> B = imresize(A,[120,NaN]);
```

Here, we have to say a few words about how MATLAB performs image resizing. The default method is cubic interpolation, but you can also use nearest neighbor or bilinear interpolation. Other valid choices could be interpolation kernels, but they go beyond our scope here. In order to specify a different interpolation method, you should add a third input in your function call. For example, if in the previous example you wanted to use bilinear interpolation, you should type in:

```
>> B = imresize(A,[120,NaN],'bilinear');
```

Note that if you want to find out more about a function and the different inputs it can accept, you can use the command line help of MATLAB by typing in the word help and the name of the function you want to investigate. You can try this by typing help imresize.

Cropping an image

Another useful tool incorporated in image editors is image cropping. In its most typical form, it consists of a manual tool for defining and placing a rectangular area; this process produces a new image that contains only the part of the original image that lies in the rectangle. Assuming you have loaded and displayed an image using imshow in the command line, you can crop it and place the results in a new matrix (let's call it cropped), by typing:

```
>> cropped = imcrop;
```

Once you do that, you will have to use the mouse to define the rectangular area to be cropped, by clicking on the left mouse button and keeping it pressed while moving the mouse, until you are happy with the resulting rectangle. Once you let go off the left mouse button, you are able to adjust its position and/or size, double-click on the left mouse button when the result is acceptable. This process stores the part of the image residing in the rectangle into matrix cropped, which will have the same dimensions as the rectangle.

Another way to crop an image would be to define the rectangle by using specific coordinates. This often happens when you know the exact area you want to crop beforehand, so you can define them as a second input to imcrop. Let's suppose that the upper left corner of the rectangular area of image A you want to crop is on pixel (x, y), where x is the row number and y is the column number. If the rectangle has a width of w pixels and a height of h pixels, you should type in the command line:

```
>> cropped = imcrop(A,[y,x,w,h]);
```

If you think that the way the MATLAB handles rectangle coordinates is impractical, you should try coming up with a way to adjust it to your needs. Suppose you want to choose a rectangle that starts at row x_min, ends at row x_max, and is bounded by the columns y_min and y_max. In that case, the second input of `imcrop` would be [y_minx_miny_max-y_minx_max-x_min].

Saving an image

Up to now, we have learned how to perform several image manipulations in MATLAB, but we haven't seen how the results can be saved using the **Command Window**. In fact, the solution is rather intuitive. Since almost everything we have seen so far had to do with calling functions with rather self-explanatory, such as `imread`, writing an image is rather unsurprisingly called `imwrite`.

Of course, like any self-respecting image processing software, MATLAB gives you a wide variety of choices regarding the type of the image you want to save. In fact, it supports most of the known image formats, such as JPEG, BMP, PGM, PNG, and TIFF. The most common way of using `imwrite` is by feeding it three inputs. For example, if we need to save an image we have stored in matrix variable `img`, as a JPEG image of the same size, we should use:

```
>> imwrite(img,'new_image.jpg','JPEG');
```

This command would result in saving a JPEG image named `new_image.jpg`, using the default quality factor. The user has the ability to choose a different quality factor, since the matter of compression is a very important one in image processing. The higher the quality factor (it may be any integer from 0 to 100) defined by the user, the less is the image degradation caused by compression. When saving a JPEG image, the user can also define the color bit depth (8, 12, or 16 for grayscale and 8 or 12 for color images), the mode of compression (lossy or lossless), and a possible comment that might have to be saved in the JPEG. By default, the saved image will be 8 bits if grayscale (8 bits/color channel, if color) with lossy compression, quality of 75, and with no comments embedded.

If we assume that we want to save our image as JPEG, but with a quality factor of 100, lossy compression, and the comment Packt embedded in the JPEG, we should type in:

```
>> imwrite(img,'new_image.jpg','JPEG','Quality',100,'Comment',
   'Packt') ;
```

As you might have understood by now, passing optional inputs in a function is a rather straightforward process, provided that you know what these inputs are called and what their supported values are (that is, what values can be accepted).

Time for action – cropping and resizing an image, then saving it as BMP

To get a better grasp of the three functions we presented in the previous three sections, we can use the example of a very common image processing drill, which is to select and crop a part of an image we would like to keep and then resize it to our desired dimensions and save it as a new image. We'll use our previous image as a start, so our first move is to load it. The whole process is described in the following steps:

1. Load the image using `imread` and save it in the variable `img`:

```
>> img = imread('my_image.bmp');
```

2. Crop the image using `imcrop` and save the result in the variable `cropped`:

```
>> cropped = imcrop(img);
```

3. Now, resize the resulting image to double its size using `imresize` and display it using `imshow`:

```
>> cropped2 = imresize(cropped,2);
>> imshow(cropped2);
```

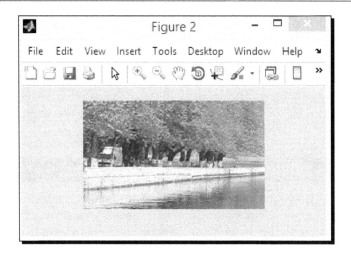

4. Now, let's see the sizes of the two images from steps 2 and 3 using `size`:

```
>> size(cropped)
ans=
    114    196
>> size(cropped2)
ans=
    228    392
```

As we see, the sizes are OK (`cropped2` is double the size of `cropped`, 114 x 196 versus 228 x 392). Now, we can save our final image as a BMP using `imwrite`:

```
>> imwrite(cropped2,'cropped_image.bmp','BMP');
```

You should now be able to see the resulting BMP image in the **Current Folder** window.

What just happened?

Well, you just performed one of the most common processes in the everyday life of an amateur photographer. You started by loading your image into the workspace of MATLAB in step 1, proceeded with selecting and cropping a rectangular area of your choice in step 2, went on to resize it to double its original size and check the resulting image size, and finally, saved your cropped and resized result to a BMP image file. Now, you are ready to move on to harder tasks.

Have a go hero – tailoring an image to suit your needs

Let's now suppose that we would like to process a photo from our holidays, by rotating it 90 degrees to have the proper orientations, cropping a specific area we want to keep, rotating this area as much as needed so that it is not crooked, and then resize it to 360 rows (say, we want to fit it in a specific space with 360 pixels of height). At the end, we would like to save our result in high quality JPEG, embedding a comment that reads I just finished Chapter 1. How would you accomplish all these things?

First of all, don't panic! All these steps have already been covered in this chapter, so it's just a matter of using the right functions in the right order.

You should start with the first and easiest step, which is loading and displaying our photograph into the **Workspace** window. The result would look something like the following screenshot:

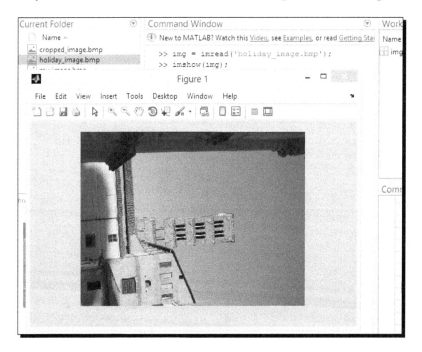

Now that your photo has been saved in a variable, you can rotate it so that it has the correct orientation. Then, use `imcrop` and select the sunny area of the image with the mouse.

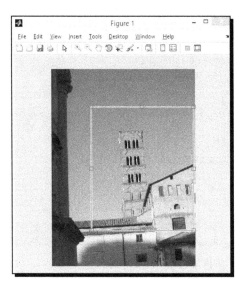

However, the resulting image is tilted! So, let's try to fix it. Here comes the trial and error process. You must try the various possible small angle values in `imrotate`, so that you find the result you are happy with. This image should look fine if you rotate it clockwise by an angle of about 5 degrees. Optionally, we can display our steps in the same figure and get the following result:

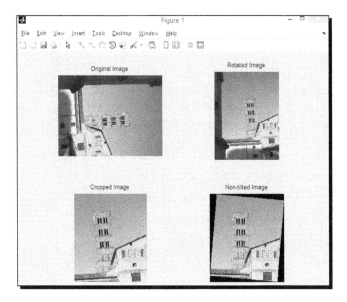

As you can see from the last image, while our final image is not tilted, it has black borders caused by the rotation by an angle that is not a multiple of 90. This means that you need yet another cropping step, to keep the image part that we actually want. When you have edited the image to your liking, proceed in resizing the image using `imresize`, and declare the number of rows you want the image to have in the second input. Finally, you can save the image in the predefined format using `imwrite`.

> The default method for rotation used in `imrotate` is nearest neighbor. This method produces rather suboptimal results, when rotating an image by an angle that is not a multiple of 90 degrees. If you want to produce a better result, you could try entering a different method as a third input, like this:
>
> ```
> >> img90c2 = imrotate(img90c,-5, 'bicubic');
> ```

Pop quiz – image processing in MATLAB

Q1. MATLAB is a very good choice for image processing purposes for various reasons. Try to answer which of the following reasons are valid:

1. MATLAB represents images as matrices and treats most variables as such.

2. MATLAB is open source and can be used by anyone.

3. MATLAB has a set of toolboxes that offer a variety of powerful and useful tools for image manipulation.

4. Function `imrotate` rotates an image in a clockwise function.

Summary

This chapter was a quick dive into the ways that MATLAB can replace your everyday image editing tool, while giving you extra parameterization choices that you wouldn't have in basic software. More specifically, you have learned the basic ways to:

♦ Load and display an image in MATLAB using the command line

♦ Load, display, manipulate, and save an image using `imtool`

♦ Rotate, flip, or mirror an image in the command line

♦ Crop and resize an image using functions

♦ Save an image in a variety of formats

These processes are core functionalities of everyday image manipulation for every amateur photographer. They provide the foundations for any complex image processing task and will be used throughout the book. So, congratulations! You have set the first stepping stone to climb to more sophisticated image processing tasks. The rest of the chapters will guide you through some more complex image processing that MATLAB offers and will then move on to video processing. Depending on your needs, you will either be able to use it as a quick reference for any of the techniques it covers, or you can read through the chapters in a sequential order, as you would do in a Media Processing course.

The next chapter will introduce you to different ways to work with grayscale image pixels and manipulate their values. On finishing it, you will be able to enhance and improve the visual quality of an image. Have fun!

2
Working with Pixels In Grayscale Images

Now you have grasped some basic visual media processes that MATLAB has to offer. You have learned how to import and export images, apply basic geometric transformations on them, and generally perform tasks that are included in most basic image editors. In this chapter, you will start building up your MATLAB skills by taking advantage of ready-made functions that allow editing of pixel values in an image. You will also start making your own small programs, save them as scripts or functions, and apply them in practical examples.

In this chapter, we will cover:

- How to manipulate one or more pixels in an image using `for loops`, or indexing
- How to perform histogram-based processing using MATLAB
- How to write our first scripts and functions for automating more complex processes

So, let's get started!

Accessing image pixels and changing their values

To gain a better understanding of how MATLAB treats images, we have to revisit the way it stores them in the **Workspace** window. In the previous chapter, we discussed the origin of MATLAB and why it is an ideal choice for processing images. So, let's start with a simple quiz to freshen your memory.

Let's start using the matrix manipulation property of MATLAB to our advantage. We have already seen how to import an image into the **Workspace** window, using the `imread` function:

```
>> img = imread('my_image.bmp');
```

Importing the image automatically generates a matrix variable in the **Workspace** window. Its dimensions (rows, columns, and colors) are the same as the original image and it also has the same depth (given in bits). In our example, the resulting matrix is `485 x 656` and its type is `uint8`, it means that the matrix has 485 rows, 656 columns, and its values are `unsigned integers` with a depth of 8 bits spanning from `0` (black) to `255` (white). The **Workspace** window also shows which are the largest and smallest pixel values in the specified image (not necessarily `0` and `255`):

In order to examine the value of a certain pixel, we should type in the command line the name of the image, followed by the row and column of the pixel we want (for example, the pixel in row `45`, and column `150`):

```
>> img(45,150)
```

The command we just typed in will produce a visible output, since we did not use a semicolon at the end. The output following the command will be as follows:

```
ans =

    63
```

Now that we see how to examine a specific pixel, it is easy for us to alter its value. Taking into account the acceptable range of values for a `uint8` matrix element `[0,255]`, we can type in the following code to change the value of the chosen pixel to `255`, thus making it white:

```
>> img(45,150) = 255;
```

Of course, the change in one pixel is hardly noticeable for the naked eyes. So how about trying to change pixel values in a wider area, for example, a window of size 20 x 20 pixels. This is where things start becoming a little more complicated, since now we have got to choose between two alternative ways to perform this task; the usual programming technique using `for loops` and the MATLAB technique, using indexing. We will address both ways, because very interesting conclusions can be drawn from this example.

Changing the pixel values of a square area using loops

For those readers who are already familiar with programming, this section shouldn't be too hard to understand. However, since the book aims at wider audiences, we will try to explain the logic behind using loops to accomplish changing pixel values.

In traditional programming languages, such as C, C++, or Java, the way to scan through every element of a vector (one-dimensional matrix) is through increasing the value of a variable, let's call it **pos**, which holds the position of an element scanned at each step, starting from the first position and ending at the last position. This variable will be used to define which element of the array we examine (or change) in each step.

For example, if we want to assign the value 255 to every element of matrix A with dimensions 1 x 5, we will write the following lines of code:

```
for pos = 1:5
A(pos)=255;
end
```

 If you are a more experienced programmer, you might find it odd that we use a variable (A) that seems to grow in size inside a loop. Furthermore, the variable is automatically generated at the first step of the loop. Both of these actions are feasible in MATLAB, however the former should generally be avoided for the sake of performance. For the time being, we are going to take advantage of the feasibility of these actions, to keep things simple.

In case of a two-dimensional matrix, for example, B of size 5 x 10, the value assigning procedure will require two for loops, one for the rows and one for the columns. In accordance with this, we should use the following code, using two variables, pos_r (to be used for rows) and pos_c (to be used for columns), to loop through the matrix:

```
for pos_r = 1:5
  for pos_c = 1:10
    B(pos_r, pos_c)=255;
  end
end
```

Now, in case we want to alter the values of the elements of matrix B in a 2 x 4 area starting at the second row and second column, we should use the following code:

```
for pos_r = 2:2+2
  for pos_c = 2:2+4
    B(pos_r, pos_c)=255;
  end
end
```

If you have experience with other programming languages, you must have noticed a significant difference in the way we number the positions in an array. While in C/C++, for example, numbering the elements of an N x 1 array starts with 0 and ends at N-1, MATLAB uses values from 1 to N.

Changing the pixel values of a square area using indexing

In the previous section, we saw a generic programming way to alter the values of the elements in a matrix. However, following this procedure is both cumbersome and inefficient. Many lines of code will be necessary to manipulate matrix values in predefined areas, while the use of `for loops` is computationally inefficient in MATLAB.

An alternative method is to use the powerful indexing method provided by MATLAB. Indexing is a flexible and expressive way for the selection of user-defined subsets of the elements of a matrix. Here, we will present the basic functionalities of indexing using the same examples we did in the previous section.

First, let's try to replace the case of setting all elements of a `1 x 5` matrix `A` to `255`. Instead of using a `for` loop, we now use indexing:

```
A(1:5)=255;
```

In this example we have achieved the same result as before, using one line of code instead of three. Imagine what happens in the case of a two-dimensional matrix, for example, `B`. Even more lines of code are now saved:

```
B(1:5, 1:10) = 255;
```

By now, you should be starting to get an idea. Instead of using the indices we want in a `for` loop, we plug them in the row and column dimensions of the matrix we want to manipulate. Following this rationale, let's alter the values of the elements in the same `2 x 4` area as before:

```
B(2:2+2, 2:2+4) = 255;
```

Writing and using scripts

Even if you have understood everything so far, you might still be wondering whether we can use the command line for all the previous processes. The answer is we can do so. If you copy and paste all the pieces of code given in the previous command line, everything should work as described. You can try it for yourself.

However, not every process should be executed through the command line. You should try to write code in files, so that you may re-use it at a later point in time. This is where the Editor comes in picture. Let's say you want to save the part of code used for the two-dimensional matrix B, with both methods, printing the result on screen, so that we can check whether the results are identical (they should be, since the methods are equivalent). What we will do is, copy and paste the following fragments of code into the Editor and then save the file with the name `MyFirstScript.m`. The extension `.m` will be added by MATLAB, so don't worry about it. You just assign the name.

```
for pos_r = 1:5
  for pos_c = 1:10
    B(pos_r, pos_c) = 255;
  end
end
B % To print the result from the loop method
clear B;  % Erase matrix B from the workspace
B(1:5, 1:10) = 255;
B % To print the result from the indexing method
```

Now, you can use your file in MATLAB, provided that you have saved it in your working directory (it should be visible in **Current Folder**). Just type the following code in the command line:

```
>> MyFirstScript
```

You should see the following result in the **Command Window**:

```
>> MyFirstScript

B =

    255    255    255    255    255    255    255    255    255    255
    255    255    255    255    255    255    255    255    255    255
    255    255    255    255    255    255    255    255    255    255
    255    255    255    255    255    255    255    255    255    255
    255    255    255    255    255    255    255    255    255    255


B =

    255    255    255    255    255    255    255    255    255    255
    255    255    255    255    255    255    255    255    255    255
    255    255    255    255    255    255    255    255    255    255
    255    255    255    255    255    255    255    255    255    255
    255    255    255    255    255    255    255    255    255    255

>>
```

As we can see, both results are identical. To verify this, we could use the MATLAB's `isequal` function, which compares two matrices used as input and output. It assigns `1` if they are equal and `0` if they are not. Let's see how it works, by comparing matrix `B` to itself:

```
>> isequal(B,B)
```

The output of the previous code is as follows:

```
ans =
      1
```

Indeed, the result was `1`. Now, let's make some holes in matrix `B` and see if they are the same. Suppose, we want to change the values of the elements residing in the area defined in the previous examples to `0`. Switch to **Editor**, erase the two lines that have to do with printing the matrix `B`, after the two methods add the following lines at the end of your previous script and then save it as `MySecondScript.m`:

```
for pos_r = 2:2+2
   for pos_c = 2:2+4
      B(pos_r, pos_c)= 0;
   end
end
B % print the result of the loop method
clear B;% Erase matrix B from the workspace
B(1:5, 1:10) = 255;% Re-create matrix B
B(2:2+2, 2:2+4) = 0;
B % print the result of the indexing method
```

This time type the following code in the command line:

```
>> MySecondScript
```

You should now be able to see the following result in your **Command Window**:

```
>> MySecondScript

B =

     255    255    255    255    255    255    255    255    255    255
     255      0      0      0      0      0    255    255    255    255
     255      0      0      0      0      0    255    255    255    255
     255      0      0      0      0      0    255    255    255    255
     255    255    255    255    255    255    255    255    255    255


B =

     255    255    255    255    255    255    255    255    255    255
     255      0      0      0      0      0    255    255    255    255
     255      0      0      0      0      0    255    255    255    255
     255      0      0      0      0      0    255    255    255    255
     255    255    255    255    255    255    255    255    255    255
```

 In the two previous examples, you might have noticed the way to insert comments in MATLAB is by using the % symbol before the comment. Whatever follows a % symbol in a line is not executed. Comments are usually used for providing explanations about the code.

Now that you know the basic theory, you should be able to tackle image processing tasks, such as making a rectangular area of a grayscale image equal to a value of your choice. So, let's see if this is true.

Time for action – whiten an area and blacken another

We will again work using `my_image.bmp`. Let's see if we can write a script that whitens a 30 x 40 rectangular area on the top-left corner of the image and blackens a 40 x 50 rectangular area at the bottom-right corner of the image. We can manage to do so, if we follow these steps:

1. First, you should open **Editor** and select **New Script**. This can also be achieved by using the *Ctrl + N* shortcut keystroke.

2. Now, write the first part of the code, which will open the image:

```
img = imread('my_image.bmp');
```

3. Then you should alter the values of the elements contained in the top-left rectangle to 255. Let's keep the original image so that we can compare it to the final result. This will be achieved using the following line of code:

```
img_final = img;
img_final(1:30,1:40) = 255;
```

4. Now, you should assign black values (equal to 0) to the elements contained in the bottom-right rectangle. In order to define the indices of the pixels you want to alter, you must use the maximum number of rows and columns. This can be easily accomplished using the generic keyword `end` as follows:

```
img_final(end-39:end,end-49:end) = 0;
```

5. You have finished the altering part. Now, it's time to display the results (both the original image and the final image), like we did in the previous chapter. The code for this will be as follows:

```
subplot(1,2,1)
imshow(img)
title('Original image')
subplot(1,2,2)
imshow(img_final)
title('Processed image')
```

6. Finally, you should save your script. Let's use the name `RectangleBrightness` (as before, the extension `.m` will be added by **Editor**).

7. To see the result, we should run your script. Go to the **Command Window** and type the following code:

```
>> RectangleBrightness
```

The result should be something like the following image:

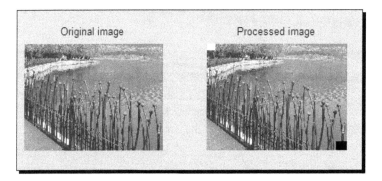

What just happened?

First of all, congratulations! You just wrote and executed your first script that alters pixel values. The commands used were not something new, but they were all executed as a batch for an image this time, producing the final result you just saw. The method used for the alteration of the pixel values was indexing, since we said that it is preferable than using `for loops`.

To select the rectangles to be altered, we had to define the top and bottom row indices and the left and right column indices. The top-left rectangle was defined in a rather intuitive manner. We used index 1 for both the top row and the left column. The indices for the bottom row and the right column were set to 30 and 40 respectively.

The tricky part was selecting the indices that should be used for the bottom-right rectangle. Again, we knew the height and width, but we should use it with respect to the height and width of the image. However, altering the width and height values for each new image would be highly impractical. This is why we used the very convenient index keyword end, which denoted the maximum valued index for each dimension. When it is used for rows, it automatically takes the value of the maximum number of rows, and when it is used for columns it takes the maximum number of columns. In our case we used it in both positions, to calculate the proper top row index (end-39) and bottom row index (end), and also to calculate the proper left column index (end-49) and right row index (end).

Thresholding an image

Now that you have learned two different ways to work with image pixels, we will present another useful and common tool found in image processing software, which is thresholding. Image thresholding can be defined as the process of creating binary images by setting pixels with values above a certain threshold to 1 and the rest to 0. It is usually used for separating the foreground from the background of an image. As we did for the previous examples, we will show three different ways to implement image thresholding in MATLAB; using for loops, a special way of indexing, and using a ready-made thresholding MATLAB function.

Image thresholding using for loops

The classic programming way to implement grayscale image thresholding is by using two nested for loops in a similar fashion to the one used in the previous sections. More specifically, the following script can be used to threshold my_image.bmp:

```
img = imread('my_image.bmp'); % Read image
subplot (1,2,1) % Open a figure for 2 images
imshow(img) % Show original image
title ('Original image') % Add title
threshold = 150; % Set threshold level
for pos_r = 1:size(img,1) % For all rows
  for pos_c = 1:size(img,2) % For all columns
      if img(pos_r,pos_c) > threshold % Check pixel value
        img(pos_r,pos_c) = 255; % Set pixels above 150 to 255
      else
        img(pos_r,pos_c) = 0;   % Set pixels below 150 to 0
      end % End if
```

```
      end % End columns for loop
   end % End rows for loop
img = logical(img); % Convert img to binary
subplot (1,2,2) % Make second image spot active
imshow(img) % Show thresholded image
title ('Thresholded image') % Add title
```

If we save this script with the name `ThresholdingUsingLoops.m` and execute it through the command line, we will get the following result:

Even though we have managed to accomplish our goal in a straight-forward manner, the method we used was very generic and does not take advantage of all the special powers of MATLAB. So, let's take a look at two alternative ways to perform thresholding.

Image thresholding using indexing

We have already mentioned that one of the great advantages of using MATLAB for matrix manipulation is indexing. Some examples of indexing have already been given, but they don't seem to be helpful for thresholding tasks. Therefore, we have to explore alternative indexing methods to perform such tasks. An interesting approach is to define the pixels we want to access using a condition instead of a predefined range of indices. This method is called logical indexing and it chooses those pixels that correspond to nonzero values in the array generated by our condition. You can find more information about logical indexing at `http://www.mathworks.com/company/newsletters/articles/matrix-indexing-in-matlab.html`.

Assuming we want to perform the same task as in the previous section, the equivalent logical indexing code replacing the two nested `for loops`, will be just two lines:

```
img = imread('my_image.bmp'); % Read image
subplot (1,2,1) % Open a figure for 2 images
imshow(img) % Show original image
title ('Original image') % Add title
threshold = 150; % Set threshold level
img(img > threshold) = 255; % Set pixels above 150 to 255
img(img <= threshold) = 0; % Set pixels below 150 to 0
```

```
img = logical(img); % Convert img to binary
subplot (1,2,2) % Make second image spot active
imshow(img) % Show thresholded image
title ('Thresholded image') % Add title
```

Saving this script as `ThresholdingUsingIndexing.m` and executing it through the command line, yields the following result:

This example reveals the power of logical indexing in MATLAB. The two highlighted lines have performed the same actions as the `for` loops they replaced. The first one chose the indices of pixels in our image that exceeded `150` and replaced the values of the pixels at those indices with `255`. The second one followed the same rationale, choosing indices of pixels with values less than or equal to `150` and replaced them with zeros. Note that thresholding using indexing method pinpoints indices in all dimensions; the same command would be used for a one-dimensional matrix and an N-dimensional matrix.

Image thresholding using im2bw

Now that you know how to programmatically threshold an image, let's see the ready-made function to perform the same thing. It is called `im2bw` and we can find more about it using the `help` command. Typing `help im2bw` in the command line will give you all the details you need to use this function. In this context, we have to make some minor adjustments in our approach.

As you may have noticed already, after the thresholding process of the previous two methods, we also performed a conversion of the result to logical form. This was done in order to follow the convention of thresholding that is the pixel values of the result should be binary (either `0` or `1`). In our case, the original image was 8 bit integer, so we used the minimum and maximum values (`0`, `255`). To convert the result to binary, the logical command was used.

When using the `im2bw` function, we should bear in mind that it is designed to work with threshold values between 0 and 1. This means, that we either have to convert our image to have pixel values in that range, or convert the threshold. The second is more practical, so we will divide the threshold value (150 in our case) by the maximum brightness level of the image (255 in the `uint8` case). Since we have compacted our code to a big extent, we can now load the image, threshold it, and display the final result in just four lines in the **Command Window**:

```
>> img = imread('my_image.bmp');
>> subplot(1,2,1), imshow(img), title('Original Image')
>> img = im2bw(img,150/255);
>> subplot(1,2,2), imshow(img), title('Thresholded Image')
```

Note that in the last part of code we gave more than one command in a single line. Since this is not a formal program, but a command-line script to perform some actions, such a style is permitted. Whenever you use this style of scripting, remember that the multiple commands should be separated by either commas (when we don't care if the output of each function gets printed on screen, or the functions don't produce an output), or semicolons when we don't want outputs to be printed on screen. Of course, you can also write these lines of code in a script and execute it through the command line, as we did before.

Image thresholding using an automatic threshold

Till here we have performed all our thresholding tasks using a predefined manual threshold (in our example, 150). Sometimes, a better threshold choice can be acquired by automatic techniques, such as the one proposed by Otsu, which chooses the threshold to minimize the intra-class variance of the black and white pixels (*Otsu, N., A Threshold Selection Method from Gray-Level Histograms, IEEE Transactions on Systems, Man, and Cybernetics, Vol. 9, No. 1, 1979, pp. 62-66*). This method is used in the function `graythresh`. The automatic threshold value estimated by `graythresh` can then be used instead of a manual value in one of the processes described previously. Let's see how this can be accomplished using `im2bw`:

```
>> img = imread('my_image.bmp')
>> subplot(1,2,1), imshow(img), title('Original Image'')
>> thresh = graythresh(img);
>> img = im2bw(img,thresh);
>> subplot(1,2,2), imshow(img), title('Thresholded Image')
```

```
Command Window
  >> img = imread('my_image.bmp');
  subplot(1,2,1), imshow(img), title('Original Image')
  thresh = graythresh(img);
  img = im2bw(img,thresh);
  subplot(1,2,2), imshow(img), title('Thresholded Image')

fx >>
```

Original Image   Thresholded Image

As we can see from the result, the automatically defined threshold value produces a very different result than the one produced by setting the threshold to 150. This means that we should always choose our threshold carefully depending on what the final goal is. If we want to see what the automatically selected threshold was, in range – to 1 and in range 0 to 255, we can type the following commands:

```
>> thresh
>> thresh*255
```

The result will be as follows:

```
>> thresh
thresh =
    0.3882
>> thresh*255
ans =
    99
```

Choosing `graythresh` works well when the image we want to threshold is bimodal. To better understand the meaning of this word, we should discuss histograms.

Calculating and displaying histograms with imhist

The histogram of an image is usually depicted as a bar graph and conveys information about the distribution of the pixel intensities in a predefined number of bins (ranges of intensities), spanning from the minimum to the maximum intensity. The information depicted in a histogram can provide a rough idea about how bright, or dark an image is. It can also give a first estimation of the optimal threshold for segmenting the pixels of an image into two or more distinct classes based on their intensities.

To calculate the histogram of an image, we may use the inherent MATLAB function `imhist`. This function outputs a one-dimensional matrix containing the distribution of the pixels in the input image in a set of bins (the default value for grayscale images is 256). The user can also give an extra input for different number of bins to be used. Let's see how this works for our previous example:

```
>> img = imread('my_image.bmp');
>> subplot (1,3,1),imshow(img),title('Original Image')
```

```
>> subplot (1,3,2),imhist(img),title('Histogram for 256 bins')
>> subplot (1,3,3),imhist(img,16),title('Histogram for 16 bins')
```

These previous commands yield to the following result:

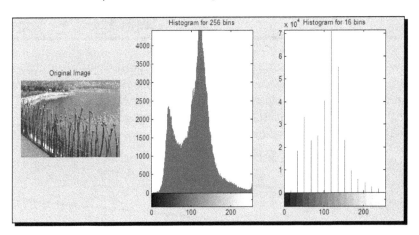

This result gives us some insight of why the automatic threshold was estimated to be
99 in the previous step, as this threshold lies between two large distributions centered
approximately at 44 and 125. We can also see what the result of the histogram for a reduced
number of bins looks like, with a higher number of pixels in the y axis, since the numbers
of 16 different bins have been summed into one.

The histogram is useful for a variety of reasons. Apart from being a useful tool for automatic
threshold selection, it can also be applied for the enhancement of images, which is the next
topic in line.

Histogram equalization for contrast enhancement

A very common method of enhancing the contrast of an image is by transforming its pixel
values so that its new histogram matches a predefined distribution. MATLAB offers a function
for this process called as histeq. The function can also be called with one input, in which
case it uses the default target histogram. Let's see what this function does, by writing the
following script:

```
img = imread('my_image.bmp');
img_eq = histeq(img);
subplot(2,2,1),imshow(img),title('Original Image');
subplot(2,2,2),imshow(img_eq),title('Equalized Image');
subplot(2,2,3),imhist(img,64),title('Original Image Histogram');
subplot(2,2,4),imhist(img_eq,64),title('Equalized Image
  Histogram');
```

Saving this script as `HistogramEqualization.m` and typing it in the command line, leads to the following result:

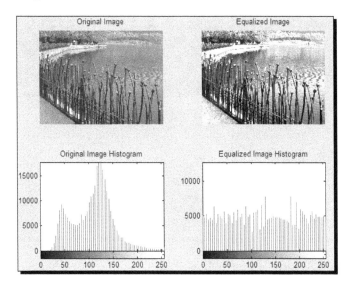

As we can see, the contrast of the image is enhanced and the values are almost evenly spread throughout the range of possible values (0 to 255). This process usually has the effect of enhancing useful details, but also at the same time enhancing unwanted noise. Therefore, this approach should be used cautiously.

Contrasting enhancement using imadjust

A more gentle method for contrast enhancement is using `imadjust`. In its default form, this function maps pixel values in the original image to new, altered values while ensuring that only a small percentage (1 percent) of the values are saturated at low and high intensities of the original image. This results in a smoother transformation that mostly enhances useful details. We can see the result of applying this method if we add some more lines to our previous script:

```
img = imread('my_image.bmp');
img_eq = histeq(img);
img_adj = imadjust(img);
subplot(2,3,1),imshow(img),title('Original Image');
subplot(2,3,2),imshow(img_eq),title('Equalized Image');
subplot(2,3,3),imshow(img_adj),title('Adjusted Intensity Image');
subplot(2,3,4),imhist(img,64),title('Original Image Histogram');
subplot(2,3,5),imhist(img_eq,64),title('Equalized Image Histogram');
subplot(2,3,6),imhist(img_adj,64),title('Adjusted Image Histogram');
```

If we save this script as `HisteqVsImadjust.m` and execute it, we get the following screenshot:

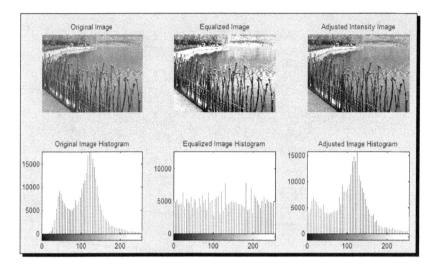

It is obvious just by looking at the histograms, that `imadjust` stretches the histogram of the image, while `histeq` spreads it almost evenly. This is why the result of `imadjust` looks more natural.

In case we want more control over the final result, we can either tweak the methods used by defining more inputs that adjust the settings. For instance, we can provide a target histogram in `histeq` or a set of lower and higher limits for values that we want to clip in `imadjust`. You can play with these settings by using **Help** to see how the two functions can be used with extra inputs and then experiment with different input values.

Contrasting enhancement using imcontrast

A tool included in the Image Processing Toolbox, which offers an extra helping hand at histogram enhancement is `imcontrast`. It can be invoked by displaying an image and then calling the `imcontrast` function with input `gcf` (get current figure):

```
>> imshow(img)
>> imcontrast(gcf)
```

This tool gives an interactive way to the user to adjust the histogram of the image by defining a maximum and a minimum value, as well as a center for the histogram of the transformed image. You can do this either by inputting the numerical values of these settings, or by dragging the three red bars on the histogram. No actions are actually performed on the original image until the button **Adjust Data** is clicked. The tool also gives you the option to clip the outliers of images (pixels with extreme values). In the default setting of **2%**, the 1 percent of minimum values and the 1 percent of maximum values are removed.

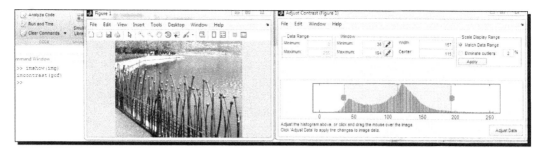

The methods described so far are quite useful for image enhancement. However, they all suffer from the same shortcoming; they are global methods, operating on the entire image. This has the obvious disadvantage of suboptimal enhancement to images with spatially variant histograms. For such cases, we need the help of locally adaptive histogram enhancement methods.

The `imcontrast` tool can also be used for interactive demonstration of thresholding results. You can see how it works if you reduce the red area of the histogram to include just one value and then drag it left or right to dynamically observe the results of thresholding using various thresholds.

Adaptive histogram equalization using adapthisteq

The advantage of `adapthisteq` is that it splits the image into small rectangular areas called tiles, and enhances the contrast of these areas by adjusting their local histograms. This method is also known as **contrast limited adaptive histogram equalization (CLAHE)** (*Zuiderveld, Karel. Contrast Limited Adaptive Histogram Equalization. Graphic Gems IV. San Diego: Academic Press Professional, 474-485, 1994*). Like almost every other MATLAB function, `adapthisteq` can be used with only one input (the image), with all other parameters set to default values. Such a usage is shown in the following script, in contrast to the `histeq` result:

```
img = imread('my_image.bmp');
img_eq = histeq(img);
img_clahe = adapthisteq(img)
subplot(2,3,1),imshow(img),title('Original Image'');
subplot(2,3,2),imshow(img_eq),title('Equalized Image');
subplot(2,3,3),imshow(img_clahe),title('CLAHE Image');
subplot(2,3,4),imhist(img,64),title('Original Image Histogram');
subplot(2,3,5),imhist(img_eq,64),title('Equalized Image
  Histogram');
subplot(2,3,6),imhist(img_clahe,64),title('CLAHE Image Histogram');
```

Saving this script as `HisteqVsClahe.m` and running it, leads to the following result:

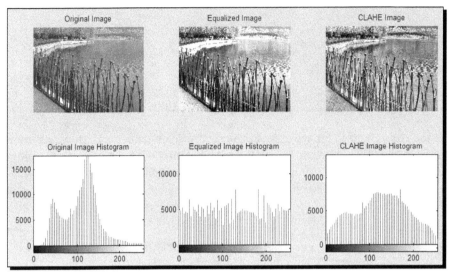

As we can see, the CLAHE method leads to a less spread result, which has an apparent positive effect especially on very bright or very dark areas. An even lesser spread histogram result can be acquired if we do not use the default, uniform, or distribution setting. Let's see what the other choices (`rayleigh` and `exponential`) look like, by running the following script (`ClaheDistributions.m`):

```
img = imread('my_image.bmp');
img_u = adapthisteq(img);
img_r = adapthisteq(img,'Distribution','rayleigh');
img_e = adapthisteq(img,'Distribution','exponential');
subplot(2,3,1),imshow(img_u),title('Uniform distribution');
subplot(2,3,2),imshow(img_r),title('Rayleigh distribution');
subplot(2,3,3),imshow(img_e),title('Exponential distribution');
subplot(2,3,4),imhist(img_u,64),title('Uniform Histogram');
subplot(2,3,5),imhist(img_r,64),title('Rayleigh Histogram');
subplot(2,3,6),imhist(img_e,64),title('ExponentialHistogram');
```

The resulting images show that the **Uniform** and **Exponential** histograms are similar, while the **Rayleigh distribution** leads to a less spread result:

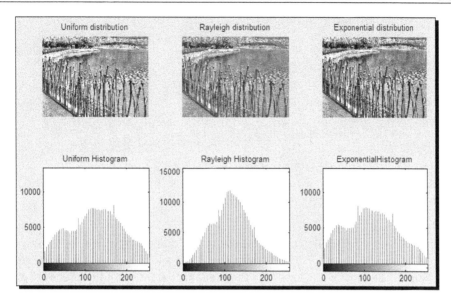

Until now, we have used functions included in MATLAB toolboxes in conjunction with basic programming techniques in order to accomplish image enhancement. Our work was facilitated by the usage of scripts; however these tools are not fully practical for more demanding tasks. Our life will become a lot easier if we begin to master the art of making custom-made functions.

Custom functions for complex tasks

A function can be thought of as a black box, which produces output results when fed with proper inputs. We have already used several ready-made functions so far, but we haven't made any functions of our own. The biggest advantage of making our own functions is that we can reuse them with different inputs to produce different results, as opposed to scripts where inputs must usually be changed by altering and resaving the source code.

To begin, let's attempt to mix all the aforementioned enhancement methods in a single function that will accept the choice of method from the input. More specifically, we will make a function that will take two inputs; an image and a number. The image will be enhanced using the method denoted by the number. After opening the Editor, we type in the following code:

```
function [output] = ContrastEnhancement(input,method)

% Function that performs image contrast enhancement with methods
% incorporated in MATLAB toolboxes
% Inputs:
%           input - Input image
```

```
%               method - Enhancement method (1: histeq, 2: imadjust,
%                                            3: adapthisteq)
% Output:
%               output - Output image (with enhanced contrast)

switch method
case 1
output = histeq(input);
case 2
output = imadjust(input);
case 3
output = adapthisteq(input);
end
```

When we are done, we can save the function using the name that is already chosen (ContrastEnhancement.m). We don't need to explain a lot here, since the basic idea is rather simple. The function includes the three enhancement methods already explained earlier. To choose which one to use on the input image, the method input must be set to 1 if we want to use histeq, 2 if we want to use imadjust, and 3 if we want to use adapthisteq. The selection is made using the switch case structure, which is a very widely used method in programming. The switch command defines which variable will be checked and the case commands check for all acceptable values and connects them to their respective tasks. To see if our function actually works, let's use it on another version of the holiday picture we used in the previous chapter:

```
>> img = imread('holiday_image2.bmp');
>> subplot(2,2,1),imshow(img),title('Original Image');
>> subplot(2,2,2),imshow(ContrastEnhancement(img,1)),title('Histeq
   result');
>> subplot(2,2,3),imshow(ContrastEnhancement(img,2)),title('Imadjust
   result');
>> subplot(2,2,4),imshow(ContrastEnhancement(img,3)),title
   ('Adapthisteq result');
```

The result reveals the very important role that adaptive histogram equalization can play in enhancing images with varying illumination.

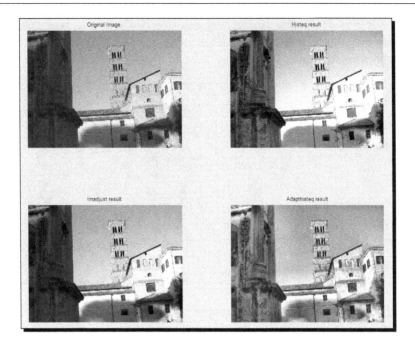

While both `histeq` and `adapthisteq` have managed to lighten the left part of the image, the latter has not only achieved a better result at it, but also has avoided saturating smooth areas like `histeq`. In order to understand this a little better, let's use `imtool` to zoom in the areas with bigger differences.

Time for action – using imtool to pinpoint differences

Now, it is time to combine the function written in the previous section with what you learned about `imtool` in the previous chapter, in order to pinpoint the areas of the image where `adapthisteq` provides superior results. The following steps will help you combine the functions:

1. First, let's load the image we will be using:
   ```
   >> img = imread('holiday_image2.bmp');
   ```

2. Then you should enhance the image using the two versions of histogram equalization:
   ```
   >> img_he = ContrastEnhancement(img,1);
   >> img_ahe = ContrastEnhancement(img,3);
   ```

3. Now, let's use `imtool` for the first and second result:
   ```
   >> imtool(img_he)
   >> imtool(img_ahe)
   ```

First, we zoom in using the magnifying glass icon with the plus sign. Once selected, we use the mouse to select the parts in the two images where `adapthisteq` enhances details more (we can enter the same zoom factor):

4.   Then, we zoom out and zoom in on again the left area of the image so that we pinpoint the shadowed areas' enhancement:

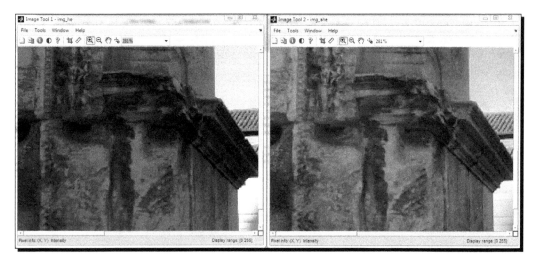

What just happened?

This time we combined knowledge acquired in this chapter, with what we learned in the previous one. First, we followed the steps shown earlier to perform two different kinds of enhancement on our image. Then, we used `imtool` to zoom into the areas where the differences between the two chosen methods are more apparent. The results strengthens our previous view, which was the CLAHE method preferable to all other methods presented in this chapter, as it provides better results both in very bright and very dark areas.

Have a go hero – writing a function to enhance an image area

Now it's time we dive into deeper waters. Let's say you want to create a function that enhances a certain area of the image, using any of the methods above. This task will need you to combine several pieces of knowledge acquired so far and also use some settings we haven't used so far.

To get you started, here is the rationale you have to follow: first, you have to find a way to cut a specific part of the image that you want to enhance. Then, you will use one of the enhancement methods on the cropped area, and finally you will have to reattach the area in its original position.

In the beginning of the function, you should crop a rectangle area of the input image while knowing the coordinates of the rectangle. Using the `help imcrop` command, you can find the following way to call the function:

```
[I2 RECT] = imcrop(...) returns the cropping rectangle in addition to
   the cropped image.
```

This description suggests that you can use `imcrop` with two outputs; the cropped image `I2` and the cropped rectangle coordinates in `RECT`. This way, you can then use matrix `RECT` to replace the selected rectangular area of the original image with the enhanced cropped image.

Let's say that your function will be named `CroppedContrastEnhancement.m`. We'll start you off with its definition, and input/output description, and you can do the rest:

```
function [output] = CroppedContrastEnhancement(input,method)

% Function that performs area-based image contrast enhancement with
% methodsincorporated in MATLAB toolboxes
% Inputs:
%          input - Input image
%          method - Enhancement method (1: histeq, 2: imadjust,
%                                       3: adapthisteq)
% Output:
%          output - Output image (with enhanced contrast)
```

To see if your function works, you could run it for our holiday image and select an area to perform histogram equalization on:

```
>> img = imread('holiday_image2.bmp');
>> img2=CroppedContrastEnhancement(img,1);
```

Then, you have to define the area you want to enhance:

Having selected the area you should be able to double-click on it to generate the result. The resulting image will be as follows:

```
>> imshow(img2);
```

Restoring old photographs

Now, we will start a process which will be continued in later chapters of this book. We will try to practice what we learned in an effort to restore, or at least improve, the appearance of old pictures.

Time for action – restoring your ancestors' photographs

First off, let me introduce you to my great-grandmother, whose picture will be used for restoration tasks. Of course, you can use your own ancestors' photographs. The following steps will help you restore your old photographs:

1. Read and show the image in the usual manner, checking also its size:

    ```
    >> ggm = imread('grandma.bmp');
    >> imshow(ggm)
    >> size(ggm)
    ```

2. Unfortunately, this image has two disadvantages; it is very large (2048 x 1536) and also it is in color (last dimension in size is equal to 3). So, let's try to make our lives a little easier for the time being, by resizing the image and transforming it to grayscale. Both steps can be done in the same command:

    ```
    >> ggm_gray = rgb2gray(imresize(ggm,0.25));
    ```

3. Now that we have a grayscale image sized 512 x 384, we can save it as `graygrandma.bmp` (just the first two inputs will suffice for `imwrite`):

```
>> imwrite(ggm_gray,'graygrandma.bmp');
```

An obvious flaw of this picture is the flash glare caused by our camera. This glow will lead to suboptimal results by our contrast enhancement methods. Till now, we haven't learned a way to remove such noise, however the thresholding techniques presented in this chapter can be used to isolate the flash. You could try verifying this on your own as a practice exercise.

4. Just so we are ready to take advantage of this result in the following chapters, we will try to perform such an isolation. It is obvious that the image brightness in the glowing area caused by our flash has very high values. Let's try to segment this area using a high brightness threshold (for example, `t=220`). This process can be performed using the following command lines:

```
>> subplot(1,2,1),imshow(ggm_gray),title(''Original image'');
>> subplot(1,2,2),imshow(ggm_gray>220),title(''Thresholded
   image using t=220'');
```

The resulting image will be:

Obviously, the image area highlighted by the segmentation process is approximately equal to the glow produced by the flash. This result will prove useful in later chapters.

5. For the time being, we should crop the image part above the flash and play with the contrast enhancement methods learned so far, to see which result we like more:

```
>> ggm_cr = imcrop(ggm_gray);
>> subplot(2,2,1)
>> imshow(ggm_cr)
>> title('Original Image')
>> subplot(2,2,2)
>> imshow(ContrastEnhancement(ggm_cr,1))
>> title('Histeq result')
```

```
>> subplot(2,2,3)
>> imshow(ContrastEnhancement(ggm_cr,2))
>> title('Imadjust result')
>> subplot(2,2,4)
>> imshow(ContrastEnhancement(ggm_cr,3))
>> title('Adapthisteq result')
```

For the time being, we will have to settle with this artistic contrast enhancement. Of course, which result is more pleasing to the eye is a rather subjective matter, but probably most people would agree that the original image is a little flat, while the one produced by imadjust looks a little more realistic, and the one produced by adapthisteq looks more artistic. The image produced using histeq has a rather disturbing high contrast and should be fine-tuned.

What just happened?

In this exercise, we have mixed some of the steps described both in this and the previous chapter in order to begin restoring an old picture, which has faded over time and been distorted by the flash of our camera. The restoration of such an image is a rather complex task, which will span in multiple chapters, but the first steps towards its completion were covered here. The image was transformed to grayscale and resized and then it was thresholded to pinpoint the area distorted by the flash glare. This area will be processed in the following chapters. Finally, the image was cropped to exclude the glare and its contrast was enhanced using the function we wrote in previous sections.

Pop quiz – contrasting enhancement methods

Q1. Which of the following facts are true?

1. MATLAB will produce an error if you have matrices growing inside a loop.

2. The histogram equalization method tends to result in evenly distributed histograms.

3. The `Imadjust` function allows a specific percentage of pixel values to be saturated at low and high intensities.

4. `Adapthisteq` performs global histogram equalization.

5. Using `for loops` is the fastest way to threshold an image in MATLAB.

6. Using `im2bw` to perform thresholding suggests that the threshold is set in the range 0 to 1.

7. An automated way to define the brightness threshold value for a grayscale image is by using `graythresh`.

Summary

This chapter included several useful techniques to manipulate the values of grayscale image pixels. At the same time, it provided a first, hopefully gentle, introduction to writing and running your own scripts and functions in MATLAB. More specifically, you have been taught:

◆ How to change pixel values in a rectangular area using `for loops`, or indexing

◆ How to write and execute a script that alters the brightness in specified rectangular areas of an image

◆ How to threshold an image using `for loops`

◆ How to threshold an image using indexing

◆ How to threshold an image using `im2bw`

◆ How to perform thresholding using an automatically derived threshold

◆ How to calculate and display the histogram of a grayscale image

◆ How to perform histogram equalization using `histeq`

◆ How to perform contrast enhancement using `imadjust`

◆ How to perform contrast enhancement using `imcontrast`

- How to perform adaptive histogram equalization using `adapthisteq`
- How to write functions that use all the methods described in this chapter on practical examples

The next chapter will introduce you to morphological operations and their importance in image processing. Some methods already presented will be combined with the morphological operations to enhance images, or segment useful areas. Once finishing it, you will be able to perform extremely useful tasks that are applied both in computational photography and in machine vision applications.

3
Morphological Operations and Object Analysis

In the previous chapters, you learned various image processing techniques related to image manipulation. In some of them, we concentrated our processing on specific regions of the images, predefined by the user. However, many processes that involve visual media enhancement need to focus on automatically specified regions of interest. In this chapter, we will present some basic techniques for selecting the regions of interest, based on image morphology. We will also revisit the manual selection of regions, presenting some more flexible tools. Then, you will be demonstrated some basic object analysis techniques such as edge, corner, and circle detection. Several examples will help you better understand how morphological operations combined with object analysis methods can help in targeting our processing on specific areas of an image.

In this chapter, we shall:

- ◆ Learn about binary images and how they are used for masking
- ◆ Learn about morphological operations and their importance
- ◆ Learn how to use MATLAB tools for **Region Of Interest (ROI)** selection
- ◆ Learn how to detect edges, corners, and circles in an image

So, let's start!

The importance of binary images

To understand the notion of morphological operations, we will have to revisit the thresholding techniques presented in the previous chapter. We have already mentioned that thresholding an image leads to binary images, which are defined by their two possible pixel values; 0 (for black) and 1 (for white). The way to convert a grayscale image to binary is through thresholding; that is, setting the pixels above a certain value to 1 and the rest to 0. Let's now explain the basic reasons for binarizing an image. The purpose of image binarization can be split into two levels. At a first level, it is used to pinpoint the pixels of an image that interest us (usually called regions of interest or simply, ROIs), thus giving us a quick and easy overview of the image content. The binary images derived, are often called **masks**. At a second level, it can be used for processing only the selected ROIs (with pixel values equal to 1) defined by the mask, leaving the rest of the image unaffected. Let's see the difference using, an example that covers both the functionalities.

Time for action – understanding the value of thresholding

In this example, we will try to separate the two useful aspects of image binarization, so that we can then use them appropriately. The first thing we will do is to locate a faulty ROI of an image and then we will try to cover it using what we have already learned. For this example, we will be again using my great-grandmother's photograph. So, let's start:

1. First, we need to load the grayscale image we have created in the previous chapter, by using `imread`:

    ```
    >> img = imread('graygrandma.BMP');
    ```

2. The second step is to perform thresholding, as we have already done in the previous chapter (using the same threshold, which was `220`):

    ```
    >> img_bin = (img> 220);   % Image img_bin is now binary
    ```

3. Now, let's perform some rough patching of the image in the specific ROI that has pixels with values over `220`. A way to accomplish this is to change these values to a grayer shade, for example, `100`:

    ```
    >> img_patched = img;
    >> img_patched(img_bin) = 100;
    ```

4. At this point, we have three images in our **Workspace**. The original one (`img`), the binarized one (`img_bin`) and the patched one (`img_patched`). Let's display them side-by-side to get a better understanding of what happened:

    ```
    >> subplot(1,3,1),imshow(img),title('Original Image')
    >> subplot(1,3,2),imshow(img_bin),title('Binarized Image')
    >> subplot(1,3,3),imshow(img_patched),title('Patched Image')
    ```

The resulting images will be as follows:

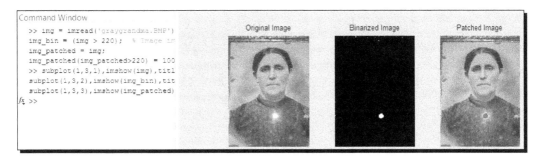

What just happened?

As explained earlier, this example pinpoints the usage of thresholded images called masks to alter the specific parts of the image. The first step, as always, is to load an image into MATLAB, using the `imread` function. We chose to use this image, because of the apparent deficiency caused by the flash of our camera. The ultimate goal is to patch up this deficiency and produce a smoother result.

The second step is to threshold the image, using a threshold value that isolates the areas with high brightness values. This was done using the threshold value as 220, as we did in the previous chapter. Typing `img_bin = (img> 220)` generates a binary image (mask) with pixels equal to 1 in the positions where the original image pixels were higher than 220. All other pixels will be set to 0.

The third step performs the actual masking process. First, we create a duplicate of our original image, and name it as `img_patched`. Then, we type in `img_patched(img_bin) = 100` to replace all pixels that are equal to 1 in our mask with the value 100 in the original image. This command actually tells MATLAB to find the positions of all pixels in the mask equal to 1 and use them to set the respective pixels of the original image to 100. This could be accomplished in many alternative ways, but this is the one that depicts the actual use of a mask, taking advantage of its size being identical to the size of the original image (or else the replacement command would result in an error message).

Our fourth step is used for verification purposes, as it shows the original image, the binary mask, and the masked image side-by-side. This way, it is easier to understand the entire masking process.

 An alternative and more compact way to get the same masking result in the preceding example, would be using `img_patched(img > 220) = 100`. This would combine the second and third step into one, but wouldn't save the mask in a new matrix.

The preceding example describes a very useful technique in its simplest form. This simple procedure has two serious flaws; one in the mask definition and one in the image masking process.

The flaw in the mask definition is the difficulty in pinpointing the specific ROI of our choice, using just the pixel values. Rarely can we isolate the region we need, by setting a specific threshold. Even in the example we saw (which is almost ideal for this simple technique), the mask derived from thresholding includes some pixels equal to 1 in other areas (for example, the frame of the picture). Also, the image masking result reveals that the area selected is a little smaller than it should be.

The flaw in the masking process is that the result is roughly patched up and just covers the area with brightness values that are closer to what would be expected. However, the ideal result would replace the bright area with something more complex than a patch of equal brightness values. This patch could be a part of an image that more closely resembles what has been destroyed by the flash.

In the rest of the chapter, we will be focusing on ways to refine the mask selection process, so that the resulting mask is more suitable to our needs. This will be accomplished using various morphological operations that will tweak our mask.

Enlarging and shrinking a region of interest

A very common technique for refining a region of interest derived using thresholding is either enlarging or shrinking it to fit our target size. This can be accomplished by the morphological operations called **dilation** and **erosion**, respectively. These operations can be implemented in MATLAB using their respective functions, intuitively named `imdilate` and `imerode`.

Explaining and analyzing the mathematical properties of dilation and erosion lie beyond the scope of this book. We will instead explain their significance using practical examples that demonstrate their importance for image processing. The basic idea that you have to understand before we start, is that the two operations can be used for enlarging or shrinking an ROI (denoted by the instances of 1 in the image) using a **structuring element**. Structuring elements can be small binary images generated by the user either arbitrarily (placing the instances of 1 and 0 in a small image), or by using the `strel` function. The choice of a structuring element should be made following two simple rules:

- The larger the structuring element, the larger the enlarging/shrinking factor
- Using a structuring element more similar to the shape of the ROI will typically give you a better result

Let's dive right in, to understand the physical meaning of all these concepts in practice.

Time for action – using dilation and erosion to refine ROIs

Since photographs from holidays are a usual target for image enhancement applications, we'll use one of these for our example, showing three large rocks in the sea. The goal is to come up with a mask that includes just them. Let's start with our usual steps:

1. As always, we'll need to load our image into MATLAB, only now we will also have to convert it to grayscale:

   ```
   >> img = imread('3Rocks.jpg');
   >> img = rgb2gray(img);
   ```

2. Now that our image is loaded and transformed to grayscale, let's show it to get a better idea of our goal:

   ```
   >> imshow(img);
   ```

3. Let's now have a go at thresholding the image. Let's set our threshold to 30, since the rocks are dark. This time, the threshold denotes the maximum value kept, meaning we will ask MATLAB to make a mask containing only the pixels with values below 30, that is, set the pixels of the image with values below 30 equal to 1 (white), and the rest to 0 (black):

```
>> img_bin = img < 30;
>> figure,imshow(img_bin)
```

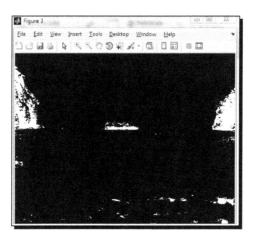

4. We can see that we have two problems; one is the inclusion of other dark objects in the scene (such as people's heads) and the other is the suboptimal selection of the rocks. First, let's take advantage of the fact that most of the unwanted areas lie at the bottom of the image. Using the data cursor, ⭒, we can see that row 705 can be used as a lower limit for the mask. So, we can set all pixels under that row to 0:

```
>> img_bin(706:end,:) = 0;
>> imshow(img_bin);
```

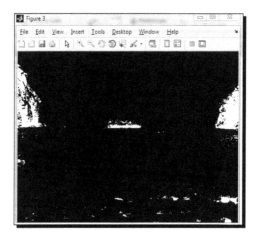

5. Now, we must do something to eliminate some sparse white dots that shouldn't be included in the mask. A possible solution is to perform binary erosion, using a small rectangular element. Let's use the second option, applying a 2x2 structuring element with all pixels set to 1:

```
>> img_bin_clean = imerode(img_bin,ones(2));
```

6. Finally, we will perform dilation with a 70x70 structuring element, with all pixels set to 1 and show the final mask:

```
>> mask = imdilate(img_bin_clean, ones(70));
>> figure,
>> subplot(1,2,1)
>> imshow(img_bin_clean);title('Image after erosion');
>> subplot(1,2,2),imshow(mask);title('Image after dilation');
```

7. Now, let's try to erase the rocks. The result will not be optimal, but it will be interesting for comprehending what masking is. We will be using the color of the sky, so we should use the data cursor on the sky to get some sample values of the brightness. A better idea is to use our `imtool`, to observe entire neighborhoods. Let's do that:

```
>> imtool(img);
```

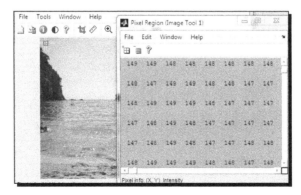

8. We observe that a good choice could be `147`, since it is a value repeated a lot near the left rock.

9. Having decided the value we want under our mask, let's try our disappearing act:

```
>> img_proc = img;
>> img_proc(mask) = 147;
>> subplot(1,2,1),imshow(img),title('Original image')
>> subplot(1,2,2),imshow(img_proc),title('Processed image')
```

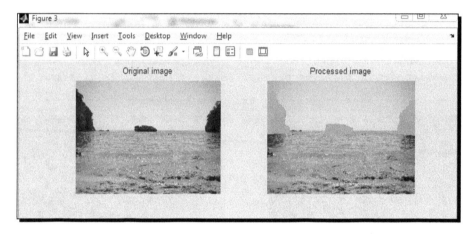

What just happened?

This example covered both dilation and erosion, combining them with techniques learned earlier. We used a user-defined threshold to acquire a first mask for our image (after we converted it from color to grayscale). Then, we cleaned the mask from unwanted spots taking advantage of their distinct location and wrapped up the cleaning process using an erosion step to eliminate small white spots. To complete the ROIs covering the three rocks, we then performed image dilation with a rectangular structuring element sized 70x70 pixels, all equal to 1. The structuring elements were created using MATLAB's `ones` function, which returns a matrix with all elements equal to 1. When the function is called with only one input, `N`, the output is a square matrix with size NxN pixels. To better understand this, let's see the result of a 3x3 matrix generated this way:

```
>> ones(3)
```

The output of the previous command is as follows:

```
ans =
     1     1     1
     1     1     1
     1     1     1
```

After creating our mask, we applied a patching-up process like the one described in the previous section. This time, our goal was to erase the rocks from the picture, replacing their pixels' values with one that is descriptive of the sky. Of course, using just one brightness value for such big areas, ends up with a flat result, which is less subtle than we would like. However, the main goal of erasing the rocks was achieved to a good extent.

> The use of `imerode` to eliminate small objects from our mask is not always a good idea, since it affects all binary objects in the image. For this example, we used it in conjunction with `imdilate`. A better choice for such tasks would be to use the `bwareaopen` function, which eliminates small objects of a predefined size from the image. In the preceding example, to eliminate objects smaller than 6 pixels, we would replace the step `img_bin_clean = imerode(img_bin, ones(2));` with `img_bin_clean = bwareaopen(img_bin, 6);`.

Choosing a structuring element

We mentioned earlier the usage of structuring elements and the two rules we must follow when choosing them. However, in our example of dilation and erosion, we used a rather simple rectangular structuring element, consisting of instances of 1. Is there a better choice? The answer is yes. The objects we want to mask are not rectangular, so the best choice is definitely not a rectangular structuring element. However, we can observe that the three rocks are not similar. The two rocks at the sides could be thought of as similar, but they have opposite orientations (that is, they look like they are mirrored). The shape of the small rock in the middle does not resemble the others. All these facts lead us to the conclusion that more than one structuring element should be used. However, we fall right into the next problem; how will we use different structuring elements for different areas? For this, we will recollect a technique we used in the previous chapter.

But first thing first; we should start with choosing the ideal structuring element for each rock. As you may already have understood from the results of the previous example, the sides of the rocks that are attached to the left and right image borders remain almost untouched. Their only alteration after `imdilate`. is being expanded at the top and bottom. The middle rock has expanded in all directions after dilation.

To make this more obvious, let's use a basic technique in binary image processing, which is image subtraction. If we subtract two binary images and observe the result, we will see which pixels have a different value in the two images. In our example, we will see which pixels were set to 1 after the dilation process, if we subtract (using function `imsubtract`) the mask before the dilation from the final mask and show the pixels that are positive:

```
>> Z = mask - img_bin; >> figure,imshow(Z)
>> subplot(1,3,1),imshow(img_bin),title('Mask before dilation')
>> subplot(1,3,2),imshow(mask),title('Mask after dilation')
>> subplot(1,3,3),imshow(Z),title('Pixels set to 1 after dilation')
```

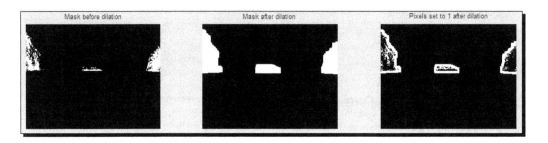

To eliminate unwanted dilation in a specific direction, we should be more careful about the structuring element we will use. The goal is to produce a structuring element that only expands our ROI in the desired directions. To achieve this, the structuring element should have instances of 1 in the pixels facing in the desired directions and instances of 0 in the rest of the pixels. One way to achieve this is by manually initializing the pixels of a matrix to fit our needs. Another way to achieve it is using a structuring element provided by MATLAB's `strel` function as a starting point and alter it to fit our needs.

Using strel to generate structuring elements

The ready-made `strel` function, provided by the **Image Toolbox** of MATLAB, offers various types of structuring elements. The supported shapes that can be used in the problem we examine, are `square`, `rectangle`, `disk`, `octagon`, `diamond`, `line` and `arbitrary`. More information can be obtained by typing `help strel` in the command line. For the time being, we shall just see some of them, by typing in the following lines:

```
>> se1 = strel('square',10); % 10x10 square
>> se2 = strel('rectangle',[12,8]); % 12x8 rectangle
>> se3 = strel('line',10,45); % line, length 10, angle 45 degrees
>> se4 = strel('disk',10); % disk, radius 10
>> se5 = strel('octagon',12);  % octagon, size 12 (must be multiple
  of 3)
>> se6 = strel('diamond',10); % diamond, size 10
>> subplot(2,3,1),imshow(getnhood(se1)),title('Square')
```

```
>> subplot(2,3,2),imshow(getnhood(se2)),title('Rectangle')
>> subplot(2,3,3),imshow(getnhood(se3)),title('Line')
>> subplot(2,3,4),imshow(getnhood(se4)),title('Disk')
>> subplot(2,3,5),imshow(getnhood(se5)),title('Octagon')
>> subplot(2,3,6),imshow(getnhood(se6)),title('Diamond')
```

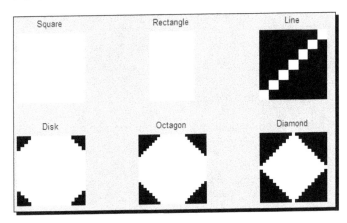

As you may have noticed in the **Workspace** window, the structuring elements are not saved as matrices, but as a special type, called **strel**. This is why in order for us to transform them into matrices, we use the `getnhood` function, which allows for them to be processed and displayed in the ways presented so far.

Altering structuring elements from strel to suit our needs

Now, let's try to solve our first problem, which was how to create different structuring elements for each rock, using the ones generated by `strel`. Observing the rocks could lead to a useful conclusion, the two side rocks can be modeled as quarters of a disk and the middle rock could be modeled as half a disk. Let's see if our assumption works well for the middle rock, in the following example.

Time for action – ROI refinement using strel

In this example, we shall see how to use the disk structuring element from `strel`, to have a better masking result for the middle rock of our holiday picture. To focus on our task, we will first crop the area we are mostly interested in. Assuming we have cleared our workspace using `clear all` (MATLAB's command to clear all the variables), we follow these steps:

1. Read our colored image, convert it to grayscale, and crop the area containing the middle rock:

```
>> img = imread('3rocks.jpg');
>> rock = imcrop(rgb2gray(img));
```

2. Threshold the cropped image using the same threshold as before (30) and show the result side-by-side with the original:

```
>> mask1 = rock < 30;
>> subplot(1,2,1),imshow(rock),title('Original image')
>> subplot(1,2,2),imshow(mask1),title('Initial mask')
```

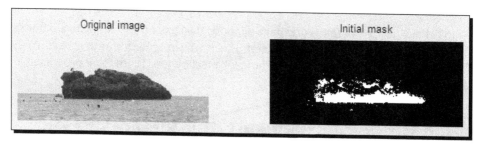

3. Perform image cleaning, using the `imerode` function:

```
>> mask2 = imerode(mask1,ones(2));
```

4. Make the structuring element for this rock, which will be the top half part of a disk. We will use a disk of radius 26 (you can experiment with other values):

```
>> se = strel('disk',26);   % Make a disk with a radius of 26px
>> se_mat = getnhood(se);   % Convert structuring element to
   matrix
>> se_mat(27:end,:) = 0;    % Make the bottom half equal to zero
```

5. Perform dilation with the processed structuring element:

```
>> mask3 = imdilate(mask2,se_mat);
```

6. Erase the rock from the original image using `mask3`:

```
>> no_rock = rock;
>> no_rock(mask3) = 200;   % Use brightness value 200
```

7. Demonstrate the results:

```
>> subplot(2,2,1),imshow(rock),title('Original image')
>> subplot(2,2,2),imshow(no_rock),title('Masked image')
>> subplot(2,2,3),imshow(mask2),title('Mask before dilation')
>> subplot(2,2,4),imshow(imsubtract(mask3,mask2)),
   title('mask3-mask2')
```

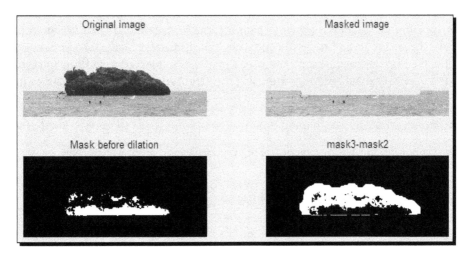

What just happened?

In the example we just did, we finished tweaking our ROI selection and masking example. After cropping our image to include only one rock, we followed the same procedure as before to get to our first mask. Then, in the most important steps of this example (highlighted code in step 4) we chose the `disk` structuring element from MATLAB, with a radius of `26` pixels, converted it to matrix form and set its bottom half to 0. Finally, we applied dilation using the structuring element we created, used the generated mask to alter the brightness of the pixels under it in the original image to 200, and displayed our results.

So, by now, you should be starting to get a good idea of how to tweak binary masks using dilation and erosion, and how these two operations actually affect your images. In a nutshell, binary masks can be used to focus your pixel processing tasks on specific areas of the image; dilation and erosion are tools used to expand or shrink your areas of interest respectively. A better structuring element selection for these operations leads to a better result.

Have a go hero – write a function to for local dilation/erosion

In the previous chapter, we saw how to write a function that performs enhancement of a rectangular area specified by the user. Can you do the same for dilation and erosion? The function should get three inputs; the original binary image, the structuring element and the selection of operation (one for erosion and two for dilation).

Well, the implementation shouldn't seem so hard now. We will more or less base our function on what we did in the previous chapter. The first step is to let the user crop the part of the image to be processed and save its coordinates. Then, we should switch to the specified operation based on the user's input. The selected operation will then be performed on the original binary image using the structuring element provided as input. The final step is to place the cropped region back on the image and return the output.

The function you should write, named `CroppedDilationErosion.m`, is defined as follows:

```
function [output] = CroppedDilationErosion(input,se,method)

% Function that performs area-based dilation or erosion with =
% a user-defined structuring element.
% Inputs:
%           input  -  Input image
%           se  -     Structuring element
%           method - Morphology operation (1: dilation, 2: erosion)
% Output:
%           output - Output image (dilated or eroded)
```

To check if your function works as expected, you can use the mask from the previous example:

```
>> img = imread('3rocks.jpg');
>> rock = rgb2gray(img);
>> mask = rock < 30;
>> mask2 = CroppedDilationErosion(mask,ones(10),2); % Erode mask
>> mask3 = CroppedDilationErosion(mask,ones(10),1); % Dilate mask
```

By selecting the following ROI in both operations:

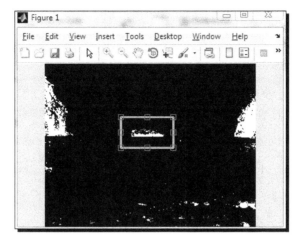

The results would be:

```
>> subplot(1,3,1),imshow(mask),title('Original mask')
>> subplot(1,3,2),imshow(mask2),title('Mask after erosion')
>> subplot(1,3,3),imshow(mask3),title('Mask after dilation')
```

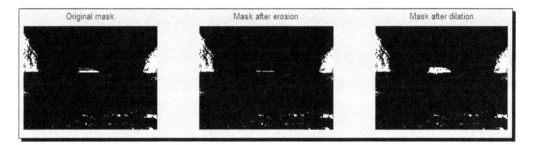

We can see that, by selecting an ROI including only the middle rock, the erosion result almost makes it disappear and the dilation result makes it grow. All the other parts of the image remain unaffected.

 You may be surprised to learn that dilation and erosion are not limited to binary images, but can also work on grayscale images generating interesting results. To have a taste, try to call the function we just made using a grayscale input instead of a binary one.

More morphological operations

Until now, we have focused extensively on the erosion and dilation operations. It would be logical for you to start thinking whether is this all that is there? Aren't there any more morphological operations? The answer is; there are plenty, but you will not be using them half as much as the two aforementioned operations, at least for everyday tasks. Also, many of the other morphological operations are based on combinations of dilation and erosion. An analytical list of morphological operations supported by MATLAB can be found at http://www.mathworks.com/help/images/morphological-filtering.html.

However, describing all the morphological operations lies beyond the scope of this book. From here on, we will use those we need and describe them at the same time, so that you can comprehend the importance of their usage by example.

Manually defining a non-rectangular ROI

Those of you who have worked with image processing tools have probably been wondering if a manual, freehand selection of a ROI is possible in MATLAB. This is an extremely useful tool, since there are many applications with ROIs, which should be very tightly defined in order to be efficiently masked. This is another area in which MATLAB doesn't fall short of competitive tools. In fact, there are two possible choices; a polygonal ROI defined by many points can be defined using roipoly, while function imfreehand can be used for accomplishing a totally free selection. Let's see how we can use them.

Using roipoly to make a mask

We will start with our three rock images in order to explain the process of making a mask using roipoly. First, we will load, convert, and crop our image (to make our results more visible):

```
>> img = imread('3rocks.jpg');
>> rock = rgb2gray(img);
>> rock = imcrop(rock)
```

Then, it is time to call `roipoly` and define the corner points of our polygon:

```
>> mask = roipoly(rock);
```

Once we have finished selecting our points, we double-click on the ROI to save our result. Let's display the result in a new figure, to verify it worked:

```
>> figure,imshow(mask)
```

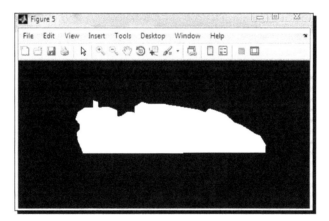

Success! The rock has been very accurately defined and our mask is probably better than anything we could generate using an automatic thresholding method. But what happens when we want even more freedom in our selection and do not wish to click on many points? Then we would have to use `imfreehand`, as we will show next.

Using imfreehand to make a mask

Once again, for the sake of comparison, we will work with the three-rocks image. Without clearing our workspace (if we have, then we must type in the first three commands of the previous example and crop the image), we type in the following commands:

```
>> figure, imshow(rock);  % Show image
>> h = imfreehand;    % Call imfreehand, using a handle as output
>> pos = wait(h);  % Save the positions of all points of the
   selection
```

After the highlighted code in the second line, we are faced with the image and we can draw the region we want to isolate by keeping the left mouse button clicked and dragging the mouse. This is accomplished by using a handle for the output of imfreehand. This handle is then used as an input to the wait function, to block the MATLAB command line, finally outputting the positions of the points selected by the user with the imfreehand function. More information on this little trick can be found at http://www.mathworks.com/help/images/ref/imfreehand.html.

When we are done defining the ROI, we let go of the mouse button and then double-click on it.

When this process is done, we type in the third command to save the row and column coordinates of all the points on the ROI perimeter in variable pos. These coordinates must then be converted into a mask:

```
>> [rows,columns] = size(rock);  % Get the size of the image
>> mask_freehand = poly2mask(pos(:,1),pos(:,2),rows,columns);
  % Make mask
>> figure, imshow(mask_freehand)
```

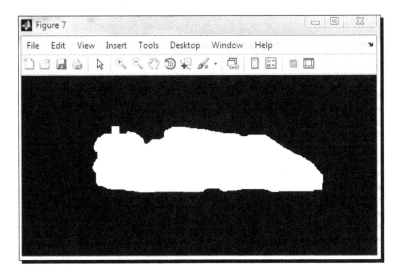

As we can see, our results are once again very precise and this technique also produces a smoother result with fewer sharp angles. Now, let's try to combine the various tools we have demonstrated into one function that can be used for erasing objects from an image.

Time for action – making a custom object eraser function

This time we are going to make a more complex tool. We'll write a function that accepts an image as an input, prompts the user to select a ROI (using either one of the two methods described previously) and then prompts the user to select a pixel with the color to be used for the erasing process. Finally, it will use the color of the pixel chosen by the user to erase the area defined by the mask. The code will be something like as follows (we'll call it FreehandMasking.m):

```
function[output] = FreehandMasking(input,method)

% Function that performs masking of a user-defined ROI
% Inputs:
%          input -  Input image
%          method - ROI selection (1: roipoly, 2: imfreehand)
```

```
% Output:
%               output - Output image (masked)

switch method
case 1
mask = roipoly(input);););% Select ROI using roipoly
case 2
figure, imshow(input)
h = imfreehand;        % Select ROI using imfreehand
pos = wait(h);
[rows,columns] = size(input);
 mask = poly2mask(pos(:,1),pos(:,2),rows,columns);
end
pix = impixel(input);    % Select pixel with eraser color
output = input;     % Set output equal to input
output(mask) = pix(1);  % Perform masking to erase selected object
```

1. Now let's test our code. We will try to erase two parts of the middle rock of our examples, using different colors. Let's first type in the commands to crop the middle rock:

```
>> img = imread('3rocks.jpg');
>> rock = rgb2gray(img);
>> rock = imcrop(rock)
```

2. Once we crop the area we want to use, we must call the function we just made, twice. We will now use the `roipoly` function for the part of the rock that is below the water level in the image and the `imfreehand` function for the part of the rock that is above the water level. First, let's mask the part below sea level (we will double-click on a pixel from the sky region to select its color for erasing the rock):

```
>> rock2 = FreehandMasking(rock,1);
```

3. Now, we will mask the part above sea level (we will double-click on a pixel from the sea for erasing the rock):

```
>> rock3 = FreehandMasking(rock2,2);
```

4. Let's see the final result:

What just happened?

The tool we just finished making is more sophisticated than the others so far. It prompts twice for user input; once for the ROI selection using the predefined method (given as input) and once for the selection of the color of the eraser. We took advantage of this functionality to repeat the example of erasing the middle rock, this time using two colors, one for each chosen ROI of the rock. The result is even better than before, since the part of the rock lying below the sea level got erased using a darker color, hence camouflaging the rock more efficiently. In the following chapters, you will see more exciting examples using the ROI selection techniques that we presented in this section.

Analyzing objects in an image

Another main function of image processing is the analysis of image content (binary or other). When analyzing an image, usually we search for the presence of edges, corners, or circles inside it. Having this information at hand, we are in the position to detect shapes and locate specific objects in our images, or enhance selected parts of the image. This has a lot to do with the subject of ROI selection that we have discussed so far in this chapter. Let's start our image analysis techniques' overview with the most popular method, which is edge detection.

Detecting edges in an image

Edge detection is a process that typically transforms a grayscale image to a binary one, denoting all the pixels belonging to lines of different orientations with instances of 1. The edge detection process is widely used and has been tackled using a variety of techniques. MATLAB has an inherent function called edge, which has incorporated most of the popular methods in an easily usable form.

To demonstrate the process, we will use an image with many lines, so that the usefulness of each algorithm is demonstrated. The one chosen is holiday_image2.bmp. To get a better idea of all the different methods supported by edge, you can type help edge in the command line. These methods are Sobel, Prewitt, Roberts, Laplacian of Gaussian (LoG), zero-cross and Canny. Let's use them all for our images and display the results. In order for the edge detection to perform faster, we will first resize our image by a scale of 0.5:

```
>> img = imread('holiday_image2.bmp');
>> img = imresize(img,0.5);
>> BW1 = edge(img,'sobel');
>> BW2 = edge(img,'prewitt');
>> BW3 = edge(img,'roberts');
>> BW4 = edge(img,'log');
>> BW5 = edge(img,'zerocross');
>> BW6 = edge(img,'canny');
>> subplot(3,3,2),imshow(img),title('Original Image')
>> subplot(3,3,4),imshow(BW1),title('Sobel result')
>> subplot(3,3,5),imshow(BW2),title('Prewitt result')
>> subplot(3,3,6),imshow(BW3),title('Roberts result')
>> subplot(3,3,7),imshow(BW4),title('LoG result')
>> subplot(3,3,8),imshow(BW5),title('Zerocross result')
>> subplot(3,3,9),imshow(BW6),title('Canny result')
```

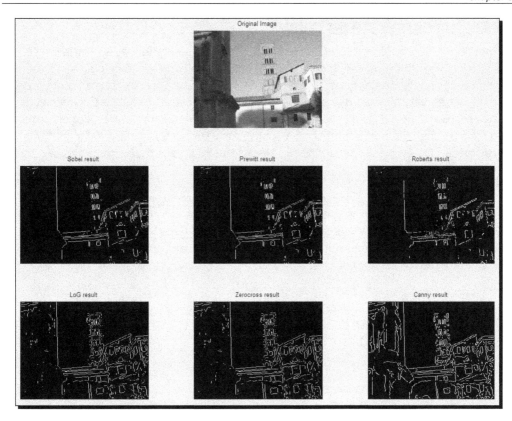

As you can see, the Canny edge detection method provides a much denser result in this case. Its main advantage seems to be the detection of edges in regions with low brightness values. The `Sobel`, `Prewitt` and `Roberts` methods appear to be the weakest, producing sparse results, detecting fewer lines than the other three methods.

The process of edge detection can be used in several ways. The two most popular applications are those of object segmentation in an image and of image enhancement. Especially in object segmentation, it is usual for edge detection to be combined with other methods such as corner detection.

Detecting corners in an image

Corner detection is another useful tool used for object segmentation, as well as in image registration algorithms (matching points in one image with corresponding points in another version of the image that has been transformed, or that has been taken at a different point of time). A general definition of a corner in the image processing domain is the intersection of two edges. As such, it is very closely connected to edge detection. MATLAB offers corner detection through the `corner` function, which in turn, supports two different algorithms; Harris corner detection method and Shi &Tomasi's minimum eigenvalue method.

Let's use the same image as before to demonstrate their usage. This time, as `corner` returns the coordinates of the detected corners, we will use `plot` to visualize them. In order for them to be projected on the original image, we will also use the command `hold on` before we call `plot`. Finally, we will use red circles for the corners detected by the Harris method and blue asterisks for the ones detected by the minimum eigenvalue method. To better demonstrate the results, we will crop a part of the image. Let's get to work:

```
>> img = imread('holiday_image2.bmp');
>> img = imresize(img,0.5);
>> img = imcrop(img);
>> C1 = corner(img);
>> C2 = corner(img, 'MinimumEigenvalue');
>> figure, imshow(img)     % Display original image
>> hold on        % Hold on the figure
>> plot(C1(:,1), C1(:,2), 'ro'); % Overlay the corners from Harris
>> plot(C2(:,1), C2(:,2), 'b*'); % Overlay the corners from Shi
```

The results show that the Shi-Tomasi method produces more results using the default settings and that most of the results coincide. However, they are not completely identical, so we must be careful when choosing which technique to use.

Detecting circles in an image

The last of the popular image processing methods we will visit, which is widely used in everyday tasks, is circle detection. Circles are a very descriptive feature of many objects that often need to be detected in an image. To name a few, circle detection can be used to localize eyes, stars, balls, coins, tires, lights, and so on. MATLAB's inherent function for circle detection is function `imfindcircles`. It can be used with several possible inputs, with the only ones necessary being the input image and the radius (or range of radii) in pixels of the circle we want to detect. Its output may be only the centers of the detected circles, or it can also contain the radii of the respective circles and the power of each circle.

We'll demonstrate its usage, using a rather funny example. The cat depicted in the photograph we will use, has a funny little piece of black fur under its nose, which looks like a human moustache. Let's try to ignore it for a while and attempt to automatically detect the cat's eyes, using `imfindcircles`. We will use the range of radii from 20 to 50 pixels. The result will be visualized using the MATLAB command `viscircles`, which is designed for such use:

```
>> img = imread('cat.jpg');
>> img = rgb2gray(img);
>> imshow(img)
```

Here is our cat. Funny little guy, right?

Let's try to locate its eyes. As we said, we will use a range of radii for our algorithm, spanning from 20 to 50 pixels (if we want to be more accurate, we can use some of the tools MATLAB provides for measuring distances in an image, for example, `imdistline`):

```
>> [centers,radii,metric] =imfindcircles(c,[20 50])
```

Now, we can observe our results produced from the last line of code which got displayed on screen, since we didn't use our semi-colon operator. A close look at the results reveals that our call to the function located three circles instead of two:

```
>> [centers, radii, metric] = imfindcircles(c,[20 50])

centers =

    1.0e+03 *

    1.0027    0.6503
    1.1901    0.6365
    1.0855    0.6364


radii =

    28.6707
    28.6164
    25.7845


metric =

    0.3377
    0.2826
    0.1630
```

Such counterintuitive results are very common when using an automated technique for object detection. This is natural, of course, since the algorithm only looks at the circularity of region, without the use of any additional knowledge to assist in refining the results. Therefore, refining the results in such tasks is usually a human's job.

Taking a closer look, we see that two of the results have almost identical radii (28.6 to 28.7 pixels). These also have a significantly higher circularity metric than the third one, so they are definitely more likely to be the cat's eyes. One last clue that could confirm our choice is the positions of the centers of the detected circles. Unfortunately, the positions in this example do not greatly vary (similar rows and close columns), so we cannot say for sure. An assumption that can be made, though, is that the first two circles detected are the eyes and the third is a smaller symmetric region between them (its center's column coordinate is near the midpoint of the two other centers), above the cat's nose. Let's see if we are right. We will visualize the two first circles using `viscircles` and then we will place a blue asterisk on the center of the third circle:

```
>> viscircles(centers(1:2,:), radii(1:2,:));
>> hold on;
>> plot(centers(3,1), centers(3,2),'b*');
```

Spot on! The circle detector indeed located the two eyes, as well as a highly symmetrical area on the top of the cat's nose. Our rationale in the post-processing phase was correct and we chose the proper centers of the cat's eyes. Not bad for a procedure based on an automatic tool, right? We will get to put this method to the test again later in the book.

Pop quiz – object analysis pros and cons

Q1. MATLAB provides several functions that implement complex object analysis tasks. Can you answer whether the following properties are true?

1. The most dense and detailed edge detection result is achieved using function `edge` with the `Sobel` method.

2. The `corner` function provided by MATLAB provides two different methods for performing corner detection.

3. The circle detection performed by `imfindcircles` can work either with one radius, or with a range of radii.

Summary

In this chapter, we presented several useful morphology-based techniques for selecting regions of interest and masking an image. After visiting several examples based on the morphology theory, we also provided an introductory presentation of some powerful object analysis tools that can be used for several image processing applications such as image enhancement, object detection, image registration, and so on. The focus of this chapter was on hands-on, practical examples demonstrating the significance of the methods presented. More specifically, in this chapter we covered:

- What binary images are and how we can create them using automatic thresholding techniques.

- How we can refine a region of interest to better suit our needs, using dilation (`imdilate`) and erosion (`imerode`) to perform enlargement and shrinking, respectively.

- What structuring elements are and how they affect the quality of dilation and erosion results.

- What masking is and how we can use it to process specific regions of interest in an image.

- How to manually select a region of interest in order to define better masks for our applications, using `roipoly` and `imfreehand`.

- How to detect edges in a grayscale image using function `edge`.

- How to detect corners in an image using function `corner`.

- How to detect circles in an image with `imfindcircles`.

In the next chapter, we will expand the methods we have discussed so far to color image processing. We will produce new functions to implement our functions to color images and provide specialized solutions that take advantage of the extra information included in these cases. At the end of the chapter, you will be able to manipulate and process color pictures to produce results that look more appealing and even apply artistic effects that give your photographs a more professional look.

4
Working with Color Images

Up to now, we have only worked with grayscale images. Even in the few cases where our photographs were in color, we first transformed them to grayscale and then processed them. However, color image processing is a much more frequent task in everyday life. It is not that different to what we have already covered; the basic thing we have to remember is that instead of two-dimensional matrices, we have to deal with three-dimensional matrices. In this chapter, we will introduce the concept of color, and expand the techniques covered so far to color images. Many of the image processing methods presented in previous chapters will be revisited, while covering specialized color image processing techniques. All these methods will be analyzed using practical examples of color image enhancement and artistic color manipulation.

In this chapter, we will cover:

◆ Some basic knowledge of color image processing and its differences from grayscale image processing

◆ How to manipulate and/or threshold the pixel values in color images

◆ How to perform color masking

◆ What color spaces are and why they are important

◆ To use color spaces other than RGB

◆ To achieve color isolation in images

◆ How to perform red eye reduction

So, let's dive right in!

An introduction to color image processing

Before we begin examining the differences of color image processing to grayscale image processing techniques, we must first understand the difference between color and grayscale images. As explained in previous chapters, a grayscale image can be represented as a two-dimensional, m-by-n matrix (m rows and n columns). Its elements, called pixels, have values spreading from 0 to 255 (in the case of 8-bit images). A value of zero represents black, a value of 255 represents white, while all the values in between represent different shades of gray.

In the case of color images, the matrices become three-dimensional. The first two dimensions, as in the case of grayscale images, are the number of rows and the number of columns (m-by-n). The difference is that the third dimension typically comprises three layers, representing colors. That is, color images are three-dimensional (usually m-by-n-by-3) matrices and can be thought of as three grayscale images combined together. Each image typically represents one of the colors (that is, Red, Green, and Blue) of the image, which is therefore characterized as RGB. These three layers are also called color channels of the color space (RGB in our case).

Similarly to the grayscale image case, when we have a case of color images of 8-bits per channel, a zero value in one channel represents non-presence of the color, while a 255 value suggests full color presence. The three color channels are mixed together to produce the final color for each pixel in the image. A pure fundamental color occurs when one of the three color channels has the maximum value and the two others are equal to zero. This means that a pixel with {R, G, B} values equal to {255, 0, 0} will be pure red. Similarly, a pixel with values {0, 255, 0} will be pure green and a pixel with values {0, 0, 255} will be pure blue. Different mixtures of values in the three basic color channels will ultimately produce different colors.

> A more extensive description of the basic concepts of RGB color images can be found in *Chapter 2*, Introduction, of the manual of the Image Processing Toolbox. It can be found freely available in pdf format on the website of Mathworks, at `http://www.mathworks.com/help/pdf_doc/images/images_tb.pdf`.

What you may have deduced from the previous description of color images, is the fact that in order to apply the methods covered in previous chapters for color image processing, we will have to repeat the same process three times (one for each color channel). This is typically correct, as we will see in the rest of this chapter. Let's start with the basic image manipulations covered in *Chapter 1, Basic Image Manipulations*.

Basic color image manipulations

Let's start with the very basics. Importing a color image and accessing its pixels is pretty much the same process as in the case of grayscale images. We can see it using the color version of the image used in *Chapter 1*, *Basic Image Manipulations*. To open both the color version and the grayscale version, we will use `imread` twice:

```
>> img_gray = imread('my_image.bmp');
>> img_color = imread('my_image_color.bmp');
```

Examining the workspace will reveal the aforementioned difference between grayscale and color images, which is the dimensionality. As we can see in the following screenshot, the grayscale version is 485-by-686 and the color version is 485-by-686-by-3.

Command Window	Workspace			
`>> img_gray = imread('my_image.bmp');`	Name ▲	Value	Min	Max
`>> img_color = imread('my_image_color.bmp')`	img_color	<485x656x3 uint8>	<Too ...	<Too ...
`fx >>`	img_gray	<485x656 uint8>	0	255

To display both the grayscale and color images, as well as the three color channels of the latter separately on the same figure, we will type in:

```
>> subplot(2,3,1),imshow(img_gray);title('Grayscale image')
>> subplot(2,3,2),imshow(img_color);title('Color image')
>> subplot(2,3,4),imshow(img_color(:,:,1));title('Red channel')
>> subplot(2,3,5),imshow(img_color(:,:,2));title('Green channel')
>> subplot(2,3,6),imshow(img_color(:,:,3));title('Blue channel')
```

The resulting image will be as shown in the following screenshot:

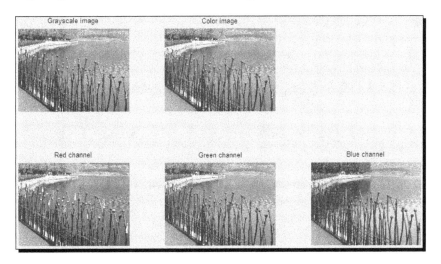

From the highlighted code shown previously, we can see that indexing in the third dimension does the trick, leading to successful displaying of the three color channels. In these images, you can better understand the meaning of separate color channels. A good point to focus on are the red tips of the fence, which have very bright red values and dark green and blue values. We can better understand this by using the **Inspect Pixel Values** option of `imtool` and clicking on a pixel of red shade:

```
>> imtool(img_color)
```

From this example, we can see that `imtool` can be used for color images in the same way we showed in the *Chapter 1, Basic Image Manipulations*. This time, the three values displayed for each pixel are not the same (as in the case of grayscale images), but instead represent the R, G, and B values of the pixel.

While `imrotate` also has the same usage as in grayscale images, `fliplr` and `flipud` do not. In fact, using them for color images in the same way we did for grayscale ones results in an error message:

```
>> figure,imshow(fliplr(img_color))
Error using fliplr (line 18)
X must be a 2-D matrix.
```

The resulting message implies that the color image is not a two-dimensional matrix, thus cannot be flipped using `fliplr`. Instead, we must use `flipdim` for all our color image mirroring tasks. Therefore, we only have the following way to perform horizontal and vertical mirroring:

```
>> img_color_lr = flipdim(img_color,2);
>> img_color_ud = flipdim(img_color,1);
>> subplot(1,2,1),imshow(img_color_lr);title('Left-right mirroring');
>> subplot(1,2,2),imshow(img_color_ud);title('Up-down mirroring');
```

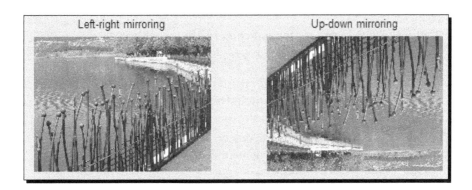

The rest of the functions we covered in *Chapter 1*, *Basic Image Manipulations*, remain almost identical when using them for color images. More specifically, `imresize`, `imcrop`, and `imwrite` can be used in the same fashion you already know. We will be using these functions as we discuss some more complicated color image processes in the rest of this chapter.

Setting a rectangular area to a specified color

The problem of altering the color of a rectangular area of our choice is a little different in the case of color images. In *Chapter 2*, *Working with Pixels in Grayscale Images*, you learned two different ways to alter pixel values in such a task; through using for loops and through indexing.

In a simple case, using the same value for all the color channels, the two aforementioned methods can still be used, but in the case of different values in each color channel, the problem becomes a little more complicated. Let's see these things using a practical example.

Time for action – repainting two areas in a color image

In this example, we will try to set the values of the pixels in the top-left corner of our image to {R, G, B} = {128, 128, 128} and the values of the pixels in the bottom-right corner to {R, G, B} = {255, 0, 0}. To see the difference, we will try to accomplish our goal using indexing. Let's start:

1. First off, we load our image and keep a copy:

```
>> img_color = imread('my_image_color.bmp');
>> img_color_orig = img_color;
```

2. Then, we will try to set our top-left corner to the specified values:

```
>> img_color(1:50,1:50,:) = 128;
```

3. Now, if we want to do the same for the bottom-right corner, we should modify our approach. Not all color channels should be set to the same value, thus each color channel must be changed separately:

```
>> img_color(end-49:end,end-49:end,1) = 255;
>> img_color(end-49:end,end-49:end,2) = 0;
>> img_color(end-49:end,end-49:end,3) = 0;
```

4. Finally, we will show our results:

```
>> subplot(1,2,1),imshow(img_color_orig);title('Original
   Image')
>> subplot(1,2,2),imshow(img_color);title('Altered Image')
```

What just happened?

We just managed to play with the colors of a color image. We used the indexing in exactly the same way you already knew, to turn an area to gray (with all color channels set to 128) and then we repeated the process for each color channel in another area to set its pixels to red. A useful observation is that three identical values in all color channels denote a shade of gray. This fact is rather intuitive, as in *Chapter 1*, *Basic Image Manipulations*, we saw that imtool represented the pixels of grayscale images as triplets of identical values. The process must be slightly altered when we want a color other than gray. This is why, in our example, we changed the values in each channel separately.

Thresholding color images

Another technique we have already covered, that is changed in the task of color image processing, is image thresholding. Color images must be thresholded in each channel separately using a proper threshold and then the results must be combined together. Let's try to do this using the automated **Otsu thresholding technique** we presented in *Chapter 2*, *Working with Pixels in Grayscale Images*.

First, the color channels should be thresholded one by one. Let's see how, writing a script under the name ColorOtsuThresholding.m:

```
img_color = imread('my_image_color.bmp'); % Load image
red = im2bw(img_color(:,:,1)); % Threshold red channel
green = im2bw(img_color(:,:,2)); % Threshold green channel
blue = im2bw(img_color(:,:,3)); % Threshold blue channel
bin_image_or = red | green | blue; % Find union using OR
bin_image_and = red & green & blue; % Find intersection using AND
subplot(1,3,1),imshow(img_color),title('Original Image')
subplot(1,3,2),imshow(bin_image_or),title('Binary Union Image')
subplot(1,3,3),imshow(bin_image_and),title('Binary Intersection
    Image')
```

Running this script gives the following result:

Note that the union of two or more binary images can be acquired using the OR operator, which in MATLAB, is denoted by symbol "|". Applying this operator to two binary images, results in an image that contains ones in those pixels that are equal to one in at least one of the two images. The AND operator denoted by symbol "&" leads to a resulting image that contains ones in those pixels that are equal to one in both images. Depending on the task, one method could be preferable to the other. Let's try to illustrate the difference with an example.

Time for action – isolating the red pixels in an image

In this example, we will try to isolate the red-orange tips of the fence in the previous image, using manual thresholding of all channels. The ultimate goal is to acquire a binary image with only pixels belonging in the area we want, being equal to one. Let's start by using `imtool` to get a better idea of what the RGB values of the pixels we want to isolate are.

1. First, we load the image and call `imtool`:

```
>> img = imread('my_image_color.bmp');
>> imtool(img);
```

Then, we will choose **Inspect Pixel Values** by clicking on the second icon from the left and placing our cursor on one of the red tips to see the RGB values of its neighbor pixels. We can repeat the process for other tips and also for getting samples from other image areas.

2. Now that we have an idea of what the RGB values are for our ROIs, we can begin the process of thresholding. By observing the color values with the help of `imtool`, we can set a general thresholding rule for our ROIs, which would be something like: "we want to keep pixels with high R values and low G and B values". The implementation of this rule could be something like this:

```
>> red_binary = img(:,:,1) > 150;
>> green_binary = img(:,:,2) < 150;
>> blue_binary = img(:,:,3) < 150;
```

Now, we can mix the three binary images using the AND operator and display the result on a new figure:

```
>> final_mask = red_binary & green_binary & blue_binary;
>> figure, imshow(final_mask)
```

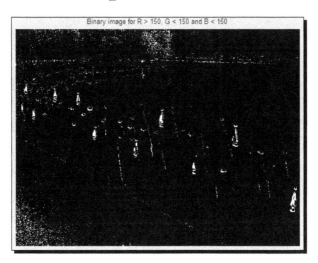

3. We can see that, while we are on the right track, our result is not optimal yet. It needs a little tweaking of the selected thresholds and perhaps, some morphology. The wise thing to do in these situations is to write a function that takes the color thresholds as inputs and returns the thresholded binary image. This way, we will be able to test several sets of threshold values with one line of code for each, instead of typing all the commands of step 2. Let's use the editor to write a function called `RGBThreshold.m`:

```
function [output] = RGBThreshold(input,thresholds)
% Function that performs color image thresholding using
% user-defined threshold values. Emphasises red areas.
% Inputs:
% input     - Input image
% thresholds - 1x3 matrix with the threshold values
%   for the R, G and B color channels.
```

```
% Output:
% output - Output image (binary)
red_bin = input(:,:,1) > thresholds(1); % Red thresholding
green_bin = input(:,:,2) < thresholds(2); % Green thresholding
blue_bin = input(:,:,3) < thresholds(3); % Blue thresholding
output = red_bin & green_bin & blue_bin; % Final image
```

4. Let's now use our new function to generate and compare results for three different sets of thresholds, that is, {R,G,B} = {150,150,150}, {160,130,130}, and {180,140,140}:

```
>> [output1] = RGBThreshold(img,[150 150 150]);
>> [output2] = RGBThreshold(img,[160 130 130]);
>> [output3] = RGBThreshold(img,[180 140 140]);
>> subplot(1,3,1),imshow(output1),title('Using [150 150 150]')
>> subplot(1,3,2),imshow(output2),title('Using [160 130 130]')
>> subplot(1,3,3),imshow(output3),title('Using [180 140 140]')
```

5. We can now choose the preferred result, so that we can tweak it using the morphology tools. Let's use the middle result, output2, which apparently needs dilation to expand the ROIs to the size we would want. First, we will set the pixels above the line 100 to zero, to exclude unneeded areas. Then, we can use imdilate with a structuring element like a diamond of size 5px, to see what happens (we'll show the result next to the original image):

```
>> output2(1:100,:) = 0;
>> final = imdilate(output2,strel('disk', 5));
>> figure, subplot(1,2,1), imshow(img), title('Original Image')
>> subplot(1,2,2), imshow(final), title('Final binary mask')
```

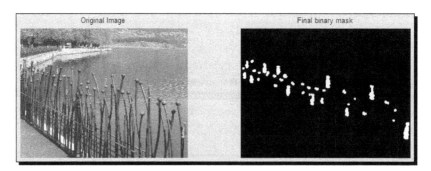

What just happened?

In this example, we combined several methods presented so far for grayscale images to generate a modified masking example for color images. We used `imtool` to acquire a feel of what the pixel values are for several regions of the image, including the region that we want to isolate. Then, we wrote a function to perform thresholding using user-defined threshold values for all the three color channels. With a trial-and-error process, we selected the most suitable thresholds (step 4), cleaned the areas we did not wish to include, and then dilated the binary result to acquire the final binary image (step 5).

A useful conclusion derived from this example would be that RGB images can be thresholded, but the process should really be performed in all color channels in order to optimize our result. This has to do with the fact that the RGB color space channels are highly correlated to each other, meaning that all three values are required to describe a given color. This results in the counterintuitive deduction, that we usually cannot just threshold the R channel to isolate red pixels, but would need to combine the R channel mask with the G and B channel masks to produce optimal results.

Achieving color masking

Since we are into masking processes, a valid question deriving from the previous section would be: since the mask we generated is two-dimensional, how can we use it to perform masking on a three-dimensional (color) image?

The answer to the question is rather straightforward; we will actually perform separate masking in each color channel, always using the same binary mask. The tricky part of this process is that after we perform separate masking in all three channels, we will have to join the results back together to acquire the final image. A very important MATLAB function, that allows us to join matrices, is `cat`. This function normally takes N + 1 inputs, where N is the number of matrices we wish to join. In the case of a color image, `cat` would be called with four inputs. The first one is the dimension along which we want the concatenation to occur and the next three inputs will be the R, G, and B color channels. Let's show this with an example:

```
>> img = imread('my_image_color.bmp');
>> R = img(:,:,1); % store R channel in new matrix
>> G = img(:,:,2); % store G channel in new matrix
>> B = img(:,:,3); % store B channel in new matrix
>> img_cat = cat(3,R,G,B); % Re-join color channels
>> img_cat_mixed = cat(3,G,B,R);  % Re-join color channels (mixed)
>> subplot(1,3,1),imshow(img),title('Original Image')
```

```
>> subplot(1,3,2),imshow(img_cat),title('Concatenated image')
>> subplot(1,3,3),imshow(img_cat_mixed),title('Concatenated image
   mixed')
```

This example demonstrates clearly, the way the function `cat` should be used. The color channels of our image are first stored separately in three different matrices and then we join them along the three-dimension, first in their normal order and then in a mixed order (first G, then B, and then R). The first result is, as expected, identical to the original, while the second one appears chromatically distorted.

Let's now use color masking to achieve a very popular image processing effect, which is color isolation. This effect is essentially the process of converting the whole color image to grayscale, while leaving our ROI untouched, which is usually of a specific color (remember the girl with the red dress in Schindler's list?). We will try to achieve this result, using the previous image.

Time for action – color isolation

Let's try to perform color isolation for our lake fence photograph. The goal will be to convert the whole image to grayscale, except the fence tips, that should remain red. Here are the steps to accomplish this:

1. First, we will load the image and generate the same mask as before, using thresholding, cleaning, and dilation:

```
>> img = imread('my_image_color.bmp');
>> [output2] = RGBThreshold(img,[160 130 130]);
>> output2(1:100,:) = 0;
>> mask = imdilate(output2,strel('disk', 2));
```

2. Then, we must use the process described above to separate the color channels:

```
>> R = img(:,:,1); % store R channel in new matrix
>> G = img(:,:,2); % store G channel in new matrix
>> B = img(:,:,3); % store B channel in new matrix
```

3. Now it is time to perform masking. We want all pixels outside our regions of interest to turn to grayscale, which can be achieved by assigning to all channels the same values (which can be acquired by `rgb2gray`). All these pixels have the value zero in our mask. So:

```
>> img_gray = rgb2gray(img);
>> R(mask == 0) = img_gray(mask == 0);
>> G(mask == 0) = img_gray(mask == 0);
>> B(mask == 0) = img_gray(mask == 0);
```

4. Finally, we have to join our new color channels to acquire our final image and display our result:

```
>> img_final = cat(3,R,G,B);
>> figure, imshow(img_final)
```

Not bad for such a quick process, right?

What just happened?

In this example, you learned how to perform color isolation in an image in a quick and quite efficient manner. We followed the same steps as before, to generate our mask for the fence tips, altering just our structuring element to achieve a less crude segmentation. Then, we split the color channels and used the inverse of our mask (the pixels having a zero value) to transform all regions, except the ones in the mask, to grayscale. To achieve this, the values of all pixels equal to zero in the mask were set to their grayscale equivalent, for all color channels. When the process was finished, we joined the resulting color channels to acquire our final image. The result may not be optimal, but it is certainly very good, considering that we did not manually choose the ROIs to be isolated, but instead we performed image thresholding to generate the mask.

The importance of different color spaces

Every color image processing task presented so far used the RGB color space, which is probably the most popular one, especially due to its broad usage in computer screens. The main disadvantage of this color space, however, is the correlation of its color channels, which makes it almost infeasible to segment specific colors just by using one of the color channels. Furthermore, the RGB color space is susceptible to shadows and illumination changes, which cause a very significant distortion in colors.

To tackle these disadvantages, different color spaces, such as HSV or CIE-L*a*b* have been proposed. These color spaces are modeled more closely to the way humans perceive colors, they are less sensitive to illumination changes and they are also more appropriate for color segmentation purposes. MATLAB provides a set of transformations between different color spaces, based on the functions pair of `makecform` and `applycform`. The combination of these two functions can convert seven different color spaces. Furthermore, MATLAB also provides three more pairs of functions for color space transformations, between RGB and HSV, NTSC, and YCbCr. Let's examine the way we can transform RGB to different color spaces, through an example.

Time for action – color space transformation

In this example, we will demonstrate the usage of inherent MATLAB functions to transform a RGB image to HSV and to CIE-L*a*b*. For the first one, we will use `rgb2hsv` and for the second one we will use `makecform` and `applycform`. The following steps will do the trick:

1. First we load our image:

   ```
   >> img = imread('my_image_color.bmp');
   ```

2. Then, we generate the HSV image:

   ```
   >> img_hsv = rgb2hsv(img);
   ```

3. Finally, we will convert our image to CIE-L*a*b*:

   ```
   >> cform = makecform('srgb2lab'); % Make the transform
     structure
   >> img_lab = applycform(img,cform); % Apply transform
   ```

4. Now, let's demonstrate our results:

   ```
   >> subplot(3,4,1),imshow(img),title('RGB image')
   >> subplot(3,4,2),imshow(img(:,:,1)),title('R channel')
   >> subplot(3,4,3),imshow(img(:,:,2)),title('G channel')
   >> subplot(3,4,4),imshow(img(:,:,3)),title('B channel')
   >> subplot(3,4,5),imshow(img_hsv),title('HSV image')
   >> subplot(3,4,6),imshow(img_hsv(:,:,1)),title('H channel')
   >> subplot(3,4,7),imshow(img_hsv(:,:,2)),title('S channel')
   ```

```
>> subplot(3,4,8),imshow(img_hsv(:,:,3)),title('V channel')
>> subplot(3,4,9),imshow(img_lab),title('CIE-L*a*b* image')
>> subplot(3,4,10),imshow(img_lab(:,:,1)),title('L* channel')
>> subplot(3,4,11),imshow(img_lab(:,:,2)),title('a* channel')
>> subplot(3,4,12),imshow(img_lab(:,:,3)),title('b* channel')
```

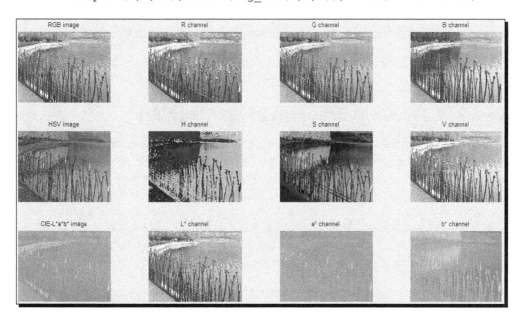

What just happened?

This was just a demonstrative example of basic color space conversions in MATLAB. The results were presented in a common figure, with each color channel isolated, so that you can get a better qualitative sense of what the alternative color spaces have to offer. Both HSV and CIE-L*a*b* separate color from brightness information. In the former case, the brightness channel is V (Value) and in the latter case, the brightness channel is L (Lightness). The remaining two channels in each color space include color information. The basic difference is that in the case of CIE-L*a*b* color space, the two remaining channels (a* and b*) are so-called color opponent dimensions. Channel a* assigns large values to red colors and low values to green colors. Similarly, channel b* assigns large values to yellow pixels and low values to blue pixels. In the case of HSV, color information is included in channels H (Hue) and S (Saturation). Hue is an angle given in degrees and Saturation is a length. Combined with Value, they define a cylinder of color shades.

It is useful to notice that the functions described previously do not produce the expected results, as they are normalized to fit the description of an image. Therefore, the color spaces produced by `applycform`, will include pixel values ranging from 0 to 255. The other three pairs of color space transformation functions (which exist also in older versions of MATLAB), will include pixel values ranging from zero to one. This should be something to beware of, especially if you try to reproduce results that are based in the original descriptions of color spaces (for example, expect the Hue to have values from 0 to 180, since it is an angle).

CIE-L*a*b* for more efficient color masking

Based on the theoretical analysis of the previous section, the alternative color spaces seem better choices for color masking tasks. This is especially true for the case of CIE-L*a*b* color space, which is particularly useful for such methods. The most important reason for this, is that CIE-L*a*b* isolates colors into its a* and b* channels in a way that is close to how humans perceive them. Therefore, in theory, we could rely on just one of the two color channels (depending on the color we want to isolate) for generating a color mask. The purer the color, the more probable it is to get the result we want. Let's revisit our previous color isolation example, using just channel a* for mask creation.

Time for action – color isolation using CIE-L*a*b*

This time we will perform color isolation for our lake fence photograph, using just channel a*. The goal will remain at converting the whole image to grayscale, except the fence tips that should remain red. For comparison purpose, we will also perform the RGB process. We will follow these steps:

1. First, we will load the image and generate the same mask as before, using thresholding, cleaning, and dilation:

```
>> img = imread('my_image_color.bmp');
>> [output2] = RGBThreshold(img,[160 130 130]);
>> output(1:100,:) = 0;
>> maskRGB = imdilate(output2,strel('disk', 2));
```

2. Let's produce the mask using CIE-L*a*b* color space:

```
>> cform = makecform('srgb2lab'); % Make the transform
   structure
>> img_lab = applycform(img,cform); % Apply transform
>> maskLab = (img_lab(:,:,2) > 150); % Threshold a* channel
```

3. Then, we separate the color channels:

```
>> R = img(:,:,1); % store R channel in new matrix
>> G = img(:,:,2); % store G channel in new matrix
>> B = img(:,:,3); % store B channel in new matrix
```

4. Now it is time to perform color isolation, using both masks. So:

```
>> img_gray = rgb2gray(img);
>> R1 = R; G1 = G; B1 = B; % Keep a copy of each color channel
>> R1(maskRGB == 0) = img_gray(maskRGB == 0);
>> G1(maskRGB == 0) = img_gray(maskRGB == 0);
>> B1(maskRGB == 0) = img_gray(maskRGB == 0);
>> R(maskLab == 0) = img_gray(maskLab == 0);
>> G(maskLab == 0) = img_gray(maskLab == 0);
>> B(maskLab == 0) = img_gray(maskLab == 0);
```

5. Finally, we have to join our new color channels for both cases to acquire our final images and display our results:

```
>> img_final_RGB = cat(3,R1,G1,B1);
>> img_final_Lab = cat(3,R,G,B);
>> subplot(2,2,1),imshow(maskRGB),title('RGB Mask')
>> subplot(2,2,2),imshow(maskLab),title('L*a*b* Mask')
>> subplot(2,2,3),imshow(img_final_RGB),title('RGB Result')
>> subplot(2,2,4),imshow(img_final_Lab),title('L*a*b* Result')
```

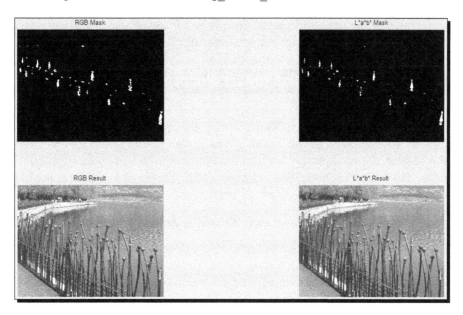

6. In order to examine the difference more closely, we could use `imtool` in both results, to zoom in on some details. The following image shows the bottom right area of the image, cropped, and zoomed to 200%. On the left, we have the RGB isolation result and on the right, the CIE-L*a*b* isolation result:

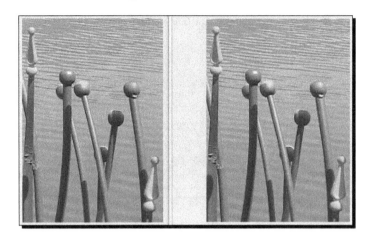

What just happened?

This example has made clear the twofold superiority of using CIE-L*a*b* for color isolation. First, the red color isolation mask is generated using just one color channel, therefore, one threshold value. Second, the final isolation result is better and more coherent; as such it does not need morphology adjustments. The process followed is identical with the one explained before, so no new methods are presented at this point.

Have a go hero – writing a function for region color isolation

You should by now have grasped the process of masking. Furthermore, we have so far written some custom-made functions to perform various tasks. So, why don't you have a go at both; write a function that will take in an image along with three color thresholds and return the isolated color image derived from the thresholds. To make your function more versatile, add two more functionalities: the support for more than one color space and the support for regional color isolation (selecting the ROI with the color we want to isolate).

You shouldn't have too much trouble writing a function defined as follows:

```
function [output] = ROIColorIsolation(input, thresh, cspace)

% Function for color isolation in a user-defined image ROI
% Inputs:
%         input  - Input image
%         thresh - Thresholds matrix ([1st 2nd 3rd])
```

```
%           cspace - Color space for mask selection (0: RGB
%                                                    1: CIE-L*a*b*)
% Output:
%           output - Output image (masked)
```

Let's test your code for correctness. You will call the function twice; once for the RGB case and once for the CIE-L*a*b* case. The channels you don't want to use in the process should have a threshold value of zero. To mix things up a little, let's use the book's cover page image to test your function. Hopefully, you will get some similar results, using the R and G channels for the RGB method (they both should have high values) and channel b* for the CIE-L*a*b* method (it also should have high values, denoting yellow color).

```
>> steps = imread('Steps.bmp');
>> [resultRGB] = ROIColorIsolation(steps,[150 150 0], 0);
>> [resultLab] = ROIColorIsolation(steps,[0 0 150], 1);
```

In both the cases, our ROI selection is around the flowers at the lower-left part of the image as shown in the following screenshot:

The results should look something like the following screenshot:

```
>> subplot(3,1,1),imshow(steps),title('Original Image')
>> subplot(3,1,2),imshow(resultRGB),title('RGB - ROI color
   isolation')
>> subplot(3,1,3),imshow(resultLab),title('L*a*b* - ROI color
   isolation')
```

Fixing illumination issues in RGB color images

Another area of image processing that has up to now been covered only for grayscale images is the one of contrast enhancement and handling of illumination problems. The basic method of generalization to color images is pretty much identical to all the other techniques presented in this chapter that is, repeating the grayscale process for all color channels. Since, the functions used in *Chapter 2, Working with Pixels in Grayscale Images*, for such tasks are used only for grayscale images (with an exception of imadjust, which also does not work for color images without defining extra inputs), we will write a function that incorporates all the contrast enhancement techniques visited so far:

```
function output = ColorContrastEnhance(input, method)

% Function for color contrast enhancement of input image
% Inputs:
% input  - Input image
% method - Enhancement method selection (0: histeq
% 1: adapthisteq
% 2: imadjust)
% Output:
% output - Output image (enhanced)
output = input;
switch method
  case 0
    for i = 1:3
```

```
    output(:,:,i) = histeq(output(:,:,i));
  end
  case 1
    for i = 1:3
    output(:,:,i) = adapthisteq(output(:,:,i));
  end
  case 2
    for i = 1:3
    output(:,:,i) = imadjust(output(:,:,i));
  end
end
```

Let's see if our function works as expected:

```
>> img = imread('Steps.bmp');
>> img1 = ColorContrastEnhance(img, 0);
>> img2 = ColorContrastEnhance(img, 1);
>> img3 = ColorContrastEnhance(img, 2);
>> subplot(1,4,1),imshow(img),title('Original image')
>> subplot(1,4,2),imshow(img1),title('Color histeq')
>> subplot(1,4,3),imshow(img2),title('Color adapthisteq')
>> subplot(1,4,4),imshow(img3),title('Color imadjust')
```

It is obvious that the histeq and adapthisteq functions lead to a color distortion in this case, so these methods should be very cautiously used in the case of per-channel processing of RGB color images. The imadjust function, on the other hand, seems to work fine, producing an acceptable result.

Fixing illumination issues in CIE-L*a*b*

The color distortion observed in the example of the previous section was caused by the high correlation between the R, G, and B channels in the case of the RGB image. This is another reason, why in many cases, a safer choice of color channel for color image processing tasks is CIE-L*a*b*. Let's try to alter the function written in the previous section, so that it converts the RGB input image to the CIE-L*a*b* color space, apply the chosen enhancement method only in the Lightness channel (so that the colors remain unaffected) and then transform the resulting image back to RGB:

```
function output = ColorContrastEnhanceLab(input, method)

% Function for color contrast enhancement of input image in L*a*b*
% Inputs:
% input   - Input image
% method – Enhancement method selection (0: histeq
% 1: adapthisteq
% 2: imadjust)
% Output:
% output - Output image (enhanced)

cform = makecform('srgb2lab'); % Make the transform structure
img_lab = applycform(input,cform); % Apply transform to L*a*b*

switch method

% Apply chosen method in the Lightness channel (img_lab(:,:,1))

case 0
  img_lab (:,:,1) = histeq(img_lab (:,:,1));
case 1
  img_lab (:,:,1) = adapthisteq(img_lab (:,:,1));
case 2
  img_lab (:,:,1) = imadjust(img_lab (:,:,1));
end

cform = makecform('lab2srgb'); % Make the inverse transform structure
output = applycform(img_lab, cform); % Apply transform to RGB
```

Now we can test our new function to see if our results have improved:

```
>> img = imread('Steps.bmp');
>> img1 = ColorContrastEnhanceLab(img, 0);
>> img2 = ColorContrastEnhanceLab(img, 1);
>> img3 = ColorContrastEnhanceLab(img, 2);
```

```
>> subplot(1,4,1),imshow(img),title('Original image')
>> subplot(1,4,2),imshow(img1),title('CIE - L*a*b* Color histeq')
>> subplot(1,4,3),imshow(img2),title('CIE - L*a*b* Color
   adapthisteq')
>> subplot(1,4,4),imshow(img3),title('CIE - L*a*b* Color imadjust')
```

Success! No color distortion this time. The `adapthisteq` result also seems to have added more detail to the original photograph this time, enhancing the shadowed areas in a way that is quite pleasing to the eye.

A practical example – red eye reduction

Now that we have presented how most of the image processing techniques met so far are translated for color images, it is time to give a very practical example mixing several of the methods. Red eye reduction is a common problem in amateur photography and has been addressed in several ways. The cause of red eyes in photographs (typically, the ones taken at night or in dark areas using flash), is the widening of our pupils. This has the effect of enlarging the area hit by the flash light, causing it to hit our retina, thus illuminating its red surface which is picked up by our camera lens.

In order to address the red eye issue after it has occurred (in the processing phase of our photograph), the most common way is to follow these two simple steps:

1. Detect the red area in the eye, either automatically, or manually.
2. Replace the R pixel values included in the detected area, by a less bright value. Usually, this value is derived from the average of the two remaining color channels (G and B), so that the result is not chromatically irrelevant to the shade of the eye.

So, in order to see if this technique really works, we should tackle a real example.

Time for action – writing a function for red eye reduction

In this example, we will use a photograph of me, to try and reduce the red eye effect. In order to be able to use this tool in other photographs as well, we should make it as generic as possible.

1. First, we should write the following function in our editor (we'll call it RedEyeReduction.m):

```
function output = RedEyeReduction(input, thresh)

% Function for red eye reduction in input image
% Inputs:
% input  - Input image
% thresh - Threshold value in channel a*
% Output:
% output - Output image (after red-eye reduction)

cform = makecform('srgb2lab'); % Make the transform structure
  img_lab = applycform(input,cform); % Apply transform to
  L*a*b*

eyes = roipoly(input);      % Select area of eyes
mask = (img_lab(:,:,2) > thresh) & (eyes > 0); % Red pixels in
  eyes

% Split the three color channels
R=input(:,:,1);
G=input(:,:,2);
B=input(:,:,3);

R(mask) = round((G(mask)+B(mask))/2); % Replace R value with
  (G+B)/2

output = cat(3,R,G,B); % Join color channels to form output
  image
```

2. Let's now test our function to see if it actually works on my picture. We will choose an area containing the eyes and use a fairly high threshold value for a* (that is, 150):

```
>> img = imread('my_red_eyes.bmp');
>> output = RedEyeReduction(img, 150);
```

3. Then, it is time to see what our function has done to the image:

```
>> subplot(1,2,1),imshow(img),title('Original image')
>> subplot(1,2,2),imshow(output),title('Image after red-eye
   correction')
```

4. The result of our red eye reduction function proved to be a huge success! Or didn't it? The truth is that, we actually haven't thoroughly tested our function. Let's change our threshold and see what happens. We'll try with a lower and a higher threshold:

```
>> output = RedEyeReduction(img, 170); % Picking a very high
   threshold
>> output2 = RedEyeReduction(img, 120); % Picking a very
   low threshold
>> figure,subplot(1,2,1),imshow(output),title('Very high
   threshold')
>> subplot(1,2,2),imshow(output2),title('Very low threshold')
```

5. The results of the previous steps reveal that our function relies very heavily on color; hence, we should very carefully choose our threshold. Now let's see what happens if we select a larger area (the results that follows show the selection and result):

```
>> output3 = RedEyeReduction(img, 150); % Picking a very large
   area
```

What just happened?

When choosing the right threshold, the results achieved in this example are very satisfying, given that we have only written less than 10 lines of functional code. The process described above was followed, that is, transforming the image to CIE-L*a*b*, choosing the area containing the eyes, combining it with our threshold to generate a mask, and then using the mask to replace R values with the average values of G and B. You should note that in order to get the average, we performed addition of the two channels, followed by division by two. This could lead to a non-integer result, so we converted it to integer using the function `round`, which rounds the result to the nearest integer value. In the last two steps, we revealed the ugly truth; our function relies too much on a proper selection of the color threshold and the eyes area from the user.

Taking advantage of eye circularity

As we can see from the problematic results described previously, the function we have written should be used very cautiously if we want to have a good output. A way to improve it would be to take into consideration additional properties of eyes, such as their radial symmetry. Since our eyes are circular, the red region should also appear circular. This can be detected using an image presented in *Chapter 3*, *Morphological Operations and Object Analysis*, `imfindcircles`. Let's see how.

Time for action – automating our function for red eye reduction

This time, we will use one extra tool in our function, removing the need for ROI selection. The rationale of the refined function will be to first check the image for circular regions in color channel a* (we must find two) and then perform masking of the pixels in these regions having high a* values. You may have noticed that we did not mention any manual ROI selection step. However, we should state the suspected radii for the circle detection.

1. Let's see if this approach works, by first writing our function:

```
function output = RedEyeReductionCircular(input, thresh, radii)

% Function for red eye reduction in input image
% Inputs:
% input - Input image
% thresh - Threshold value in channel a*
% radii - 2x1 matrix with lowest and highest radius
% Output:
% output - Output image (after red-eye reduction)
```

```
cform = makecform('srgb2lab'); % Make the transform structure
  img_lab = applycform(input,cform); % Apply transform to
  L*a*b*

a = img_lab(:,:,2); % Isolate a* channel
[I,r] = imfindcircles(a,radii); % Detect circles in ROI

mask = zeros(size(a)); % Make a mask full of zeros

if size(I,1) ~= 2   % If we don't detect a pair of eyes
  disp('No pair of eyes detected in ROI!')
  % In case of failure, revert to the manual function
output = RedEyeReduction(input, thresh);
else
  mask(round(I(1,2)),round(I(1,1)))=1; % First eye center
  mask(round(I(2,2)),round(I(2,1)))=1; % Second eye center
  average_radius = round((r(1)+r(2))/2); % Find average eye
    radius
  mask = imdilate(mask,strel('disk',average_radius)); % Enlarge
    ROIs
  mask = (mask > 0) & a > thresh; % Keep pixels with high a*
    values
  % Split the three color channels
  R=input(:,:,1);
  G=input(:,:,2);
  B=input(:,:,3);

  R(mask) = round((G(mask)+B(mask))/2); % Replace R value with
    (G+B)/2

  output = cat(3,R,G,B); % Join color channels to form output
    image
end
```

2. This time, the results are computed automatically, so if we have chosen proper values for the threshold and radii, the result should be correct. Let's check if this is true. First, we load our image and call the function with the proper inputs:

```
>> img = imread('my_red_eyes.bmp');
>> output = RedEyeReductionCircular(img, 150, [10 25]);
```

3. Now, it is time to visualize our results:

```
>> figure,subplot(1,2,1),imshow(img),title('Original image')
>> subplot(1,2,2),imshow(output),title('Automatic red eye
   reduction')
```

4. So far, so good. Our function seems to be working like a charm! But what happens when wrong radii are chosen? Will our function revert to the manual method, or will it fail completely? Let's see what happens if we give very large radii values:

```
>> figure; % Open new figure
>> output = RedEyeReductionCircular(img, 150, [40 45]);
```

The output of the previous code is as follows:

```
No pair of eyes detected in ROI!
Warning: Image is too big to fit on screen; displaying at 33%
> In imuitools\private\initSize at 72
  In imshow at 283
  In roipoly>parse_inputs at 184
  In roipoly at 81
  In RedEyeReduction at 13
  In RedEyeReductionCircular at 22
```

5. The result of the previous action was as expected. The warning message is nothing to worry about; it comes up every time the image we try to display is very large to fit on the screen. After the warning message, our image is displayed at 33% of its size and we must, as before, select the ROI of the eyes:

6. After selecting our ROI, we can display the results:

```
>> figure,subplot(1,2,1),imshow(img),title('Original image')
>> subplot(1,2,2),imshow(output),title('Automatic red eye
   reduction')
```

What just happened?

You have just mastered the secrets behind a simple automated red eye reduction. The process of ROI selection is no longer needed, as we use the proper MATLAB function to detect circular objects. We also included a safety check, so that the function does not do anything if no pair of eyes is detected (or if more than two circular objects are detected). In this case, we use `disp` to display an error message in the command line and then we return the input as output. In case there is a pair of circular objects detected, we locate the coordinates of their centers, create an empty mask of equal size to our image, and set the pixels of the centers equal to one. Then, we find the average radius of the two eyes, round it to the nearest integer, and use it to make a disk structuring element to dilate the centers. This process leads to an almost perfect mask creation. The mask is then refined using the color thresholding process used in the previous example and finally, we replace the red pixels as already described. In the case that no pair of circles is detected, our function falls back to the previous method implemented and uses the selected threshold and a user-selected ROI to perform red eye reduction.

Pop quiz – working with color

Q1. Which of the following sentences are true?

1. A pixel with RGB values equal to {0,255,0} is red.

2. If we set all the pixels of the first dimension, of a three-dimensional matrix representing an image equal to zero, we will have no red pixels left.

3. HSV and CIE-L*a*b* handle illumination fluctuations more efficiently, because they have separate channels for brightness and color information.

4. Using `histeq` is the best out-of-the-box method to correct the illumination of an RGB image.

5. Red eye reduction can be handled efficiently just by thresholding the red channel of the picture.

Summary

This chapter was dedicated to the presentation of color image processing techniques that build upon the grayscale methods of previous chapters. The meaning of color was explained, accompanied by an introduction to color image manipulation. Then, color image thresholding in various color channels was visited with examples, denoting the significant of a proper color channel. Several techniques for color image illumination enhancement were also presented and compared to their grayscale versions. Finally, two alternative ways for red eye reduction in photographs were developed and explained. More specifically, this chapter covered:

- What color images are and how they can be manipulated
- How we can manipulate color images in ways using functions, such as `imrotate`, `imresize`, and `flipdim`
- How to change pixel values in all, or selected color channels
- How we can apply color image thresholding using `im2bw`
- What the steps for performing color isolation are and how we can achieve it in RGB or CIE-L*a*b*
- How to enhance color image illumination in RGB and CIE-L*a*b*
- How to perform red eye reduction in manually selected regions of your photographs
- How to perform automatic red eye reduction in your photographs

In the next chapter, we will present various image filtering techniques, that can be used either for repairing flawed images or to achieve artistic results. Spatial and frequency filters will be explained, using practical examples, to understand their importance. Several usual image processing problems will be addressed using combinations of filtering methods and other techniques that you have learned so far in this book.

5
2-Dimensional Image Filtering

Up to this point, you should be able to use MATLAB at a novice level, to perform various useful image processing operations. It is now time to move on to more advanced image filtering processes and revisit some of the already covered ones. In this chapter, we will dig a little deeper into the image filtering theory and use some more complicated techniques to enhance our images. We will also provide some more information about the processes that you have already learned, so that you take a look behind the curtains and see what they really do. All the methods we will present, will once more be accompanied by hands-on examples that demonstrate their significance in both typical and more advanced image processing tasks.

In this chapter, we shall learn:

- The basic theory on image filtering and processing pixel neighborhoods
- How we can filter an image using convolution
- Alternative ways to filter an image
- Creating image filters in MATLAB
- Using filters for image blurring
- How to remove noise from images
- Enhancing edges in images
- Filtering only specific ROIs in an image

So, let's get started!

An introduction to image filtering

The truth is that, even though we did not explain the notion of filtering thoroughly, you have already performed several image filtering processes throughout the previous chapters. Morphological operations and edge detection are actually types of image filtering, even though we used them in a black box sense, without really looking under the hood. Hopefully, this approach will get you accustomed to the details of image filtering a little faster.

First of all, let's give a general definition of image filtering; it can be explained as the process of modifying the values of the pixels using a function that is typically applied on a local neighborhood of the image. In many situations, applying the function on a neighborhood involves a special operation, called **convolution**, with an operand called **kernel**. In this sense, you have already applied such a process in the case of erosion or dilation and even in the case of edge detection. The former processes used the `strel` function to create a kernel, while the latter used a kernel based on your choice of the edge detection method. But let's not get ahead of ourselves. We will try to take things one step at a time, starting by explaining neighborhood processing.

Processing neighborhoods of pixels

In the previous paragraph, we mentioned that the filtering process typically takes place on a specific neighborhood of pixels. When this neighborhood process is applied for all pixels, it is called **sliding neighborhood operation**. In it, we slide a rectangular neighborhood window through all possible positions of the image and modify its central pixel using a function of the pixels in the neighborhood.

Let's see how this is done, using a numeric example. We'll start with something simple, like a linear filtering process, that is, **averaging**. Let's suppose that we have a small image, sized 8x8 pixels and we want to modify its pixel values, so that they get assigned with the rounded average of the pixels' values in their 3x3 neighborhoods.

This will be easier to explain by using a real numeric example. Let's explain what happens in the step shown in the following image, in which the central pixel of the highlighted 3x3 neighborhood (in the fourth row and sixth column) will be replaced by the average value of all the pixels in the neighborhood (rounded to the nearest integer):

132	101	101	107	115	121	110	92
120	124	122	120	129	123	121	129
134	146	144	134	134	132	134	138
143	147	136	121	121	115	107	107
145	147	138	129	119	113	113	122
162	155	152	149	142	129	118	122
127	122	115	113	117	102	95	94
67	74	78	80	89	89	107	109

132	101	101	107	115	121	110	92
120	124	122	120	129	123	121	129
134	146	144	134	134	132	134	138
143	147	136	121	121	121	107	107
145	147	138	129	119	113	113	122
162	155	152	149	142	129	118	122
127	122	115	113	117	102	95	94
67	74	78	80	89	89	107	109

Let the image be called *I*, the result in pixel *I(4,6)* will be:

$$I(4,6) = \frac{I(3,5) + I(3,6) + I(3,7) + I(4,5) + I(4,6) + I(4,7) + I(5,5) + I(5,6) + I(5,7)}{9}$$

Substituting the values of the pixels, we can calculate the average value:

$$I(4,6) = \frac{134 + 132 + 134 + 121 + 115 + 107 + 119 + 113 + 113}{9} = \frac{1088}{9} = 120.89$$

Hence, the value of the central pixel of the neighborhood will become 121 (the closest integer to 120.89).

By repeating the process described previously for all the pixels of the image, we get a result commonly known as **mean filtering** or **average filtering**. The final result of the entire process is shown in the following figure:

132	101	101	107	115	121	110	92
120	124	122	120	129	123	121	129
134	146	144	134	134	132	134	138
143	147	136	121	121	115	107	107
145	147	138	129	119	113	113	122
162	155	152	149	142	129	118	122
127	122	115	113	117	102	95	94
67	74	78	80	89	89	107	109

53	78	75	77	79	80	77	50
84	125	122	123	124	124	122	80
90	135	133	129	125	124	123	82
96	142	138	131	124	121	120	80
100	147	142	134	126	120	116	77
95	140	136	130	124	116	112	74
79	117	115	115	112	110	107	72
43	65	65	66	66	67	66	45

You may be wondering now; the choice of neighborhood, for the example, was very convenient, but what happens when we want to change the value of a pixel on the borders of the image such as let's say pixel *I(1,4)*? Why was it set to 77 as shown in the image?

This is indeed a valid and natural question, and you are very intuitive if you already thought about it. The answer is that the way to tackle this problem when you want your resulting image to be the same size as your original image is to involve only the neighboring pixels that exist in your calculations. However, since in our example, the calculation that has to be performed is averaging the neighborhood pixels, the denominator will still be 9, hence, it will be like we pad the rest of the neighborhood with zeros. Let's demonstrate this example as well:

	0	0	0								0	0	0			
132	101	101	107	115	121	110	92		132	101	101	77	115	121	110	92
120	124	122	120	129	123	121	129		120	124	122	120	129	123	121	129
134	146	144	134	134	132	134	138		134	146	144	134	134	132	134	138
143	147	136	121	121	115	107	107		143	147	136	121	121	115	107	107
145	147	138	129	119	113	113	122		145	147	138	129	119	113	113	122
162	155	152	149	142	129	118	122		162	155	152	149	142	129	118	122
127	122	115	113	117	102	95	94		127	122	115	113	117	102	95	94
67	74	78	80	89	89	107	109		67	74	78	80	89	89	107	109

As shown in the previous image, the central pixel value gets evaluated as follows:

$$I(1,3) = \frac{I(0,3) + I(0,4) + I(0,5) + I(1,3) + I(1,4) + I(1,5) + I(2,3) + I(2,4) + I(2,5)}{9}$$

Of course, since there is no 0th line, the first three operands of the addition are non-existent, hence set to zero:

$$I(1,3) = \frac{0 + 0 + 0 + 101 + 107 + 115 + 122 + 120 + 129}{9} = 77.11$$

Therefore, the result of the averaging process for the aforementioned neighborhood will be equal to 77 (as shown in the image). This approach is not the only one we have for the image borders. We could assign the maximum possible value (255 for our example) to the non-existent pixels, or assign them the mean value of the rest of the neighborhood, and so on. The choice we make affects the quality of the borders of the image, as we will see in real pictures later on.

The basics of convolution

The process described previously was performed in overlapping neighborhoods of the image, but no use of a **kernel** was mentioned. So, what is this all about? And how does the **convolution** fit in this framework? Well, the truth is that the process described previously is actually describing the essence of convolution, which is passing a kernel over all possible equally sized neighborhoods of the image and using it to modify the value of the central pixel. The only problem in our case is that we did not use a specific kernel in the process described. Or did we? Let's try to find out using MATLAB code to perform two-dimensional convolution.

The 3x3 neighborhood we used for the described process can be replaced by a 3x3 kernel, as long as the final result remains the same. The kernel that accomplishes this effect is a 3x3 matrix with all pixels set to 1/9. Convolving this kernel with the original image produces the same result as the aforementioned example. To demonstrate the process, we can use the two-dimensional convolution MATLAB function `conv2` as follows, to get the result:

```
>> original = [132  101  101  107  115  121  110   92
   120  124  122  120  129  123  121  129
   134  146  144  134  134  132  134  138
   143  147  136  121  121  115  107  107
   145  147  138  129  119  113  113  122
   162  155  152  149  142  129  118  122
   127  122  115  113  117  102   95   94
    67   74   78   80   89   89  107  109];       % Create original
   image
>> kernel = ones(3,3)*(1/9);          % Create kernel
>> conv_result = conv2(original, kernel,'same'); % Perform
   convolution
>> final_result = round(conv_result)          % Rounding of result
```

The final result obtained is as follows:

```
final_result =
      53      78      75      77      79      80      77      50
      84     125     122     123     124     124     122      80
      90     135     133     129     125     124     123      82
      96     142     138     131     124     121     120      80
     100     147     142     134     126     120     116      77
      95     140     136     130     124     116     112      74
      79     117     115     115     112     110     107      72
      43      65      65      66      66      67      66      45
```

As expected, the result is the same as the one calculated using the analytical process described before. The convolution kernel has done its job. In our process, we used a 8x8 original image and a 3x3 kernel with the values of all pixels as 1/9 (this is what happens when you get a 3x3 matrix with all instances of 1 and multiply it by 1/9, as we did) and finally ordered the `conv2` function to produce the result using the padding process described earlier for the borders, hence calculating a result with the same dimensions as the original.

But how did it do it? What exactly is convolution? Now it is time to fully understand convolution. But first, you must get acquainted with its mathematical equations. Since learning math is not the purpose of this book, we will try to give you just the basics, so that you get an idea of what this operation is all about, as it is invaluable for image filtering.

The ugly mathematical truth

Let's start with the mathematical definition of convolution for discrete functions (since in digital image processing all functions are discrete). To form our problem in a signal processing sense, we can define it as passing an input image *I*, through a **Linear Space Invariant** (**LSI**) system, performing convolution with a kernel *h* (also called a filter), to produce an output image, *g*. Hence, we get the following block diagram:

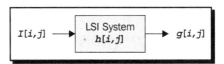

This process is described mathematically by the following equation:

$$g[i,j] = I[i,j] * h[i,j] = \sum_{k=0}^{m-1} \sum_{l=0}^{n-1} I[k,l] \cdot h[i-k,j-l]$$

where $*$ is the symbol for convolution and the large Σ denotes a sum. The reason we have two sums is because our process is two-dimensional. Without going into too much detail, we can summarize the process described previously using the following steps, which are also followed in the implementation of `conv2`:

1. Rotate the convolution kernel by 180 degrees to abide by the process in the double sum of the equation.

2. Determine the central pixel of the neighborhood. This is straightforward when the neighborhood has an odd number of rows and columns, but must be based on some rule if either of the dimensions is even.

3. Apply the rotated kernel to each pixel of the input image. This is a multiplication of each pixel in the rotated kernel by the corresponding pixel on the image neighborhood processed. It can be thought of as the weighted sum of the neighborhood pixels.

The result of `conv2` can be either of the following choices:

- ◆ `full`: Larger than the original image, taking into account all the pixels that can be computed using the convolution kernel, even if their center falls out of the image. This is the default choice for the function.

- ◆ `same`: Same size as the original image, using zeros to calculate border pixel values.

- ◆ `valid`: Smaller than the original image, so that it uses only pixels that have full valid neighbors in the computations.

This means that when you want to produce a convolution result with the same size as the original image, you will have to use `same` as an input, as we did in our previous example.

By now, those of you that are not very much into math may be tempted to stop reading. So, let's stop the mathematical jargon and dive into the practical examples. We know what a convolution does and we have seen an example on the pixels of a very small image, using an averaging convolution kernel. So, what does this process really do to an image?

Time for action – applying averaging filters in images

We will start off with an easy-to-follow example, so that all the theory described previously is demonstrated. For our purposes, we will be using one of the images from the previous chapters. In this example, we will also introduce some new MATLAB functions, to facilitate your understanding. Let's start:

1. First, we load our image, which is `holiday_image2.bmp`:

```
>> img = imread('holiday_image2.bmp');
```

2. Then, we generate our convolution kernel, using function `fspecial` and then rotate it 180 degrees:

```
>> kernel = fspecial('average',3);
>> kernel = rot90(kernel,2)
```

3. The output of the code will be as follows:

```
kernel =
    0.1111    0.1111    0.1111
    0.1111    0.1111    0.1111
    0.1111    0.1111    0.1111
```

4. Now, it is time to use the three different ways of convolving our image:

```
>> con1 = conv2(img,kernel);           % Default usage ('full')
>> con2 = conv2(img,kernel,'same');    % convolution using
   'same'
>> con3 = conv2(img,kernel,'valid');   % convolution using
   'valid'
```

5. In the previous step, you probably got a warning saying:

```
Warning: CONV2 on values of class UINT8 is obsolete.
Use CONV2(DOUBLE(A),DOUBLE(B)) or CONV2(SINGLE(A),SINGLE(B))
 instead.
```

6. This actually means that UNIT8 type will not be supported by conv2 in the future. To be on the safe side, you might want to use the suggestion by MATLAB and convert your image to single prior to convolving it:

```
>> img = single(img);
>> kernel = fspecial('average',3);   % Create 3x3 averaging
   kernel
>> con1 = conv2(img,kernel);          % Default usage ('full')
>> con2 = conv2(img,kernel,'same');   % convolution using 'same'
>> con3 = conv2(img,kernel,'valid');  % convolution using
   'valid'
```

7. Now, we can show our results in one figure, along with the original image. This time, we are going to use an empty matrix as the second argument in imshow, to avoid having to convert our results to UNIT8:

```
>> figure;subplot(2,2,1),imshow(img,[]),title('Original')
>> subplot(2,2,2),imshow(con1,[]),title('full')
>> subplot(2,2,3),imshow(con2,[]),title('same')
>> subplot(2,2,4),imshow(con3,[]),title('valid')
```

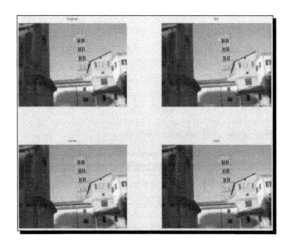

8. It is obvious that the three results are identical, but there is a small detail. Their size is not. So let's see if we got what we expected. In the **Workspace** window, you can see the difference in sizes:

Name	Value	Min	Max
con1	<476x642 uint8>	2	237
con2	<474x640 uint8>	4	237
con3	<472x638 uint8>	6	237
img	<474x640 uint8>	0	253

9. Let's now discuss the physical, qualitative meaning of averaging an image. What does it exactly do? The answer is; it performs blurring of the image. To examine this effect, we can crop the tower from our original and averaged image and display the result. The tower can be cropped using the following coordinates:

```
>> tower_original = img(51:210,321:440);
>> tower_blurred = con2(51:210,321:440); figure
>> subplot(1,2,1),imshow(tower_original),title('Original
   tower')
>> subplot(1,2,2),imshow(tower_blurred),title('Blurred tower')
```

10. The original image and the blurred image are as follows:

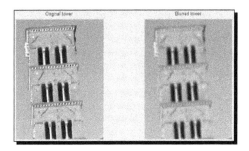

What just happened?

The process described in the previous example demonstrated the usage of convolution in its various implementations, using the averaging kernel produced using `fspecial`. This function is designed to generate kernels for popular filtering tasks, as we will further analyze in the following sections. In our case, we created a 3x3 kernel of values equal to 1/9 (which is almost equal to 0.1111, hence the result in step 2). Then, the three different choices of convolution were applied and the results were displayed along with the original image. Of course, a detail such as the size of the borders cannot be easily observed in full scale, so we observed the difference in the sizes of the results. Finally, we displayed a part of the original image next to the same part of the `same` convolution result, to prove that the result of the averaging process is a blurring of the image.

Alternatives to convolution

Convolution is not the only way to perform image filtering. There is also **correlation**, which gives us the same result. Filtering an image using correlation can be accomplished by using the MATLAB function called `filter2`, which performs, as its name implies, a two-dimensional filtering of two images. The first input in this case is a kernel (filter) and the second input is an image (or in a more general case a two-dimensional matrix). We will not go into detail here, just point out that one main difference between the two methods is that correlation does not need the kernel to be rotated. The border issue remains, having the same three approaches as in the case of convolution using `conv2`. A demonstration on the equivalence of the two functions is given if we type in the following commands:

```
>> img = imread('holiday_image2.bmp');
>> img = img(51:210,321:440);
>> kernel = fspecial('average',3);
>> kernel180 = rot90(kernel,3);
>> conv_result = conv2(img,kernel180,'same');
>> corr_result = filter2(kernel,img,'same');
>> subplot(1,3,1),imshow(img),title('Original')
>> subplot(1,3,2),imshow(uint8(conv_result)),title('Blurred - conv2')
>> subplot(1,3,3),imshow(uint8(corr_result)),title('Blurred -
   filter2')
```

The result of the preceding code is displayed as follows:

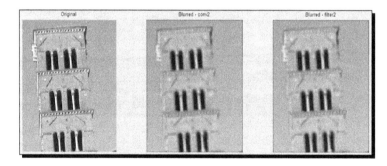

 In our example, the two kernels used for `conv2` and `filter2` are identical, since the averaging filter used is square (3x3) and all its elements are equal. The generalized process shown will be useful when we have a more complex kernel.

Using imfilter

The two alternative solutions for performing image filtering presented so far have their origin in general two-dimensional signal processing theory. This means that they should be expanded for three-dimensional signals when we have to deal with colored image filtering. The process is pretty straightforward and involves repeating the process for all three separate colored channels. But why do that, when we have a function that takes care of checking the image before applying the filter and then selecting the correct method?

This specialized function is called `imfilter` and it is designed for handling images, regardless if they are grayscale or color. This function can implement both filtering methods described in previous paragraphs and it can also define the result to be `same` or `full`. Its extra functionality comes in the selection of the way it handles boundary values, and the automatic processing of color images. Furthermore, this function performs the needed conversions, in case the image input is integer-valued. Combined with the `fspecial` function, this will probably be your most valuable tool in MATLAB when it comes to image filtering.

Creating filters with fspecial

So far you have seen the averaging filter kernel, which can be generated in any method possible that can produce a mxn matrix with all its values equal to 1/mn.

The `fspecial` function used in our previous examples is one way to produce the averaging kernel mentioned. However, it can be used to produce several other filtering kernels. A simple call to the `help` of MATLAB on this function shows us its usage in the first few lines of the result:

```
>> help fspecial
```

The call to the help command of MATLAB will give following output:

```
fspecial Create predefined 2-D filters.
   H = fspecial(TYPE) creates a two-dimensional filter H of the
   specified type. Possible values for TYPE are:
     'average'   averaging filter
     'disk'      circular averaging filter
     'gaussian'  Gaussian lowpass filter
     'laplacian' filter approximating the 2-D Laplacian operator
     'log'       Laplacian of Gaussian filter
     'motion'    motion filter
     'prewitt'   Prewitt horizontal edge-emphasizing filter
     'sobel'     Sobel horizontal edge-emphasizing filter
     'unsharp'   unsharp contrast enhancement filter
```

This means that `fspecial` can create nine different filters, depending on the input choice of the user. If we want to categorize them according to their functionality, we will have to use three broad categories:

- **Image smoothing** or **Blurring**: This is a process that is performed using low-pass filters. The ones that `fspecial` provides are **average**, **disk**, **motion** and **gaussian**. The filters of this type are generally called low-pass because they only let image areas with low frequencies (smooth areas without much detail) be unaffected.

- **Edge detection filters**: These are the core filters used for the edge detection techniques visited in *Chapter 3, Morphological Operations and Object Analysis*. The ones supported by `fspecial` are **laplacian**, **log**, **prewitt** and **sobel**. All these filters suppress the pixel values in areas that do not have many edges and enhance the edges in the image. When they are thresholded, they produce results like the ones generated by `edge`.

- Finally, `fspecial` can create a filter that is used for high-pass filtering, that is, the enhancement of areas that contain much detail. This has the opposite effect from the first group of filters and can be accomplished using an **unsharp** kernel.

In the rest of the chapter, we will try to check the functionality of some of these filters, using real and practical examples.

Different ways to blur an image

Image blurring or smoothing, can be accomplished in many ways. Three of the most popular techniques can be accomplished using `imfilter` and `fspecial`. Since the tower from the previous example contains enough detail to show the effect, we will use it for our example.

Time for action – how much blurring is enough

Just like we did in previous chapters, we will write a custom function that incorporates a combination of MATLAB functions to make our lives easier. This time, our function will perform image blurring, hence will be called `BlurImage.m`:

```
function [output] = BlurImage(input,kernel_choice,kernel_size,method)

% Function for image blurring
% Inputs:
%         input - Input image
%         kernel_choice - User's choice of filter
%         (1: disk
%          2: average
%          3: gaussian)
```

```
%          kernel_size - User's choice of kernel size
%                        ([radius] for disk,
%            [rows, columns] for average,
%            [rows, columns, standard deviation] for Gaussian)
%          method - User's choice of filtering method
%          (1: correlation
%           2: convolution)
% Output:
%          output - Output image (after bluring)

switch kernel_choice
  case 1
    kernel = fspecial('disk',kernel_size);
  case 2
    kernel = fspecial('average',kernel_size);
  case 3
    kernel = fspecial('gaussian',kernel_size);
end

switch method
  case 1
    output = imfilter(input,kernel,'conv');
  case 2
    output = imfilter(input,kernel,'corr');
end
```

Now we can test our code. Let's filter the same image using three different filters, using two different sizes:

1. First, we will load and crop our image:

    ```
    >> img = imread('holiday_image2.bmp');
    >> img = img(51:180,321:440);
    ```

2. Then, we will apply the three filters with selected size 3x3:

    ```
    >> f1 = BlurImage(img,1,1,1);
    >> f2 = BlurImage(img,2,[3,3],1);
    >> f3 = BlurImage(img,3,[3,3,1.5],1);
    ```

3. Let's do the same for kernels of size 5x5:

    ```
    >> f4 = BlurImage(img,1,2,1);
    >> f5 = BlurImage(img,2,[5,5],1);
    >> f6 = BlurImage(img,3,[5,5,1.5],1);
    ```

4. Finally, we will display all images in the same figure, next to the original:

```
>> subplot(2,4,1),imshow(img),title('Original')
>> subplot(2,4,2),imshow(f1),title('Blur by disk of radius 1')
>> subplot(2,4,3),imshow(f2),title('Blur by 3x3 averaging
   kernel')
>> subplot(2,4,4),imshow(f3),title('Blur by 3x3 Gaussian
   kernel')
>> subplot(2,4,6),imshow(f4),title('Blur by disk of radius 2')
>> subplot(2,4,7),imshow(f5),title('Blur by 5x5 averaging
   kernel')
>> subplot(2,4,8),imshow(f6),title('Blur by 5x5 Gaussian
   kernel')
```

5. The result will be as follows:

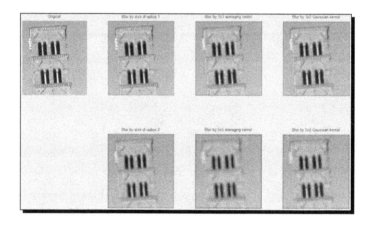

What just happened?

We have just created a tool that can be useful for the one-step blurring of images. All three blurring methods are included and you have the choice of filter parameters. The three methods were then demonstrated, for different kernel sizes, and the effect they have on an image became obvious. From this example, the pros and cons of each choice are not very apparent. The only thing that is very apparent is that they all cause a loss of detail, which could be useful in special cases.

Time to make art using blurring

Losing information by blurring an image is not always bad; many photographers use this effect to add an artistic touch to their images. A common effect is called **bokeh** and it is the blurring of out-of-focus areas in a photograph. Let's see how we can create an out-of-focus effect in one of our photographs. We will use a panoramic night photograph of the city I grew up in, Ioannina. Let's try the disk kernel with a radius of 25:

```
>> img = imread('Ioannina.jpg');
>> kernel = fspecial('disk',25);
>> for i=1:size(img,3),
bokeh(:,:,i) = imfilter(img(:,:,i),kernel);
end
>> subplot(2,1,1),imshow(img),title('Original image of Ioannina')
>> subplot(2,1,2),imshow(bokeh),title('Bokeh image of Ioannina')
```

Now, we will try to add such an effect to our images, by writing a function that will let the user define the Region Of Interest (ROI) that will remain in focus and then perform blurring using the disk kernel.

Time for action – creating the bokeh effect in an image

We will now work on another night image taken in Berlin, Germany. We will try to isolate the light bulb soldier and perform blurring in the other areas of the image. The function we will use will be able to handle both grayscale and color images. Let's see the function:

```
function [output] = Bokeh(input, radius)

% Function that performs blurring on the whole image except a user
defined
% ROI,using a disk kernel. The effect resembles the bokeh effect.
```

```
% Inputs:
%         input   - Input image
%         radius  - User's choice of radius for the disk kernel
% Output:
%         output  - Output image (only user-defined ROI stays in focus)

kernel = fspecial('disk',radius);      % Create disk kernel
disp('Select area to keep in focus!')  % Display message to user
mask = roipoly(input);                 % User selects area of interest
output = [];                           % Start with an empty image
for i = 1:size(input,3)                % Covering the case of color images
    cropped = input(:,:,i);            % Perform per-channel processing
    channel = input(:,:,i);             % Replica of channel
    cropped(mask == 1) = 0;             % Keep only ROI outside mask
    cropped = imfilter(cropped,kernel); % Perform blurring out of ROI
    channel(mask==0) = cropped(mask==0); % Only keep ROI unaffected
    output = cat(3,output,channel);    % Concatenate channels
end
```

Now, we can use our function on the image described:

1. Let's start by loading our image:

    ```
    >> img = imread('soldier.jpg');
    ```

2. Then, we must call our Bokeh function, giving it the input image name and the radius of the filter (we will use 15 pixels):

    ```
    >> [output] = Bokeh(soldier,15);
    ```

    We get the following message displayed by our function:

    Select area to keep in focus!

3. Now we select the area we want to keep in focus:

4. Now, let's show our original image and our artistic result next to each other:

```
>> subplot(1,2,1),imshow(img),title('Original')
>> subplot(1,2,2),imshow(output),title('Bokeh effect')
```

What just happened?

In this example, you got to learn a new way to process your images so that you add an artistic effect to them. The process of ROI selection covered in previous chapters was used so that we select a region we want to remain unaffected. Then, for all channels of the image (whether it has one or three), we perform blurring with a disk kernel, which is a good approximation of the bokeh effect caused by the rendering of out-of-focus light sources by a photographic lens. This way, you can make the area outside your selection seem naturally out-of-focus. In a similar manner, you can add other effects in selected parts of your image. You just have to be careful of what regions you select to take place in the processing (set to 1 in your mask) and which ones you want to keep unaffected (set to zero in your mask).

Have a go hero – add a motion effect in your image

Now it is your turn to take the wheel. Try to alter the Bokeh function we wrote to perform blurring using the motion filter instead of the disk kernel. The motion filter adds a feel of motion to your images; the larger the kernel, the faster the motion. Wouldn't it be fun if the cars in our soldier image seemed to move? Let's try it. You could base your code on the function we created earlier. Its definition is given below:

```
function [output] = Motion(input,len)

% Function that performs motion blurring on a user defined
% ROI,using the motionkernel. The effect resembles a local motion.
% Inputs:
%        input   - Input image
%        len     - User's choice of length for the motion in pixels
```

```
%         theta  - User's choice of angle for the motion in degrees
% Output:
%         output - Output image (only user-defined ROI appears to
   move)
```

To check if your function works, you should type:

```
>> img = imread('soldier.jpg');
>> [output] = Motion(soldier,25,0);
```

Then, you should be able to use the mouse to define the ROI you want to appear as moving:

When displayed next to the original image, the final result should look something like this:

Removing noise using blurring

Another very popular image processing task in which blurring is used, is removing noise from images. Images can be distorted because of various reasons such as, for example, from their scanning process, where the film grain adds unwanted noise, but the scanner could also introduce noise, or the photograph to be scanned might have aesthetic marks on it (such as scratches). Furthermore, even digital photographs may have noise in them, for example, due to their CCD detectors. Transmitting images over electronic mediums may also corrupt them, leading to a noisy result. Many types of additive noise have been implemented in the **Image Processing Toolbox** of MATLAB and they can be used to simulate some of the aforementioned image corruptions. The function that is used for adding noise to an image is called `imnoise`. Its usage can be explored using `help`. Let's see the first lines of the result:

```
>> help imnoise
```

The output of the preceding command is as follows:

```
imnoise Add noise to image.
    J = imnoise(I,TYPE,...) Add noise of a given TYPE to the intensity
image
    I. TYPE is a string that can have one of these values:
        'gaussian' Gaussian white noise with constant mean and variance
        'localvar' Zero-mean Gaussian white noise with an intensity-
dependent variance
        'poisson'  Poisson noise
        'salt & pepper'  "On and Off" pixels
        'speckle'  Multiplicative noise
    Depending on TYPE, you can specify additional parameters to
imnoise. All
    numerical parameters are normalized; they correspond to operations
with
    images with intensities ranging from 0 to 1.
```

This means that we can add five different types of noise to an image. Each type corresponds to some physical source of noise and this should be taken under consideration in your chosen course of action for removing noise from an image.

In this section, we will try to get a rule of thumb on which filter should be used for each type of noise.

Time for action – trying to remove different types of noise

Let's go back to our holiday in Rome picture. We will add different types of noise to it and then filter the noisy result with our blurring kernels:

1. Once again, we will start with loading our image:

```
>> img = imread('holiday_image2.bmp');
```

2. Now let's add four kinds of noise to it (we'll use the default settings):

```
>> gauss = imnoise(img,'gaussian');
>> poiss = imnoise(img,'poisson');
>> speck = imnoise(img,'speckle');
>> snp = imnoise(img,'salt & pepper');
```

3. First, we will write a small function that takes the original image, the distorted image, and the type of noise as input; performs filtering with our three filters and displays the results. We'll name our function `DenoiseAndPlot.m`:

```
function DenoiseAndPlot(original,distorted,type)

% Function that performs filtering of the distorted image with %
three different kernels and displays the results
% Inputs:
%       original  - Original image
%       distorted - Image distorted by noise
%       type      - Type of noise
%       (1: Gaussian, 2: Poisson, 3: speckle, 4: Salt & Pepper)

switch type
  case 1
    message = 'Noisy image (Gaussian)';
  case 2
    message = 'Noisy image (Poisson)';
  case 3
    message = 'Noisy image (speckle)';
  case 4
    message = 'Noisy image (Salt & Pepper)';
end
f1 = BlurImage(distorted,1,2,1);
f2 = BlurImage(distorted,2,[5,5],1);
f3 = BlurImage(distorted,3,[5,5,2],1);
subplot(2,3,1),imshow(original),title('Original image')
subplot(2,3,2),imshow(distorted),title(message)
subplot(2,3,4),imshow(f1),title('Filtered by disk kernel')
subplot(2,3,5),imshow(f2),title('Filtered by averaging kernel')
subplot(2,3,6),imshow(f3),title('Filtered by Gaussian kernel')
```

4. Now, we will call our function for the case of Gaussian noise:

```
>> DenoiseAndPlot(img,gauss,1);
```

5. The result of the preceding code is as follows:

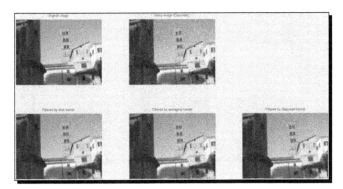

6. We can observe that all three filters have a comparable result, with the average filter causing more detail loss.

7. Now, we'll try to remove the Poisson noise using our known filters:

```
>> DenoiseAndPlot(img,poiss,2);
```

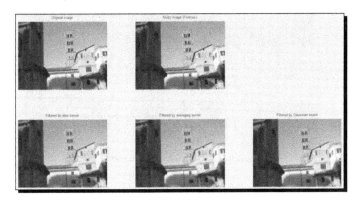

8. Once again, all three filters have a comparable result, with the average filter causing more detail loss.

9. It's time for the third type of noise, which is speckle noise. Once more we execute:

```
>> DenoiseAndPlot(img,poiss,3);
```

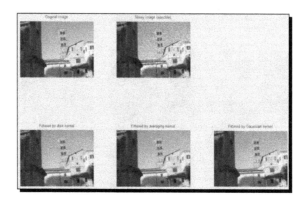

10. The results are again similar to previous cases of noise.

11. Let's finally try the salt & pepper noise:

```
>> DenoiseAndPlot(img,snp,4);
```

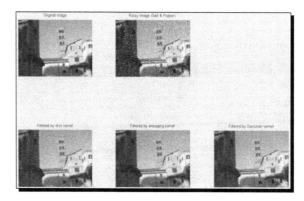

12. The result accomplished for the salt and pepper case appears quite noisy for all three filters. This gives us a hint that maybe these three blurring filters are not equally successful for all types of noise. The deduction is really intuitive, but still, we would have to find another filter that works better, at least for the salt and pepper noise.

What just happened?

First of all, we made a very wise choice by writing a function that performs the repeating parts of our code, which were quite lengthy. The only thing that changed according to our choice of filter was the title of the noisy image. Hence, we included a `switch` clause to change our message depending on the type of noise. All other lines in our function are pretty straightforward. We passed the noisy image through all of our filters using the `BlurImage` function we made earlier and displayed all the results in the same figure as the original and noisy images.

The results we got were decent for all cases, except the case of salt & pepper noise. Nothing exceptional and perfect, but the resulting images were generally an improvement over the noisy ones.

Hence, these three filters can be used for denoising purposes in cases of:

- Image sensor noise in the brighter parts of an image, which normally resembles the Poisson noise. This kind of noise is usually called **shot noise**.
- Image sensor noise in the darker parts of an image, which normally resembles the Gaussian noise. This kind of noise is usually called **amplifier noise**.
- Film grain noise, which also can be modeled by Gaussian noise.
- Noise that appears in **SAR (Synthetic Aperture Radar)** images, which is granular and appears like speckle noise.

However, the case of noise added by **A/D (Analog to Digital)** conversion or by errors in image data bits during transmission cannot be handled very effectively by these filters. This is why we will now visit another very important filtering method, called **median filtering**.

The importance of the median filter

The median filter is also a neighborhood filter resembling the averaging filter, but instead of calculating the average value of the neighborhood it processes, it finds their median value and assigns it to the central pixel. This difference causes the process of median filtering to be less sensitive to outliers. Since the salt & pepper noise is essentially a collection of randomly placed outlier (black or white) pixels, the median filter should work better on this type of noise. Let's see if this is true, using the function `medfit2`.

Time for action – removing salt & pepper with medfilt2

We will start in the usual way and try to remove the salt & pepper noise from our image, using the median filtering function offered by MATLAB.

1. Let's load our image and add salt & pepper noise to it:

```
>> img = imread('holiday_image2.bmp');
>> snp = imnoise(img,'salt & pepper');
```

2. Now, let's filter it and show the results:

```
>> denoised = medfilt2(snp,[5,5]);figure
>> subplot(1,3,1),imshow(img),title('Original image')
>> subplot(1,3,2),imshow(snp),title('Noisy image
   (Salt&Pepper)')
>> subplot(1,3,3),imshow(denoised),title('Denoised image')
```

What just happened?

This is much better. It seems that we have found our preferred filtering solution for the case of salt and pepper noise. The only thing we did was to apply median filtering to our image that was distorted by salt and pepper noise, using a 5x5 kernel.

Have a go hero – denoising real images

Now that you have learned most of the filters for noise removal, it is time to put them to the test with real noise. You should download problematic pictures, for example, taken with a high ISO setting, or bad JPEG compression artifacts and then try to find which filter can de-noise them more successfully. A simple search for noisy images on the internet should provide a multitude of examples to work on.

Bringing back the details

Up to now, we have been using filters that subtract details from the images. There is a way to do the opposite, which is to highlight details. This can be done using the edge enhancement kernels available, or the **unsharp** kernel provided by the `fspecial` function. The second option is quite straightforward and involves only filtering the image using the contrast enhancement filter. The first option though, is a little trickier and demands an understanding of the edge enhancement filtering results. Let's first try to understand these results, using an example.

Time for action – enhancing the edges in our images

We will now try to get a feel of what edge enhancement is all about. We will use our holiday image to perform grayscale enhancement and our soldier image to perform color enhancement (remember that the edge detection techniques of *Chapter 3, Morphological Operations and Object Analysis*, involved only grayscale images):

1. First, we will load our two images in two matrices:

    ```
    >> gray = imread('holiday_image2.bmp');
    >> color = imread('soldier.jpg');
    ```

2. Now, let's prepare our kernels (we'll use their default settings):

    ```
    >> lp = fspecial('laplacian');
    >> lg = fspecial('log');
    >> pr = fspecial('prewitt');
    >> sb = fspecial('sobel');
    ```

3. Next, we apply the filters to both images (in the same line to save space):

    ```
    >> g1 = imfilter(gray,lp); c1 = imfilter(color,lp);
    >> g2 = imfilter(gray,lg); c2 = imfilter(color,lg);
    >> g3 = imfilter(gray,pr); c3 = imfilter(color,pr);
    >> g4 = imfilter(gray,sb); c4 = imfilter(color,sb);
    ```

4. And now, let's show our grayscale results on the same figure:

```
>> subplot(3,2,1),imshow(gray),title('Original grayscale
   image')
>> subplot(3,2,2),imshow(g1),title('Grayscale Laplacian
   result')
>> subplot(3,2,3),imshow(g2),title('Grayscale LoG result')
>> subplot(3,2,4),imshow(g3),title('Grayscale Prewitt result')
>> subplot(3,2,5),imshow(g4),title('Grayscale Sobel result')
```

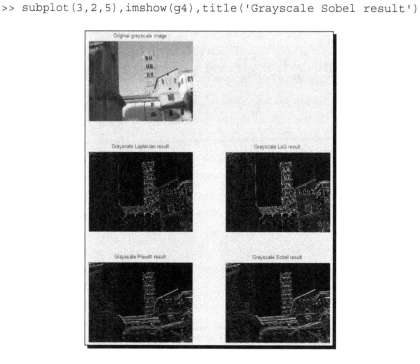

5. Finally, let's show our color results on the same figure:

```
>> subplot(3,2,1),imshow(color),title('Original color image')
>> subplot(3,2,3),imshow(c1),title('Color Laplacian result')
>> subplot(3,2,4),imshow(c2),title('Color LoG result')
>> subplot(3,2,5),imshow(c3),title('Color Prewitt result')
>> subplot(3,2,6),imshow(c4),title('Color Sobel result')
```

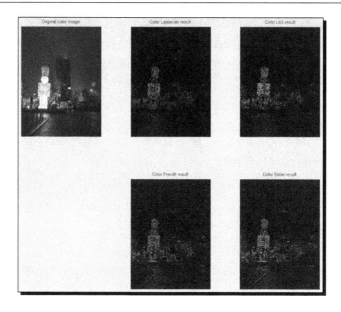

What just happened?

You just performed edge enhancement using all the filters available by the `fspecial` function. In step 2, we prepared the kernels and in step 3 we filtered our images (loaded in step 1) with each one of the kernels. Note that, to save space in our text, we took advantage of the fact that we can give multiple commands in one command line, just by separating them with the semi-colon symbol (or the comma if we do not care about the result being printed on screen). The same trick has always been used in the case of plotting, so you must have understood the logic by now. The results generated in step 4 show that the edge enhancement filters produce a very interesting effect; in grayscale images they enhance the areas with sudden transitions between dark and bright (high frequencies) and in color images, they have the same effect in each color channel, therefore enhancing bright lights in night scenes. This is an interesting effect, right?

Brighten up the lights

Now, we will take advantage of the last conclusion of the example we just performed, to brighten the lights in our soldier picture. We already saw that the color edge enhancement in night scenes has the effect of enhancing light sources. So, what would happen if we used this result to amplify the lights in our image by adding the result of the edge enhancement filter to the original image? Normally, we would have to worry about the values after the addition exceeds 255 (the maximum brightness value of an 8-bit image). However, MATLAB will automatically truncate these results and make them equal to 255. Therefore, the only thing we need to be careful about will be to not let many pixels get assigned the maximum value, as this would give us an unnatural result. Let's see all these things with an example.

Time for action – brighten up the lights in our soldier picture

Once again we will work with our color image depicting the light bulb soldier. The results can be visible even in the grayscale form of the image, so you could convert it to grayscale before applying the technique:

1. Let's start off with loading our image and creating the filter. We'll use the `prewitt` kernel (in its default value it will emphasize horizontal edges):

    ```
    >> img = imread('soldier.jpg');
    >> kernel = fspecial('prewitt');
    ```

2. Then, we will apply our filter to the image and add the result to our original:

    ```
    >> edges = imfilter(img,kernel);
    >> brighter = img + edges;
    ```

3. Now, let's see the result side-by-side with the original:

    ```
    >> subplot(1,2,1),imshow(img),title('Original image');
    >> subplot(1,2,2),imshow(brighter),title('Brightened image');
    ```

4. To get a better idea of the effect, let's crop the left part of the images, containing Christmas light bulbs on trees:

    ```
    >> imcrop(brighter);
    >> imcrop(img);
    ```

5. It should be obvious that the left image is the brightened one, as it has even enhanced some light bulbs that seemed dim in the original image (on the right). Furthermore, we must note once more that the Prewitt filter we used emphasized just the horizontal edges. On the down side, we have a side-effect of minor, unimportant details in the sky also being enhanced. A possible way to tackle that would be to enhance only the pixels with values higher than a certain (either manual or automatic) threshold. This will be left to you as an exercise, since the way to do it is already covered in previous chapters.

Pop quiz – image filtering in 2-dimensions

Q1. Which of the following are true?

1. Convolution and correlation use identical filtering kernels.
2. When you use valid as a filtering choice in `conv2`, you end up with a smaller resulting image than the original.
3. Filtering an image with the `laplacian` kernel results in blurring it.
4. Salt and pepper noise is best removed by the Gaussian filter.
5. Using the `unsharp` kernel to filter an image results in enhancing details.

Summary

This chapter gave you a rather detailed tool of two-dimensional filtering in MATLAB. The basic mathematic ideas behind image filtering were explained and practical examples were given. You got to see various techniques for using two-dimensional filtering in everyday problems such as removing noise from images, or enhancing areas that are blurred. You also learned some artistic effects caused by image filtering and practiced on ways to use them in your images. More specifically, this chapter covered:

◆   An introduction to neighborhood-based operations on an image

◆   An explanation of what convolution is and why it is important

◆   The alternative way to perform filtering, by using correlation

◆   The usage of `imfilter` for performing image filtering

◆   How you make kernels with `fspecial`, for image filtering usage

◆   How to blur images and why it is important

◆   How to create artistic effects using blurring

- How to remove noise using blurring

- How to enhance edges in an image, why it is important, and how it is connected to edge detection

- How to brighten up light sources in a night image using edge enhancement

In the next chapter, we will get to discuss exciting and practical examples about artistic and scientific implementations of image processing. We will work on examples of multispectral images, panoramas, and HDR images. We will also discuss other artistic effects by mixing some of the techniques you've learnt so far. All our examples will be accompanied by hands-on tasks, as always.

6
Mixing Images for Science or Art

In the previous chapters, we covered how many of the common techniques, used for image processing, can be implemented using MATLAB. This chapter is a little bit more advanced in terms of the complexity of the algorithms covered, but we will present them in a gentle, introductory manner. The results will be more than interesting, since you will get to learn how to mix, or combine multiple images to create new ones, either for scientific purposes, or for pure artistic results. More specifically, in this chapter, we will cover how you can work with multispectral images in MATLAB, to unveil hidden details.
We will move on to **panorama stitching** *for the creation of beautiful panoramic images and then we will show blending techniques to combine masked areas in an image with another image. Finally, we will cover the production of* **High Dynamic** *Range (HDR) images using MATLAB. All these techniques will be demonstrated in the simplest possible ways, using hands-on examples.*

In this chapter, we will cover:

- ◆ What the importance of mixing images is
- ◆ What multispectral images are and how we can manipulate them in MATLAB
- ◆ How we can create composite images in MATLAB
- ◆ How we can blend selected areas of images to create interesting visual results
- ◆ What High Dynamic Range (HDR) images are and how we can create and process them in MATLAB
- ◆ How we can stitch images to create panoramas in MATLAB

So, let's get started!

The importance of mixing or combining images

An obvious question for a beginner in the field of image processing, would be about what the importance of mixing images is. The answer is that the basic idea behind mixing or combining images is to enrich them and achieve the following results:

◆ Enhance the information included in multimodal images, that is, images acquired from different sensors or scanners, to detect regions of interest. This is a technique often used in medical imaging applications, such as brain CT/MRI images or body PET/CT images.

◆ See more than the eye can see, by combining images of the same subject, taken at different frequencies of the electromagnetic spectrum. This is a way to extract information that is not normally visible to humans, such as for example, infrared wavelengths.

◆ Blend two or more images together to end up with an artistic result.

◆ Combine images of the same subject taken using different exposure levels, to end up with a resulting image with a higher dynamic range.

◆ Stitch together multiple images that partially overlap each other, to produce a larger, panoramic image of the photographed scene.

In the rest of this chapter, we will show how we can achieve many of the examples mentioned previously, using MATLAB.

Using multispectral imaging

Multispectral imaging is a highly sophisticated technique that proves invaluable in a multitude of scientific applications. It is widely used in the following fields:

◆ In the interpretation of Synthetic Aperture Radar (SAR) images, which are a little tricky to analyze. Combining the information extracted from them with the information derived by the multispectral images of the same area, we can come to many useful conclusions.

◆ In the determination of the techniques used by painters and the condition of paintings; by a thorough examination of the visible, infrared, ultraviolet, and X-ray pictures of the paintings.

◆ In fingerprint image acquisition devices, to capture the relationship between the visible fingerprint patterns that lie on the skin surface with subsurface patterns that are invisible to the eye and can be detected using ultrasonic imaging. This way, the fingerprint acquired is much more detailed.

Loading and manipulating the multispectral images

The multispectral images can be stored in various formats. A common format that is often used to store geospatial map data gathered from satellites is the ERDAS LAN format, which uses the extension .lan. MATLAB can read these kinds of files using the function multibandread. Since the files are multiband, in order for us to be able to visualize it in RGB, we must be able to limit the channels to three. This can be done in a single line of code, since multibandread can define the bands that will be read into MATLAB. More details about using this function can be given using our usual tool, which is the help command:

```
>> help multibandread
```

The output of the previous code is as follows:

```
multibandread Read band interleaved data from a binary file
    X = multibandread(FILENAME,SIZE,PRECISION,
                      OFFSET,INTERLEAVE,BYTEORDER)
    reads band-sequential (BSQ), band-interleaved-by-line (BIL), or
    band-interleaved-by-pixel (BIP) data from a binary file, FILENAME.
X is
    a 2-D array if only one band is read, otherwise it is 3-D. X is
returned
    as an array of data type double by default.  Use the PRECISION
argument
    to map the data to a different data type.
```

The rest is rather lengthy, so we will leave it at that. The most important thing is that the function is rather complex and uses several inputs to define how it works. We will try to demonstrate its use with some useful multiband image processing techniques.

Let's use one of the .lan files included in the Image Processing Toolbox to demonstrate some basic processing steps. Since, the documentation of MATLAB covers the Landsat imagery of Paris, France, we will use another example. But first, let's see our choices.

The images included in MATLAB 2012b for use in the examples given in the documentation are placed in the folder home\toolbox\images\imdemos, where home is the installation directory of MATLAB. In our case, this is c:\MATLAB\2012b\. Hence, we can have a look at the images included in this directory, using the following, DOS-like, line of code:

```
>> dir('C:\MATLAB\R2012b\toolbox\images\imdemos\*.lan')
```

This leads to the following result:

```
Command Window
  >> dir('C:\MATLAB\R2012b\toolbox\images\imdemos\*.lan')

  littlecoriver.lan   montana.lan       rio.lan
  mississippi.lan     paris.lan         tokyo.lan

fx >>
```

In general, the function `dir` is the same as in DOS; it lists the directories of the current directory. When it is called with a specified path as an input, it lists the contents of the directory specified. The use of the wildcard symbol (*) in our example, asks `dir` to list all the files in the specified path ending with `.lan`.

Now that we know there are six different landsat images included in MATLAB, we can choose which one we want to use in our example. Let's use Rio, Brazil.

Time for action – visible spectrum from a multiband image of Rio

We will use the file `rio.lan` for this example and try to manipulate its visible spectrum bands. The file contains seven bands, from which the third contains red color, the second green one, and the first blue one. Let's use the following steps to import and process just these three bands in MATLAB:

1. First, we load the multiband image using `multibandread` (`imread` could still be used, in the possible case, where the multiband image is of type `.tif`):

```
>> image = multibandread('rio.lan', [512, 512, 7],...
'uint8=>uint8',128, 'bil', 'ieee-le', {'Band','Direct',[3 2
   1]});
```

2. The previous step saves the red, green, and blue bands of the image in a matrix with 8-bit integer values, which can be now displayed as a RGB image, in the usual way:

```
>> figure,imshow(image),title('Original RGB image')
```

3. However, the image derived from step 2 has very little contrast and its color bands are highly correlated with each other. This is why, the resulting image seems like it is monochromatic, that is, includes only the shades of one color. To enhance the image and acquire a more decent and life-like result, we can adjust the contrast of all the three channels. A way to accomplish this is:

```
>> for i=1:size(image,3)
adjusted(:,:,i) = imadjust(image(:,:,i));
end
>> subplot(1,2,1),imshow(image),title('Original RGB image')
>> subplot(1,2,2),imshow(adjusted),title('Adjusted RGB image')
```

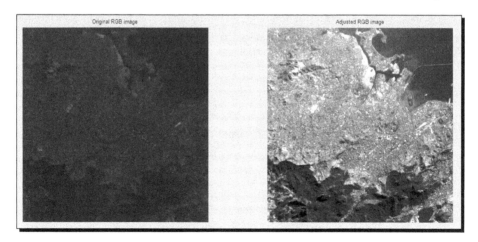

4. Sometimes we will need to have a result that is even more pronounced, for example, have the vegetation of a landsat image denoted with a very bright color. This can be achieved using a so called decorrelation stretch, that produces an image with high correlation among its bands.

5. Contrast stretches can easily be achieved using MATLAB's decorrstretch function, followed by a linear contrast stretch performed by defining the fraction of the image 'Tol' to be saturated at low and high intensities:

```
>> stretched = decorrstretch(image,'Tol',0.01);
```

6. Now, we can display our resulting image next to the original:

```
>> subplot(1,2,1),imshow(adjusted),title('Adjusted RGB image')
>> subplot(1,2,2),imshow(stretched),title('Stretched RGB
   image')
```

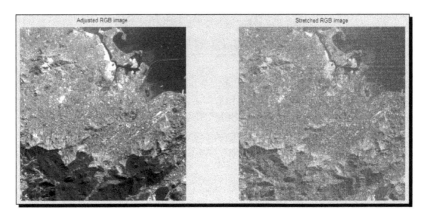

What just happened?

You just got acquainted with multiband images. The first step was to import a binary file, rio.lan, which is a multiband **BIL (Band Interleaved by Line)** satellite image of Rio, into MATLAB. The function used to accomplish this was multibandread, which used the following as inputs:

- the name of the binary file ('rio.lan')
- the number of rows, columns, and bands of the image ([512 512 7])
- the format used for reading the data from the binary file (integer, that is, 'uint8=>uint8')
- the offset, that is, the number of bytes after the beginning of the file, where the data begins (128)
- the format in which the data is stored ('bil')
- the byte ordering in which the data is stored ('ieee-le' for little endian)
- the subset, which is a cell that describes the way the data will be imported from the binary file (in our example, {'Band','Direct',[3 2 1]} denotes reading the visible bands of the spectrum, which are the third (red), second (green), and first (blue))

Then, we displayed the imported image and saw that it seems monochromatic, and so fixed this defect by adjusting the contrast of each color channel separately. To offer an alternative solution that can further enhance differences in the land surface, we performed decorrelation stretching, followed by linear stretch of the contrast of the resulting image. Such techniques might be used as the foundations for geospatial analysis systems that either automatically or semi-automatically, classify the areas depicted in satellite imagery into various terrain classes. In the next example, we will see how we can use more bands of the same multispectral image.

Time for action – working with invisible spectrums

This time, we will not import just the bands belonging to the visible spectrum, but all seven bands. We will play around a little bit with the resulting images, trying to justify the importance of the bands. Let's start:

1. First, we will import our image, but this time without specifying just three channels:

```
>> multi = multibandread('rio.lan', [512, 512, 7],...
'uint8=>uint8',128, 'bil', 'ieee-le');
```

To prove that we have indeed loaded all seven channels, let's check the size of our resulting matrix:

```
>> size(multi)
```

The output of the previous code is as follows:

```
ans =
   512   512     7
```

2. Since we have a matrix containing seven bands, let's make our RGB image using another method. We know the mirroring of color channels to bands is R:third, G:second, and B:first, so we will use an appropriate concatenation method, followed by the same contrast adjustment technique as before:

```
>> rgb = cat(3,multi(:,:,3),multi(:,:,2),multi(:,:,1));
>> for i=1:size(rgb,3)
adjusted(:,:,i) = imadjust(rgb(:,:,i));
end
```

3. Now, what about the rest of the seven bands? To get a good idea of what they are, let's display them along with the visible bands and the adjusted RGB image we created. As you can see from the names assigned, the rest of the bands contain infrared spectral ranges, with the larger wavelength being the sixth band (thermal infrared):

```
>> subplot(2,4,1),imshow(multi(:,:,1)),title('Band 1: Blue')
>> subplot(2,4,2),imshow(multi(:,:,2)),title('Band 2: Green')
>> subplot(2,4,3),imshow(multi(:,:,3)),title('Band 3: Red')
>> subplot(2,4,4),imshow(adjusted),title('Contrast adjusted
   RGB')
>> subplot(2,4,5),imshow(multi(:,:,4)),title('Band 4: Near-IR')
>> subplot(2,4,6),imshow(multi(:,:,5)),title('Band 5: Short-IR
   1')
>> subplot(2,4,7),imshow(multi(:,:,6)),title('Band 6: Thermal-
   IR')
>> subplot(2,4,8),imshow(multi(:,:,7)),title('Band 7: Short-IR
   2')
```

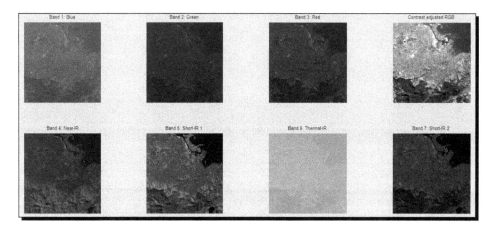

4. The first practical way to use the invisible bands is to construct a near infrared color image, which in theory will make the vegetation appear reddish and the water appear dark. This can be achieved by creating an RGB image from the concatenation of the fourth, third, and second band:

```
>> nearIR = cat(3, multi(:,:,4), multi(:,:,3), multi(:,:,2));
```

5. Before showing our resulting image, let's create a shortwave infrared image as well. This kind of image emphasizes changes due to moisture and it is very important for scientists. It can be created by combining the seventh, fourth, and second bands:

```
>> shortwIR = cat(3, multi(:,:,7), multi(:,:,4), multi(:,:,2));
```

6. Now, let's see our results next to the adjusted RGB image:

```
>> subplot(1,3,1),imshow(adjusted),title('Contrast adjusted
   RGB')
>> subplot(1,3,2),imshow(nearIR),title('Near Infrared')
>> subplot(1,3,3),imshow(shortwIR),title('Shortwave Infrared')
```

What just happened?

In this example, we worked on the manipulation of more than the visible bands. We loaded all seven bands of the file into one matrix and then mixed some of them to create resulting images that make valuable details more visible. The purpose of this section was not to make you a geospatial imagery expert, but to provide you with some insight into what the invisible layers of an image might be. Furthermore, we tried to offer an alternative solution to the analysis of geospatial data, since MATLAB can also be used for these applications. Since you got the idea on how to visualize these images, you can mix the techniques presented here with some of the methods described in previous chapters to enhance, filter, or even mask the results. The sky is the limit!

The characterization of the bands is based on information found here: http://landsat.usgs.gov/best_spectral_bands_to_use.php. You can visit the page to find a little more information about the usefulness of each band. Some more ideas on how to work with these images can be found at http://zulu.ssc.nasa.gov/mrsid/tutorial/Landsat%20 Tutorial-V1.html.

Creating composite images

If you got bored with all the science, now it's time for you to dive into the more fun part of image mixing. A very popular technique that is handled very efficiently by popular image processing suites is compositing two or more images, to make selected elements in them appear in the same scene simultaneously. When performed successfully, this technique can lead to beautiful artistic results, or even hilarious or odd scenes. But before getting to work on compositing, we should first get to know the tools we will be using in MATLAB.

Using imfuse to create a composite image

The most useful function you will use when it comes to compositing tasks is `imfuse`. This function takes two images as input and returns a fused version of these images as output. The function can also accept extra optional inputs, such as spatial referencing information for the two input images, fusion method selection, intensity scaling option, and output color channel for each of the two images. The main output will be the composite of the two input images. Having the composite image available as an output means we can also save it using the `imwrite` function presented in previous chapters.

Using imshowpair to inspect a composite image

Usually, before saving an image, we want to make proper adjustments or experimentations. Even more so, in the case of compositing, the mixing process normally needs a lot of tweaking in order to produce the desired result. The tweaking process can be performed using the `imshowpair` function, which has the same functionality as `imfuse`, only without producing an output image.

Let's start with a small, straightforward example of blending two images using the aforementioned functions. We will use two pictures of the same seagull, taken only a few seconds apart.

Time for action – cloning the seagull

In this example, we will demonstrate how we can perform image blending without actually preprocessing the two input images. Let's start:

1. As always, our first step is to import the two images in MATLAB. As already mentioned, we will use the two images that do not need preprocessing, named `seagull1.jpg` and `seagull2.jpg`:

    ```
    >> A = imread('seagull1.jpg');
    >> B = imread('seagull2.jpg');
    ```

2. Now that we have loaded our images, we can display them next to each other, to see if they fit our purpose:

```
>> figure,imshowpair(A,B,'montage');
```

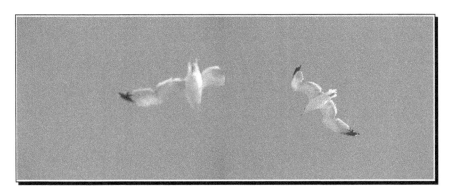

3. It is apparent that the images are quite suitable for our purposes. They have almost identical backgrounds and the seagull is at a different part of the image in each picture. So, we can give it a go, by asking MATLAB to blend the two images:

```
>> imshowpair(A,B,'blend');
```

4. Let's now say that we want to achieve a more psychedelic result, with pseudo colored elements. Well, I have good news for you! MATLAB provides this without requiring any complex preprocessing steps. All you have to do, is to omit the `'blend'` input and let MATLAB use the default choice (`'falsecolor'`), which is to show the two images overlaid in different color bands:

```
>> imshowpair(A,B);
```

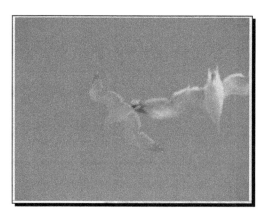

5. If we prefer to alter the predefined colors used in the previous step, we can also alter them. This is done via the `'ColorChannel'` input. This input can assign the default (`'green-magenta'`) choice, the `'red-cyan'` choice, or any arbitrary choice that can be generated using a [R G B] vector. Let's try the `'red-cyan'` choice:

```
>> imshowpair(A,B,'ColorChannel','red-cyan');
```

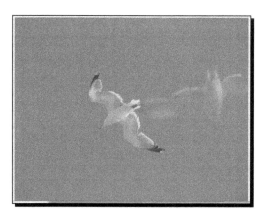

6. Now that we have a rough idea of what we are doing, let's save our last result into a new image, which we will call `'RedCyanSeagulls.jpg'`:

```
>> C = imfuse(A,B,'ColorChannel','red-cyan');
>> imwrite(C,'RedCyanSeagulls.jpg');
```

What just happened?

With this example, you have started to get a grasp on some of the powers of MATLAB that are really easy to use. The only thing that we really did was to pick two pictures with the same size, very similar backgrounds, and non-overlapping (or to be more precise, minimally overlapping) objects in them and blend them using several ready-made choices of the function pair `imshowpair-imfuse`. Once we were happy with the result, we saved it in a new JPEG file using `imwrite`.

Note that the predefined `'green-magenta'` and `'red-cyan'` choices for the color channels can also be accomplished using the [R G B] triplets. The first one is [2 1 2], meaning that red and blue (magenta) were used for the second image and green was used for the first image. The second one is [1 2 2], meaning that green and blue (cyan) were used for the second image, while red was used for the first image. It's time for you to try out some of this now, so that you create a work of art with four different versions of the seagull composite picture.

Have a go hero – playing Warhol with your pictures

In this exercise, you should try to create four different false-color composite versions of the seagull pictures. Try whichever combinations of [R G B] that you wish and then concatenate the four images in order to make a large 2x2 grid that contains all of them.

Using the functions `imread`, `imfuse`, `flipdim`, and `cat`, you should be able to make a picture that looks like the following screenshot:

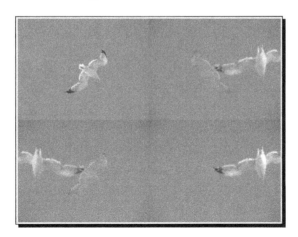

This was not exactly difficult, right? Of course, your choices in tweaking the result are almost unlimited, since only your imagination can dictate what choices you would like to make in designing a work of art. You are free to try other choices of inputs, as well as applying various filters on your results to see what happens.

In this exercise, you created a quite interesting visual result using just two plain images. Playing with the `falsecolor` method setting and different mixtures of the three color channels, led to four different variations of the blended image. Flipping two of the images along the vertical axis led to a more symmetrical outcome. You could experiment with other kinds of transformations, such as rotation, to further customize your resulting image.

One step beyond – blending selected image regions

In the previous section, we examined ways to produce a composite image from two pictures, without applying any preprocessing to them. Now, it is time to bring forward some of the techniques covered in previous chapters, so that we make our resulting images more sophisticated. Let's start with an easy example. We will try to blend two images of the same size, by first setting a part of their pixels to zero. We will use two pictures taken in a subway station of Berlin. Let's first load and see them:

```
>> A = imread('bench1.jpg');
>> B = imread('bench2.jpg');
>> imshowpair(A,B,'montage')
```

As you can observe in the montage of these images, the closer bench (in the right picture) seems to have its upper edge just above the railway ridge of the left picture. If we place a **Data Cursor** (tenth icon) at its upper edge, we see that it is located at approximately the 796th row. Now, we can try our trick: we will make all pixels below the 796th row of the left image equal to zero and also make all the pixels above the 795th row of the right image equal to zero. Then, we will blend the two images and display the result:

```
>> A(796:end,:,:)=0;
>> B(1:795,:,:)=0;
```

```
>> C = imfuse(A,B,'blend');
>> figure,imshow(C);
```

The result is quite pleasing to the eye, but because of the blending, its intensity is low. We can easily fix this by multiplying the result with two:

```
>> C = C*2; imshow(C)
```

The result is quite good for such an easy process. But this time, we got lucky. The two images were meant for each other. But what happens when we want to accomplish a harder compositing task? What if the areas we want to mix are not so easily distinguishable? We will see such an example in the next exercise.

Time for action – directing a threatening scene

This time we will aim at a task that is a little more difficult than the previous ones. We will try to blend two images taken at the zoo, so that we create a threatening scene. More specifically, the first picture is portraying a team of penguins, standing peacefully in their dome and the second one is portraying a polar bear, strolling in her yard more than 500 meters away. Now, what if we brought the bear closer? This would look alarming, especially if the blending process is performed correctly. Let's start by loading our pictures, as always:

1. Our two pictures are called `penguins.jpg` and `bears.jpg`, so we will load them and display them next to each other:

```
>> peng = imread('penguins.jpg');
>> bear = imread('bear.jpg');
>> imshowpair(peng,bear)
```

2. Now, these photographs have almost nothing in common, so the prospects of mixing them don't look very good. Not all hope is lost though. The first step is to crop both pictures, aiming at having the bear and the penguins roughly at the same height, without overlapping each other. So, we should call `imcrop` twice and try our best, so that our result looks something like this:

```
>> bear = imcrop(bear);
>> peng = imcrop(peng);
>> subplot(1,2,1),imshow(peng);title('Penguins after cropping')
>> subplot(1,2,2),imshow(bear);title('Bear after cropping')
```

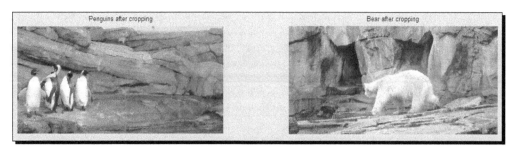

3. However, we are not ready yet. Even if your cropping skills are perfect, the two images could not be exactly the same size. This means that in order for us to be able to use `imfuse` properly, we should resize one of them to fit the other. The best selection is to resize the bear image, since it is larger and we will not cause much distortion. In order to resize it to the size of the penguin image, we type in:

```
>> bear = imresize(bear, [size(peng,1) size(peng,2)]);
>> imshowpair(peng,bear,'montage');
```

4. Apart from the fact that our sizes are now OK, we now see that the images could actually blend together well. We just have to find a way to perform the most seamless blending possible. Let's try to crop the area of the bear, so that we make a proper mask (we will also include the rock hiding the front foot, so that it does not seem unnatural):

```
>> mask = roipoly(bear);
```

5. Our next step is to use the mask to keep only the areas we want from the two images. This means that we will keep the area from the bear picture that has a mask value equal to one and the area from the penguins' picture that has a mask value equal to zero. Since we are using color images, we have to perform the masking in every channel. First, we make two new, three-dimensional masks, that is, by concatenating the mask matrix.

```
>> bear_mask = cat(3,mask,mask,mask); % Construct bear mask
>> peng_mask = 1- cat(3,mask,mask,mask); % Construct penguin
   mask
```

6. Then, we will multiply each mask element-by-element (dot multiplication) with the image we want to mask, after we have converted its type to single (so that the multiplication is feasible).

```
>> bear_img = single(bear).*bear_mask; % Masking of bear
>> peng_img = single(peng).*peng_mask; % Masking of penguins
```

7. Finally, we will convert the result back to uint8 and display the results. Let's see how:

```
>> bear_img = uint8(bear_img); % Convert result to uint8
>> peng_img = uint8(peng_img); % Convert result to uint8
>> figure, imshowpair(peng_img, bear_img,'montage');
```

8. Now, for the last step, we need to perform blending of the two images:

```
>> pengbear = imfuse(peng_img,bear_img,'blend');
>> figure, imshow(result)
```

9. The final touch will be to repair the contrast of the resulting image. Composite images created with `imfuse`, appear to have half their original contrast. A way to fix this would be to multiply the result with a factor of two. A better way to handle it is to use some contrast stretching method. In order for the result to be more vivid, we can use the `imadjust` function in each color channel separately. To do this, we type in:

```
>> for i = 1:size(result,3)
result(:,:,i)=imadjust(result(:,:,i));
end
>> imshow(result)
```

And this is the result. Poor penguins! Lucky for them, it's just an illusion.

What just happened?

This example mixed a lot of what you have learned so far in this book. We wanted to create a rather challenging composite image, from two images with very few similarities. The only thing in our favor was the non-overlapping positioning of the penguins and the bear after we cropped the two images. Cropping the images was necessary also for the better alignment of the two target areas (penguins and bear) in the vertical axis. Once we did that, we chose to transfer the bear to the penguin territory, since the bear was larger and could be down-sized to fit in the other image without losing quality. After down-sizing the bear, we manually defined a ROI around it to form a mask. The inverse mask was selected for the penguin picture. Then, we performed masking on the two images, using the respective masks in step 5. The resulting images were blended and consequently, the result was filtered in each of its channels using `imadjust`, to enhance its intensity.

 Sometimes, too much information is not necessarily a good thing. If you look closely, some areas of the blended image at the edges of the bear's legs give away the fact that our image was processed. A trick that can be used to reduce this effect is applying a median filter to smooth the image. This way, the resulting image would be less crisp, but its imperfections would be camouflaged. To apply the median filter to a color image, you would need to do it in each channel separately.

Creating High Dynamic Range images

So far, we talked about mixing different spectrums or different images. A relatively new technique that involves mixing different versions of the same scene is High Dynamic Range photography. In this technique, we mix multiple shots of the same scene, taken at different **Exposure Values (EV)**. EV, in camera settings, denotes a combination of exposure time and relative aperture. Rules and suggestions about the optimal EV settings for different subjects are extensively covered in the theoretical books and websites about photography and are not really within the scope of this book.

What is within the scope of this book, is to understand what the mixture of multiple EV pictures can accomplish. In a nutshell, it makes the resulting photograph have a greater dynamic range between dark and bright areas in the image. However, to use this technique to its full power, the images that will be mixed should not be 8-bit, since the range of 256 values per color contained in them normally produces artefacts.

Since the average reader of this book normally has access to 8-bit images, we will use such an example for our demonstration of the method. But first, we will say a word or two about how to shoot the required images.

First off, you should have a camera that supports manual settings. Second, you should find the setting for **Auto Bracketing**, which will allow you to shoot with multiple exposures. Some cameras give you a choice of three different EV values (usually -2, 0, 2, or -1, 0, 1), while others have more stops available. An alternative is to manually adjust your preferred ISO and f-setting and then, using a steady tripod (and ideally a remote control, so that you do not move your camera at all) to shoot with at least three different exposures. Immobility is of the essence, since moving the camera or shooting mobile subjects will result in blurred areas.

After you have taken your three shots, you will have to use the MATLAB's `makehdr` function to compose the HDR image and then use `tonemap` to render the resulting image for viewing purposes. Let's see an example that demonstrates all these.

Time for action – composing your own HDR images

Now that we know the theory, let's dive into a real life example. For the purposes of this exercise, we shot three pictures of a scene with a wide range of brightness, in an office, using three different EV settings: -2, 0, and 2. The names of the three images are `image_-2.jpg`, `image_0.jpg`, and `image_2.jpg`. So, in order to use them to make an HDR image, we will follow the steps as shown:

1. Save the names of the three images in a cell and the respective EV choices in a matrix:

```
>> filenames = {'image_-2.jpg', 'image_0.jpg', 'image_2.jpg'};
>> expValues = [-2, 0, 2];
```

2. In order to get an idea of what these images look like, we can optionally load them and display them:

```
>> im1 = imread('image_-2.jpg');
>> im2 = imread('image_0.jpg');
>> im3 = imread('image_2.jpg');
>> subplot(1,3,1),imshow(im1),title('EV: -2')
>> subplot(1,3,2),imshow(im2),title('EV: 0')
>> subplot(1,3,3),imshow(im3),title('EV: 2')
```

3. Now, we will use the two variables created in step 1 to make our HDR image:

```
>> hdr = makehdr(filenames, 'ExposureValues', expValues);
```

4. The HDR image now needs some postprocessing to be ready for viewing purposes. This can be done using `tonemap` with its default values, which will result in converting the HDR result to a lower dynamic range RGB image:

```
>> rgb = tonemap(hdr);
```

5. The result is clearly more detailed, but it includes some grain noise and also some small blocking effect in smooth areas (such as the desk surface) due to the JPEG compression and the limited bit depth:

```
>> rgb = tonemap(hdr);
```

6. The grain noise mentioned previously, can be reduced using a median filter. A 7x7 median filter will suffice, without causing great degradation of the quality of the image. For color images, we must use the filter separately in each channel. Combining this filter with contrast adjustment, leads to:

```
>> for i=1:size(rgb,3)
filtered(:,:,i) = medfilt2(imadjust(rgb(:,:,i)),[7 7]);
end
>> subplot(1,2,1),imshow(im2);title('Original image at 0EV')
>> subplot(1,2,2),imshow(filtered);title('Final HDR result')
```

What just happened?

This was a basic example of how to shoot and process an HDR image in MATLAB. The use of JPEG images may not particularly help in getting the full idea of what HDR images can offer, but you have certainly acquired the basic knowledge on how to create them. Our process comprised the declaration of the names of our images and the respective exposure values, followed by a call of the function `makehdr`. Then, the High Dynamic Range is converted to RGB using `tonemap` and if we want, we perform some further preprocessing steps to acquire our final result.

When we want to create HDR images from action scenes, the process described previously is usually problematic, because of the subject's movement. In these situations, we can use cameras that capture raw images of higher color depth (12, or even 16 bit) and artificially create our three different exposures from a single shot, using techniques similar to the ones presented here:

http://captainkimo.com/single-exposure-hdr/

Stitching images for the creation of panoramas

So far, we have presented image mixing techniques performed by overlaying one image on top of the other(s). Now, it is time to discuss what happens when we want to make a panoramic image; that is, combine partially overlapping images to make a larger one. This technique is often called panorama stitching and it has gained much attention during the last decade. Nowadays, some modern cameras come with internal stitching algorithms.

To create such an image in the simplest possible way, we need to do two things, namely, detect (either manually or automatically) some corresponding points in adjacent images and use them to transform the images, so that their geometry is correct. Blending the images, so that the connection areas are smoother, might also be needed.

For the purpose of our beginner level tutorial, we will show a manual way to perform panorama stitching. In our example, we will not make any transformation to the resulting images, so that we show why this method is not optimal.

Time for action – basic approach to panorama stitching

In this example, we will use three photographs taken from the same point in space, just by rotating the camera in the horizontal axis. Let's see the steps needed:

1. First, as always, we will load and display our images:

```
>> L = imread('Left.jpg');
>> M = imread('Middle.jpg');
>> R = imread('Right.jpg');
>> subplot(1,3,1);imshow(L);title('Left image')
>> subplot(1,3,2);imshow(M);title('Middle image')
>> subplot(1,3,3);imshow(R);title('Right image')
```

2. Now, let's pick two pairs of points that we will use for the connections (remember: we will not use any geometric transformations here). For the selection, we will use the **Zoom In** and the **Data Cursor** tools. First we do it for the left and middle image:

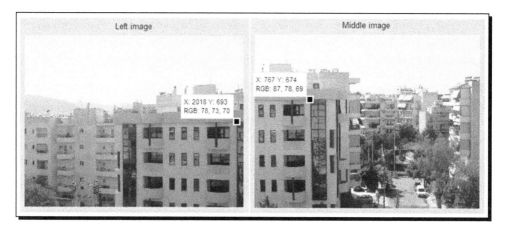

Then, it is time to pick a pair of points for the middle and right image:

Having pinpointed the two points that will be matched to connect the two images, we now have to move on to stitching.

3. Let's start with the left and middle images. The point we selected in the left image is on row 693, column 2018. In the middle image, the same point resides on row 674, column 767. This means that the left image should be raised by 693 - 674 = 19 pixels (so that the points are on the same row). We can accomplish this using `circshift`. This function shifts the elements of a matrix in the dimension stated by the user in a circular fashion; that is, the pixels that fall out of the picture due to the shifting process, re-appear at the other end:

```
>> Lr = circshift(L,-19);
```

Now, we must connect the two images at the vertical line passing through the common point:

```
>> First = cat(2,Lr(:,1:2018,:),M(:,767:end,:));
```

4. Now, the resulting image can be combined with the right one, but first, we must perform an alignment like the one in step 3. The point selected in the middle image is at row 587 and column 1767, while in the right image, it resides on row 618, column 466. This means that the right image must be shifted upwards by 618 - 587 = 31 pixels:

```
>> Rr = circshift(R,-31);
```

Now, we must connect the two images at the vertical line passing through the common point:

```
>> All = cat(2,First(:,1:3019,:),Rr(:,466:end,:));
```

5. Let's see what we have accomplished:

```
>> imshow(All)
```

6. A closer look at the result reveals that several things went wrong; some alignments, especially in the connection of the middle image to the right one, appear too distorted. Some experimentation reveals that minor adjustments to the shifting process and the vertical coordinate for the middle-right connection can improve things, but even better results will come, by also performing median filtering:

```
>> Rr = circshift(R,-21);
>> All = cat(2,First(:,1:3019,:),Rr(:,450:end,:));
>> for i = 1:size(All,3)
panorama(:,:,i)=medfilt2(All(:,:,i),[5 5]);
end
>> figure,imshow(panorama)
```

What just happened?

In this example, we demonstrated the simplest possible approach to panorama stitching. For acceptable results with minimal effort, this approach is not bad, but the demanding user should look for more complicated methods; combining feature detection with geometrical image transformations. The approach presented here, started with the manual selection of the common points between the images and the usage of their coordinates for aligning and stitching the images. Some refinement of the exact coordinates is commonly needed, as well as some postprocessing filtering step, such as median filtering. The final result still has artefacts, but it is certainly acceptable for such an easy and straightforward process. The blue sky areas that have appeared at the bottom of the image after the shifting commands, can either be blacked out, or cropped to achieve a better result.

Pop quiz – image mixing details

Q1. Which of the following is true?

1. Using bands four through seven of a lan image, adds information that is not visible to the human eye.

2. Blending two images using `imfuse`, results in an image that is very bright.

3. We can perform masking of a color image, by dot multiplying it with a two-dimensional mask.

4. HDR images should be constructed using uncompressed images of a higher depth than 8-bits.

5. The only thing needed for a good panoramic image is to concatenate the images at the correct column.

Summary

In this chapter, we combined many of the methods presented so far with some new techniques, to produce results that have scientific or artistic value. Since the methods visited in this chapter involve some very complex theories for a beginner, we chose to follow a learn-by-example approach and introduced all the techniques with hands-on exercises on multispectral imaging, image compositing, HDR imagery, and panorama stitching. More specifically, this chapter covered:

◆ An introductory presentation on mixing methods and their importance

◆ A presentation of basic multiband image processing techniques in MATLAB

◆ The basic MATLAB tools for performing image blending (`imfuse` and `imshowpair`)

◆ A thorough explanation of image blending with practical and artistic examples

◆ Applications of image compositing using selected areas of the images to create fiction images

◆ How the notion of image blending can go further into combining many low dynamic range images to create an HDR image

◆ A presentation of panorama stitching, with a simplified example, that produces acceptable results

In the next chapter, we will discuss video processing, by first combining sequences of still images to create time-lapse videos. We will explain the notions of frame rate and motion and we will introduce you to the basic MATLAB tools for creating video objects, adding frames to them, and watching your videos. You will also get hands-on experience of how to make your own time-lapse videos.

7

Adding Motion – From Static Images to Digital Videos

In all the previous chapters, we have focused on ways to import, manipulate, process, and save static images using MATLAB, in numerous manners and for various goals. Now, it is time to slowly indulge in the peculiarities of video processing, using MATLAB as our only tool. We will start with explaining the nature of videos and the ways they can be created. Some necessary theoretical details about videos will be explained, followed by instructions on how to load and view videos in MATLAB. Then, we will continue with ways to create video streams using static images. These are the fundamentals of time-lapse videos, so by the end of this chapter you will be able to make your first time-lapse video using MATLAB. Finally, we will provide another way to save your time-lapse sequence, which is in gif format.

In this chapter, we will learn:

- ◆ The basic principles of digital video processing
- ◆ The significance of frame rates
- ◆ How we can load videos in MATLAB
- ◆ How we can playback videos in MATLAB
- ◆ How we can create videos using static images
- ◆ How we can inspect all or some of the frames in a video, using MATLAB
- ◆ How to use `implay` to playback a video
- ◆ How we can create and save time-lapse videos in MATLAB

So, let's start working with videos!

An introduction to digital videos

To build a solid foundation for this chapter, as well as the next ones, we must first take some time to present the fundamental concepts of digital videos. Once again, the theory will be explained in a very practical way, using hands-on examples wherever possible.

Videos are practically created by joining several still images, called **frames**. The joining of the images is performed by adding an extra dimension to hold the sequence. Since, as you already know by now, grayscale images are two-dimensional and color images are three-dimensional, grayscale videos will be three-dimensional and color videos will be four-dimensional.
For example, if we join 100 grayscale images of size 1080 rows and 1920 columns, we will get a matrix that is 1080 x 1920 x 100. Similarly, if we join 100 color images of the same size, the resulting matrix will be 1080 x 1920 x 3 x 100.

The most usual and natural way to create a digital video is to use a video capturing device, for example, a video camera. Modern photographic cameras also have the capability of shooting digital video. Moreover, since a video can be thought of as a sequence of consecutive still images, it can also be created using photographs, or even sketches. This is a technique that can also be used to create animated `.gif` files, as we will see in this chapter. But first, we should try to explain some important aspects of video processing, always bearing in mind that all the descriptions pertain to uncompressed videos.

The meaning of frames

This is a trick question, since it can be interpreted in two ways; how many frames do I need for a video of a certain duration or what is the **frame rate** needed for a certain amount of motion to be clearly portrayed?

For both questions to be answered satisfactorily, we first need to talk about two very important properties of videos; interlacing and frame rates.

Interlaced versus progressive

The first important choice when shooting a video is whether we will shoot it in interlaced or progressive mode. Interlaced videos contain two kinds of frames; those containing odd lines and those containing even lines. When displaying these frames consequently (first odd then even) at a high enough frequency, the viewer cannot distinguish the empty lines and therefore perceives the video as sequential full frames. Progressive (or non-interlaced) videos on the other hand, display full frames (all lines appear at each frame). From the description of these two types of videos, it can be deduced that a progressive video will demand twice the size of an interlaced video of the same length and resolution. Another interpretation of this property is that the frame rate of an interlaced video that the human spectator perceives, is double that of an equally sized progressive video. Which brings us to the frame rate question; what is it and what does it affect?

Frame rates and their importance

The concept of frame rate denotes the number of frames that will be shot (and consequently displayed) in a second and thus it is measured in **frames per second** (**fps**). The number of frames per second defines the quality of motion capturing in a video, as high frame rates can capture more changes per second than low frame rates. This is particularly useful in videos containing lots of motion, for example, sports videos.

The frame rate of a video is highly dependent on the camera used to shoot it and the type of media it is shot for. Another very important feature of videos that affects the way the frame rates are described, is whether they are progressive or interlaced. The most widely used frame rates are:

- ◆ 24 fps progressive, or 24p, as it is more commonly known. A frame rate of 24p means that every second, 24 frames will be shot (or displayed). This frame rate is the typical standard for the film industry.

- ◆ A similar frame rate, used mostly in PAL video, is 25p. As its name denotes, this is a 25 fps frame rate of progressive video. This format is preferred in countries with an electrical current of 50Hz, as it is divides the frequency evenly. A common practice is to shoot PAL video at approximately 23.98 fps, slowing it down by a factor of 1000/1001. This leads to an easier transfer process of the video to the NTSC format, which is described next.

- ◆ In the U.S.A. and Canada, as well as some other countries which have a 60Hz power grid, the usual frame rate used is 30 fps progressive, that is, 30p. This video format is called NTSC and it is usually a better choice when the video will be viewed on computer monitors, as they are likely to have a refresh rate of 60Hz, which is divided evenly by 30. It is worth noting that the actual frame rate used for most NTSC videos is 29.97 fps. This should be taken into account when processing a video, because in these tasks accuracy matters a lot.

- ◆ Lately, Hollywood moviemakers started experimenting with a frame rate of 48p, with the first movie to be filmed at this frame rate being **The Hobbit**.

- ◆ The interlaced equivalents of PAL and NTSC videos mentioned previously are called 50i and 60i respectively. While they are generally better than the progressive alternatives at half the frame rate (for example, 60i over 30p) in depicting fast movements (such as in sports videos), they tend to blur details because only half of the information exists in any given frame.

- ◆ Higher frame rates are also feasible in modern systems such as 50p, 60p (or 59.94 fps for better compatibility with NTSC), or even 120p. These formats are slowly being spread beyond the field of industrial applications where they were first used because of their property of capturing high speed processes with great detail.

Calculating number of frames

Now, let's get back to one of our original questions; how many frames do I need for a video of certain duration of, let's say 20 minutes?

Well, assuming that we shoot in 25p (PAL), the number of frames will be equal to the number of seconds multiplied by the number of frames per second (25). Since each minute consists of 60 seconds, we will need:

(20 minutes) x (60 seconds/minute) x (25 frames/second) = 30000 frames.

Now, if we were to shoot our video in classic NTSC format (29.97 fps), we'd need:

(20 minutes) x (60 seconds/minute) x (29.97 frames/second) = 35964 frames.

This is quite a lot of frames, right? This is why video processing is one of the most time-consuming tasks you can use to stress test a PC. It is also the reason why compression is a definite must when it comes to storing videos, if you want to avoid having to buy hard disks regularly.

Some thoughts on choosing frame rates

Selecting the proper frame rate for your video has a lot to do with its intended use. Common sense dictates that the higher the frame rate, the better the quality of the video in terms of temporal smoothness (capturing motion details). This is the reason that older silent movies that were shot at frame rates below 24 fps appear to have an unnatural and jerky motion at times.

However, even 24 or 30 fps do not necessarily guarantee a perfect, fluid capturing and display of motion. The speeds of the depicted objects, as well as the detail in each of them also play important roles in choosing a high enough frame rate for your videos and generally speaking, when having a choice you should go with the higher frame rates, always minding the peculiarities of conversions between formats.

On the other hand, when dealing with animated sketches, the choice is usually very common; most of them are drawn to be played at 24 fps. However, the process of drawing 24 sketches for each second of an animated film is extremely time-consuming and exhausting. The solution to this issue, is for the designers to draw half, or even a quarter of the images needed and repeat them as many times as needed to fill the missing frames (for example, when drawing 12 frames for a second, each frame is shown twice to achieve a 24 fps frame rate).

Another important consideration in the aforementioned problem is the sensitivity of human visual perception. The visual system that we possess is quite complex and cannot be analyzed easily in a way that would favor a certain frame rate over others. While our eye-brain combo can be fooled into believing that a hand-drawn cartoon with only 12 unique frames per second moves smoothly, on the other hand it can detect light flashes that last way less than 1/25th of a second. This perception can also be affected by the viewing angle; that is, peripheral vision is even more sensitive to light flickering.

Loading videos in MATLAB

Before we start discussing how to create our own videos, it is important to first see how MATLAB handles videos. In fact, video processing is one of the areas in which MATLAB has been evolving a lot over these past years. As opposed to image processing, where `imread` was introduced in early versions of the software and could be used for loading most popular image formats, the respective function for video loading has been changed a lot. The main reason behind the changes was the differences in video compression formats, which did not allow for a single efficient function that could handle opening every possible one. In this section, we will present the different functions that can be used in MATLAB for video importing. This way, readers with previous versions of MATLAB will be able to use the function they feel most comfortable with.

Loading videos with aviread

The first function used for reading videos in MATLAB was `aviread`. This function still exists in Version 2012b, but it is scheduled to be removed in future versions. Furthermore, it has a limited functionality with respect to the video types that it can read, since it is only designed to open `.avi` files. A typical usage of `aviread` is shown as follows, using one of the videos included in MATLAB (`singleball.avi`):

```
>> A = aviread('singleball.avi');
```

This command gives the following result:

As you can see, the resulting variable, A, is of type `struct`. Its size is equal to the number of frames comprising the video. Luckily, the number of frames was not big, so we had no problem importing all of them in our workspace. Imagine if we tried to import a 25p video with one hour duration. Then, we would have needed to store 90000 frames! This would lead to a certain memory problem, especially if our video was high resolution.

To avoid this problem, it is common to first inspect the videos we are about to process and then decide on a strategy for importing them. To do this, we can use `aviinfo`, a function that complements `aviread` and aims at drawing information from a video file. To use it, we just type it in the command line with the video filename as input:

```
>> aviinfo('singleball.avi');
```

```
>> aviinfo('singleball.avi')
Warning: AVIINFO will be removed in
a future release. Use VIDEOREADER
instead.
> In aviinfo at 67

ans =

              Filename: [1x58 char]
              FileSize: 23405568
           FileModDate: [1x20 char]
             NumFrames: 45
       FramesPerSecond: 30.0001
                 Width: 480
                Height: 360
             ImageType: [1x9 char]
      VideoCompression: 'none'
               Quality: 0
     NumColormapEntries: 0
```

Now, let's say that we want to import just the first 10 frames of our video. The only thing needed is to identify the frames we want to load in `aviread`:

```
>> A = aviread('singleball.avi', 1:10);
```

It can be easily deduced that adding a step of 2 in the frames vector, that is, using `1:2:10` instead of `1:10`, would lead to skipping even numbered frames, leading to a speed-up of our image if the playback rate is kept steady.

Since the video imported is stored in a `struct`, we must find a way to manipulate it using what we know, that is, multi-dimensional matrices. If we type the name of our `struct` in the command line, we get:

```
>> A
```

The output of the preceding command is as follows:

```
A =
1x10struct array with fields:
cdata
colormap
```

This means that the `struct` has two fields; `cdata` and `colormap`. The `colormap` field is useful only in the case of videos with indexed images as frames (no color information is stored in the pixel data). If the color information is directly stored in the pixel data of the frames (called **truecolor** images in this case), as in all the cases we have seen so far in this book, `colormap` will be an empty matrix. The `cdata` field holds all pixel information.

If we want to access the 5th frame of our imported video, we will have to use the following command:

```
>> frame5 = A(5).cdata;
```

If, however, we want to read all 10 frames to a four-dimensional matrix, we will have to use a `for` loop:

```
>> for i = 1:10, vid(:,:,:,i) = A(i).cdata; end
>> size(vid)
```

The output of the preceding code is as follows:

```
ans =
   360    480     3    10
```

The second line of code was used to see the size of our result, which is normal, as it shows that our generated matrix has 360 rows, 480 columns, 3 colors, and 10 frames.

> A big disadvantage of `aviread` for Unix users is that it can only handle uncompressed `.avi` files. This is why external toolboxes for video processing were extensively used in the past. The most important one is VideoIO, which is still well-maintained and can be found at `http://sourceforge.net/projects/videoio/`

Loading videos with mmreader

The next attempt for a video reading function in MATLAB was `mmreader`. This function (or class) was part of the introduction of object oriented programming methods in MATLAB and it supported more video formats than `aviread`. On the downside, the speed of video importing, using `mmreader` was reduced. This function will be abandoned in future releases of MATLAB, so it would be wise not to use it extensively in your work.

As already mentioned, `mmreader` is an object oriented function, meaning that its output is a multimedia reader object that can be used to import video data from a file. The function that will then import the video from the constructed object is called `read`. The process that must be used to achieve the same results shown in the previous paragraph for `aviread`, is as follows:

```
>> vObj = mmreader('singleball.avi');
>> videoA = read(vObj);        % read in all frames from video object
>> videoB = read(vObj,[1 10]); % read in only the 10 first frames
```

This process leads to the following result in our workspace:

```
Command Window                              ⊙   Workspace
  >> vObj = mmreader('singleball.avi');        Name ▲          Value
  videoA = read(vObj);       % read in all fram   vObj          <1x1 mmreader>
  videoB = read(vObj,[1 10]); % read in only the  videoA        <4-D uint8>
  Warning: MMREADER will be removed in a future   videoB        <4-D uint8>
  release. Use VIDEOREADER instead.
  > In mmreader.mmreader>mmreader.mmreader at 120
fx >>
```

As you can see in the figure, the object constructed has an `mmreader` type, while the two imported videos are four-dimensional 8-bit integer matrices (**rows** x **columns** x **colors** x **frames**). `VideoB` should be identical to the `vid` matrix generated in the previous example (you can check it using the `size` function). Once again, MATLAB produces a warning about `mmreader`, having to do with its removal in future versions.

In case we need to inspect our video file before we load it in MATLAB, we can take advantage of the fact that we have to create a video object first and use the `get` function to inspect it. This can be performed as follows:

```
>> get(vObj)
```

```
>> get(vObj)
  General Settings:
    Duration = 1.5000
    Name = singleball.avi
    Path = C:\MATLAB\R2013a\toolbox\vision\visiondemos
    Tag =
    Type = VideoReader
    UserData = []

  Video Settings:
    BitsPerPixel = 24
    FrameRate = 30.0001
    Height = 360
    NumberOfFrames = 45
    VideoFormat = RGB24
    Width = 480
```

Loading videos with VideoReader

The `VideoReader` function (or class) has almost identical usage to `mmreader`. The only visible differences are that it generates a `VideoReader` object and it usually performs a little faster. To achieve the same results as in previous paragraphs, we have to type in the following:

```
>> vObj = VideoReader('singleball.avi');
>> videoA = read(vObj);        % read in all frames from video object
>> videoB = read(vObj,[1 10]); % read in only the 10 first frames
>> size(videoB)
```

The output of the preceding code will be as follows:

```
Command Window                                    Workspace
  >> vObj = VideoReader('singleball.avi');      Name ▲              Value
  videoA = read(vObj);           % read in all fr▒  ans              [360 480 3 10]
  videoB = read(vObj,[1 10]); % read in only the    vObj             <1x1 VideoReader>
  >> size(videoB)                                   videoA           <4-D uint8>
                                                    videoB           <4-D uint8>
  ans =

     360    480     3    10
```

As you can see from the results of the previous commands, the results are identical
to previous methods. The second video also has the same number of frames as in previous
tries. Of course, this time we had no complaints from MATLAB about our selection of
function, since VideoReader is the most recently introduced function for video file reading.
Using get on the result of VideoReader will, as you can easily prove yourself, produce the
same result as the one produced for the mmreader result. If we want to use some of the
fields produced by get, for example the number of frames, we can do it by typing:

```
>> numOfFrames = get(vObj,'NumberOfFrames')
```

The preceding command will give the following result:

```
numOfFrames =
    45
```

Choosing which function to use for video reading

The choice of the best video reading function for your needs is usually made taking into
account three basic parameters; the version of MATLAB you have access to, the format
of the video file you want to process, and the desired speed of processing.

The first parameter cannot be covered extensively here, since the book is based on MATLAB
version 2012b. However, you should take into account that versions of MATLAB prior to
2007b included only aviread. Versions from 2007b to 2010b supported both aviread
and mmreader, and finally since 2010b, all three functions can be used. However, as already
mentioned, you should cautiously use the two oldest functions because they have been
scheduled to be replaced in future versions.

Now, let's see what are the formats that each function supports. As its name implies, `aviread` only reads `.avi` video files, which can only be uncompressed in Unix systems. The two other functions have pretty much the same functionality when it comes to video formats. This can be proven using the `getFileFormats` method that is available in both `mmreader` and `VideoReader`. To see them, we can type in the following commands:

```
>> mmreader.getFileFormats()
>> VideoReader.getFileFormats()
```

Both these calls have the same result, which in Windows looks like as follows:

```
Video File Formats:
    .asf - ASF File
    .asx - ASX File
    .avi - AVI File
    .m4v - MPEG-4 Video
    .mj2 - Motion JPEG2000
    .mov - QuickTime movie
    .mp4 - MPEG-4
    .mpg - MPEG-1
    .wmv - Windows Media Video
```

Regarding the speed of processing, the improvements are neither so spectacular nor so definitive that they will dictate the use of either one of the two new functions. The faster of the three is `aviread`, but as it is nearly obsolete and it does not support a variety of formats it should be avoided.

Taking all these facts into consideration, your choice of the appropriate function should probably be the most recent function supported by your version of MATLAB. Therefore, from now on we will be using `VideoReader` for all the video importing tasks we will demonstrate.

Playing back videos in MATLAB

Now that you know how to load a video, it is time to learn how to play it back. As you can recall, images can be displayed in an open figure, using `imshow`. However, playing back a movie is a slightly more complex process. The function that can be used for this process is called `movie`. This function takes the name of the variable as input, in which we have stored the video frames, and plays it back in the current axes (if there aren't any, it creates them). The process described has two issues; one is that the variable containing the video must be a movie struct (similar to the one generated by `aviread`) and the other is that the figure that will be used to display the movie must be resized to exactly fit the video dimensions. Otherwise, we may have a result that will include a visible white part of the axes apart from the video.

Movie can also use extra inputs that define playback details. More specifically, it can get the number of times the movie will be played, the order in which the frames will be displayed, and the frame rate. Let's see all of these with an example.

Time for action – reading and playing back a video

It's time for our first hands-on example in video processing. Let's use the following steps to import and play-back the video we used before (`singleball.avi`):

1. First, we import the video in a matrix, using `VideoReader` followed by `read`:

```
>> vObj = VideoReader('singleball.avi');
>> video = read(vObj);  % read in all frames from video object
```

2. Now, it is time to use the number of frames to create a video structure like the one that is generated by `aviread`. Remember, for truecolor frames, it consists of a `cdata` field with all the pixel values and an empty `colormap` field:

```
>> numOfFrames = get(vObj, 'NumberOfFrames');
>> for i = 1:numOfFrames,
vid(i).cdata = video(:,:,:,i);   % Frames are stored in cdata
vid(i).colormap = [];    % Colormap is empty
end
```

3. Since we have stored our video in the necessary format, we can now create the figure in which we have to display it and then call `movie`:

```
>> hf = figure;
>> movie(vid)
```

The last frame of the played-back video will look like as follows:

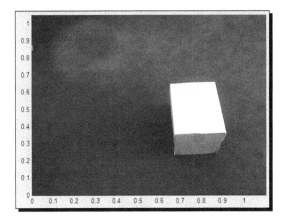

4. Even though we managed to play back our video, there are a couple of things that are not optimal. One of them is the frame rate. The default frame rate used by movie, when we have not specified something different, is 12 fps. The other thing is that we have left the choice about the size of the window for the playback. Let's try to fix these things by specifying both the attributes, while at the same time ask MATLAB to playback the video five times. We'll start again from where we left off at step 2:

```
>> hf = figure;
>> set(hf,'position',[200 200 vObj.WidthvObj.Height]);
>> movie(hf,vid,5,vObj.FrameRate)
```

5. The result is, as expected, a loop of five consecutive playbacks of our video, at its proper frame rate.

What just happened?

You just got a first glimpse at some of the things MATLAB is capable of when it comes to video. First we loaded an .avi video into our workspace as a four-dimensional matrix and then we converted it to a video structure so that it can be played back properly using movie. Finally, we fine-tuned our code to make sure that the position and dimensions of the playback window will be appropriate for our video and then we asked for a five-times repeat of the video at its original frame rate (specified by vObj.FrameRate). The call to movie was made with all possible inputs, which are in order of appearance; the handle to the figure we want our video to be played back in, the name of the video struct variable, the number of times we want the video to be played back, and the frame rate of the playback.

Making videos from static images

So, now that we know how to import and play back videos in MATLAB, it is time to discuss how to make our own videos, by stitching together continuous still images. We have already mentioned that videos are essentially a sequence of static images called frames, which, when displayed in the proper frame rate portray the sense of motion to the viewer. Therefore, it is feasible to use sequentially taken photographs to construct a video, provided that their resolutions and bit-depth are the same. When we have gathered all our photographs in one place, we can import them in MATLAB using imread, construct a VideoWriter object with the function of the same name and then use the function writeVideo to add frames to our video. Let's see all these with an example.

Time for action – constructing and saving a video

For this example, we will use a sequence of images derived from a driving video. The frames must be read into MATLAB and then added to a video object in chronological order. Let's see how this works:

1. First, we will change our working directory to the directory that contains our `.jpeg` image sequence. In our example, this directory is called `E:\Videos\seq`. Of course in your system the directory containing the sequence may be different, so you should change the path accordingly. When in this directory, we will save the filenames of the image sequence to a new struct variable, named `contents`:

```
>> cd ('E:\Videos\seq');
>> contents = dir('*.jpeg');
```

2. Then, we must create a video object to store our video in. Let's call it `vid.avi`:

```
>> outputVideo = VideoWriter('vid.avi');
>> outputVideo.FrameRate = 15;
>> open(outputVideo);
```

3. Now that we have our filenames stored in the `contents` variable and we have opened a video file, we can loop through the filenames of the pictures so that we load each of them once:

```
>> for i = 1:length(contents)
im = imread(contents(i).name);
writeVideo(outputVideo,im);
end
close(outputVideo);
```

4. At this point, our brand new video is created. The only thing left is to check our results. We will once again follow the process described in the previous example to make the video struct that will be used to play back the video:

```
>> newVid = VideoReader('vid.avi');
>> for i = 1:newVid.NumberOfFrames
mov(i).cdata = read(newVid,i);
mov(i).colormap = [];
end
```

5. Now, we must create the playback window. We will use the width and height of our video to set the dimensions of the window and then display its first frame:

```
>> set(gcf,'position', [300 300 newVid.Width newVid.Height])
>> set(gca,'units','pixels');
>> set(gca,'position',[0 0 newVid.Width newVid.Height])
>> image(mov(1).cdata,'Parent',gca);
>> axis off;
```

6. Finally, we will play back the video at the proper frame rate:

```
>> movie(mov,1,newVid .FrameRate);
```

7. The output will be as follows:

What just happened?

This time we got to construct a video using a sequence of still images. In the first step of the process, we changed our working directory to the one containing our images and saved the filenames in a `struct` variable using function `dir`. We used the input `*.jpeg` because all of our images were in that format. Since we are already in the folder containing the images, in step 2 we proceed to create a video object called `outputVideo`, which will be used to add our images as frames in a video called `vid.avi`. In the same step, we also set the video frame rate to 15 and open the video object for writing. In step 3, we go over all the filenames saved in the first step, use them to load the respective images in the workspace and then add them to our video object. After we have added all the frames to our video, it is time to close it so that it is ready to be played back in MATLAB, or any other video-playing software.

The second part of this example takes over playing back the video we just created. The prevailing function from our previous sections, `VideoReader`, is used to load our video to a video reader object, which is then traversed through all its frames using a for loop. In this loop, each frame is saved in a struct variable called `mov`. Step 5 creates the figure in which our video will be displayed. The position of the bottom-left corner of this figure is placed 300 pixels higher and 300 pixels right of the bottom-left corner of the monitor. The size of the figure is equal to the size of the video we just opened. The second and third line of code set the axes to be placed at the exact same place and dimensions as the figure. Then, the first image of the sequence (also first frame of the video) is displayed in the figure, and the ticks and labels of the figure are switched off. Finally, in step 6 we use the `movie` function to play back the whole video.

Have a go hero – make a video with a fade in/fade out effect

Now that you know how to make a video out of still images, let's try to spice things up a little. You should try to include a fade out effect, followed by a fade in effect. To accomplish this, you should choose a frame to start your fade out and then lower the values of its pixels by a constant number (for example, 20). This number should double in the next frame, triple in the next one, and so on. Make sure that negative values are set to zero. The opposite process will accomplish the fade in effect, but it is a little trickier, since you have to start from a dark frame and gradually brighten up the next ones.

Inspecting a video using montage

A useful tool for when we want to inspect all the frames of a video or all the images of a sequence at the same time, is montage. Its usage will be explained with a simple example that will demonstrate its importance.

Time for action – don't wait for the ball

In one of our previous examples, we used the video called singleball.avi, which is included in MATLAB as a demo. This video portrays a static box and a green ball that enters from the left of the frame and passes underneath the box to exit from the right part of the frame. Of course, without inspecting the video, we have no idea when the ball enters our frame. It could be at the beginning of the video, or maybe we would have to wait a while until we see it. So let's inspect all the frames to get a better idea:

1. First off, we load the video using VideoReader:

    ```
    >> vObj = VideoReader('singleball.avi');
    >> video = read(vObj);  % read in all frames from video object
    ```

2. Now, we have our video stored in a four-dimensional matrix. This is enough for montage to take over:

    ```
    >> montage(video,'Size',[5 9]) % Using a 5x9 grid for 45 frames
    ```

3. The result of the preceding steps is as follows:

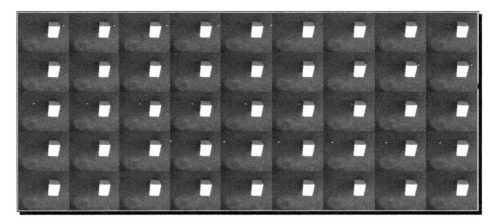

What just happened?

Now we are in a position to pinpoint the frames that are most useful for us. As we can remember from the previous example in which we used the same video, it comprises of 45 frames. Thus, our call to montage with a 5 x 9 grid as input is rather intuitive, since it will fit all frames without leaving any empty spaces. As you can easily observe, the ball enters our scene at the 13th frame and exits at the 42nd frame. Of course in this example the number of frames we would exclude knowing this information is small (12 at the beginning and 3 at the end), but it still is 1/3rd of the entire video. However, imagine a long video with only a few frames containing motion. This overall inspection tool would be a lifesaver in terms of time and effort. It can also be invaluable in artistic or other video editing tasks, since we can quickly skim through chunks of frames and pinpoint the ones we want to process.

A tool just for your playback needs – implay

Until now, we have demonstrated ways to display videos in MATLAB that are quite useful for adding processing steps in the loop, but are somewhat difficult in comparison to standard video-playing software. However, MATLAB also provides a tool aimed at those that do not want to get their hands dirty with frame-by-frame processing. Its name is implay and it has a pretty straightforward usage. It can be used in three different ways; as a standalone GUI-based video player, as a function that plays back a given image sequence stored in a matrix and as a function that loads and plays a video given its filename. Let's see how these work.

Using the GUI of implay

This is the most common way to use this tool. It is invoked by typing in its name:

```
>> implay
```

This opens the following window:

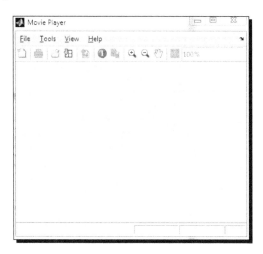

This GUI gives you the following choices:

- To open up a new player (clicking on the first icon from the left)
- Printing your frames (using the second icon from the left)
- Opening a video file (using the third icon from the left)
- Opening an image sequence from a matrix in the workspace (fourth icon)
- Exporting the current frame to `imtool` for processing (fifth icon)
- Inspecting information about the open video (sixth icon)
- Inspecting pixel values by placing a crosshair cursor inside the frame, like we did in the `imtool` (seventh icon)
- Zooming in/out (eighth/ninth icon)
- Dragging image to pan (tenth icon)
- Resizing the frame to fit the window (eleventh icon)
- Resizing the frame to a given ratio (textbox at the top right corner)

When we load a video, a second toolbar opens up beneath the first one:

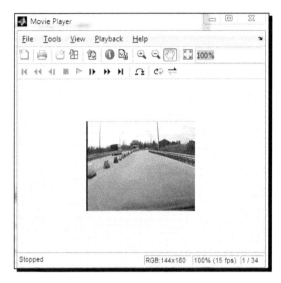

This second toolbar will probably look familiar to anyone that has used video players of any kind. Its functionalities are:

◆ Go to first frame (first icon)

◆ Jump 10 frames back (second icon)

◆ Step back one frame (third icon)

◆ Stop video (fourth icon)

◆ Play video (fifth icon)

◆ Step forward one frame (sixth icon)

◆ Jump 10 frames forward (seventh icon)

◆ Go to last frame (eighth icon)

◆ Jump to a frame of your choice (ninth icon)

◆ Repeat on/off (tenth icon)

◆ Forward/backward playback (eleventh icon)

All these functionalities give the everyday users of MATLAB a handy tool to playback their videos. Let's see how they can be combined with what we have already shown.

Using implay to play a video file

Instead of clicking on the third icon of the GUI, we can call `implay` with the filename of the video we want to play as input:

```
>> implay('singleball.avi');
```

We can also use a different frame rate:

```
>> implay('singleball.avi',20);
```

Using implay to play an image sequence

Combining it with a function such as imread and a loop that goes through all the filenames of images in a directory, we can also playback an image sequence such as the driving scene presented in an earlier example:

```
>> cd ('E:\Videos\seq');        % Change working directory
>> contents = dir('*.jpeg');    % Get names of jpeg images
>> for i = 1:length(contents)   % Loop through all images
images(:,:,:,i) = imread(contents(i).name); % Import and save them
end
>> implay(images,15); % Play back the video sequence at 15 fps
```

Creating time-lapse videos

Until now, we have covered all that we need to make our own time-lapse videos. Time-lapse is essentially the art of capturing video frames at a very low frame rate. When these frames are combined and played back at a regular frame rate (say, 25 fps), the viewer gets a sense that time is moving at a higher speed than normal, hence the term **lapse**. When the frames are captured using high resolution photographic cameras or even HDR images, then the results can be spectacular. Effects such as watching a flower bloom in seconds, or seeing the sun set or rise in a small time frame can become reality.

Lately, time-lapse photography has become one of the most used modern artistic effects in documentaries, or even movies. To achieve the impressive time-lapse videos you see in such cases, complex rigs that move the camera very slowly are combined with devices called **Intervalometers** (special devices which are programmed to get the camera to shoot several pictures at given intervals), to achieve the required precision.

Time for action – time-lapsing a regular video

Making a time-lapse video can also be as simple as skipping several frames from a video, to keep only the number of frames per second that will achieve the desired effect. Let's see how we can achieve this.

1. Our first step will be to use `VideoReader` to import a 2-minute driving video called `car2min.avi` into MATLAB:

```
>> E=VideoReader('car2min.avi');
```

2. Then, we will loop through our video using a large step (12 frames) and save the frames we visit into a new matrix:

```
>> k = 1;  % This will be used as a counter for the frames we
   keep
>> for i = 1:12:E.NumberOfFrames  % Visit every 12th frame
v(:,:,:,k)=read(E,i);  % Save the frame in the kth position of
   v
k=k+1;  % Increase the counter by 1
end
```

3. At this point, we have our video, comprising 104 frames, saved in matrix v. We can now inspect it using `montage`:

```
>> montage(v,'Size',[7 15])
```

4. The result will be as follows:

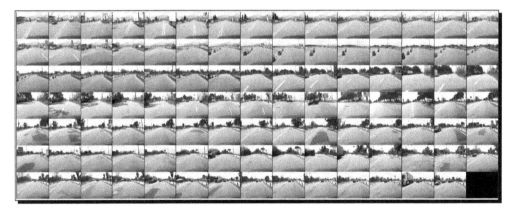

5. Now we can save our time-lapse in a new video, using what we have already learnt:

```
>> lapse = VideoWriter('timelapse.avi');
>> lapse.FrameRate = 15;
>> open(lapse);
>> for i = 1:size(v,4)
writeVideo(lapse,v(:,:,:,i));
end
close(lapse);
```

6. If you want to preview your video, you can use `implay`:

```
>> implay('timelapse.avi')
```

What just happened?

Congratulations! You have just made your first time-lapse video. Of course, it was a little less sophisticated than the average videos you might have seen in the documentaries, but nevertheless, it is a first step. You have achieved it by first importing a regular video and then selecting a large enough step to take sample frames from this video and save them in a new matrix. Finally, after inspecting all the frames of your newly constructed matrix using `montage`, you looped through all the frames to save them in a new video file with a frame rate of 15 fps. In the following chapters, we will get into the details of how to shoot the frames for a time-lapse using a photographic camera, a USB cable and a laptop with MATLAB.

Have a go hero – spinning our time-lapse

So, now that you know how to make a time-lapse, why not use another little trick to make it spin? You should try to rotate each frame by a fixed, arbitrary angle, and then save the result using the process you have already learned. If you do it correctly, the size of each frame will remain unaffected and you will have in your hands, a spinning timelapse video. Make sure that the angle you choose is not very small, or very large, so that the result is as smooth as possible.

Saving your time-lapse videos in a gif file

Another very popular format that incorporates motion is the **graphics interchange format**, shortly known as **gif**. This is a widely used file format, which supports up to 8-bits per pixel for each color channel. It can be used for still images, but also for animation. Gif files are very frequently used in the internet due to their simplicity and portability, which allows for easy production of animations made from photographs, plots, or sketches. In MATLAB, we can make a gif file using `imwrite`.

To save our time-lapse video generated in the previous example in a gif file, we have to repeat step 4, this time using `imwrite`:

```
>> fl = 'gifTimelapse.gif';
>> for i = 1:size(v,4),
[imind,cm] = rgb2ind(v(:,:,:,i),256);   % Change rgb frame to indexed
  image
if i==1,
imwrite(imind,cm,fl,'gif', 'Loopcount',inf);
else,
imwrite(imind,cm,fl,'gif','WriteMode','append');
end
end
```

The file we created, called `gifTimelapse.gif`, can be opened using any photo editor that supports animated gif files. Its frame rate in this example is dependent on the frame rate of the original video. In general, the playback frame rate of gif files can be affected by other factors as well, for example, the browser that plays the gif.

Pop quiz – image filtering in 2-dimensions

Q1. Which of the following are true?

1. `implay` is a tool supporting image processing tasks.
2. A gif file is a static image format that is rarely used.
3. Interlaced videos have double the information that progressive videos of the same size and frame rate have.
4. A higher frame rate leads to a smoother depiction of motion.
5. A `struct` variable can be a matrix containing fields of different types.
6. Function `aviread` can read compressed videos in Unix systems.
7. Function `VideoReader` is the most recent video reading function in MATLAB and therefore it is the safest choice for such tasks.

Summary

This chapter gave an introduction to videos and basic video processing tools contained in MATLAB. A brief explanation of the various properties of the videos that affect their quality has been provided in the first half of the chapter, followed by a presentation of the basic functions used to load videos in MATLAB. Then, ways to playback videos and video sequences using the command line were demonstrated and the process of video creation from static images was explained. In the rest of the chapter, two useful tools for inspecting and playing back videos were discussed and then the creation of time-lapse videos in both `.avi` and `.gif` formats was shown in detail. More specifically, this chapter covered:

*   An introduction to digital video basics
*   A presentation of interlaced and progressive videos
*   A discussion on frame rates and their importance
*   Some thoughts and examples on choosing a frame rate
*   Loading videos in MATLAB using `aviread`
*   Loading videos in MATLAB using `mmreader`
*   Loading videos in MATLAB using `VideoReader`
*   Selecting the best function for reading a video

- ◆ Playing back videos in MATLAB using `movie`
- ◆ Making videos from static images
- ◆ Inspecting a video using `montage`
- ◆ Using `implay` to playback videos, or image sequences
- ◆ Creating time-lapse videos from regular ones
- ◆ Saving your videos in gif format

In the following chapter, we will extensively cover ways in which MATLAB can be used for the acquisition phase of videos or image sequences. We will present `imaqtool` in detail and use it to create beautiful time-lapse videos. We will also discuss issues related to disk space preservation in video processing tasks. Finally, we will show how to process video frames in small chunks, aiming at producing a new video with enhanced colors and intensity.

8

Acquiring and Processing Videos

Now that you are acquainted with the processes of importing videos in MATLAB and creating new ones from still images, it is time we explore another aspect of MATLAB video processing, which is video acquisition. In this chapter, we will learn how you can use MATLAB to acquire videos, or sequences of images, which are saved on your computer rather than the storage of the camera. Furthermore, we will learn about the storage space problems faced everyday by video processing professionals and discuss compression issues and tricks, so that we mitigate this problem. Finally, some difficulties of real-time video processing in MATLAB will be presented and explained. Various tips on speeding up such processes will also be given. While learning all these, we will investigate hands-on examples that will help you comprehend various implementation techniques.

In this chapter, we will cover:

- ◆ How we can record videos in MATLAB, using the Image Acquisition Tool
- ◆ What video compression is and why it is important
- ◆ How we can work with uncompressed videos in MATLAB
- ◆ How we can make a time-lapse video in MATLAB
- ◆ How we can process videos in real time

So, let's start!

Using MATLAB for digital video recording

Till now we have used MATLAB as a powerful and versatile image processing tool. In the previous chapter, we also started exploring its video reading and writing capabilities. You may be surprised to find out that MATLAB has another useful functionality. It can be used to capture and record images and videos shot either by external cameras connected to a PC, or by internal cameras embedded in laptops. The tool that supports these capabilities is included in the Image Acquisition Toolbox and it is called Image Acquisition Tool.

The Image Acquisition Tool is a simple, yet effective, **Graphical User Interface (GUI)** that enables MATLAB to turn your PC to a **Digital Video Recorder (DVR)**. It is invoked by simply typing its function name in the command line as follows:

```
>> imaqtool
```

Once it is called, the window that appears looks like the following screenshot:

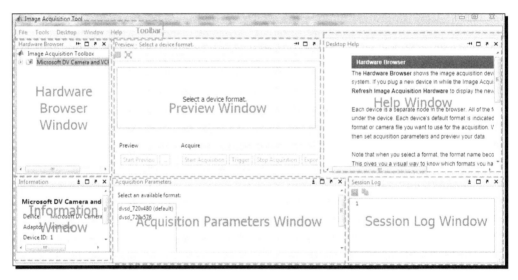

In the **Image Acquisition Tool** window, there are several subwindows that are used for acquisition purposes. We will briefly learn their properties here, so that you know your way around when we start using this tool.

The Hardware Browser window

The **Hardware Browser** window contains the list of acquisition devices that can be used by the Image Acquisition Tool. If your computer does not have a camera connected to it, or an embedded camera, this list will be empty. When a camera is detected by the **Hardware Browser** window, then its name, followed by its supported video formats are listed in the window. In our case, just one video camera with two supported formats was connected to the PC, so expanding its list of supported formats looked like the following screenshot:

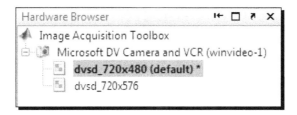

The default video format was highlighted and written in bold, so that we know that it is preselected for us. Of course, we can choose the alternative format just by clicking on it.

The Information window

The **Information** window is used to provide additional information about whichever part of the list in the **Hardware Browser** window you have clicked on. In our case, clicking sequentially on the first three items of the list, leads to the following results:

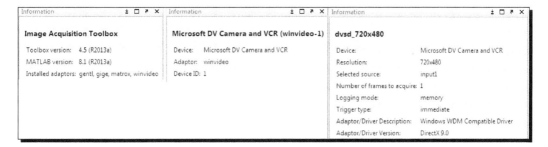

The Desktop Help window

The **Desktop Help** window contains helpful information about all the other windows in the GUI. It will change its contents depending on the window you have chosen to click on.

The Preview window

The **Preview** window is the part of the tool that provides a visual guide for you on what the camera is capturing. You can start or stop previewing what your camera sees, by clicking on the **Start Preview** or **Stop Preview** button respectively. From here, you can also start or stop the acquisition process, by clicking on the **Start Acquisition** or **Stop Acquisition** button respectively. There is also a **Trigger** button that may be used when you have set the acquisition trigger to be manual (through the **Acquisition Parameters** window) and finally there is an **Export Data...** button to save the acquired video, or sequence of images. This option allows you to export the video to a MAT-file, to the MATLAB **Workspace**, to the **Movie Player**, or to a video file using VideoWriter. All previews are displayed in a figure embedded in the **Preview** window, the size of which changes dynamically when you change the size of the window.

The Acquisition Parameters window

The **Acquisition Parameters** window is the panel in which all the settings for the acquisition process are defined. It contains five different tabs, named **General**, **Device Properties**, **Logging**, **Triggering**, and **Region of Interest**. Let's see what their settings are.

The General tab

The **General** tab is used to define two things:

- The number of **Frames per trigger** that will be acquired (either a user-defined integer number or infinite).

- The **Color space** tab that will be used for the acquired frames. It can be **rgb**, **grayscale**, or **YCbCr**.

The Device Properties tab

The **Device Properties** tab will be useful only in cases where your acquisition device allows it. In our examples it won't be the case, since our camera did not support its properties to be set. Other cameras may give you the choice of setting properties such as its exposure, or frame rate.

The Logging tab

The **Logging** tab allows you to define where the acquired frames will be saved, under which filename, how high your allowed memory limit will be set, and finally the output file format you want to use. More specifically:

- The **Log to** setting defines where the acquired frames will be saved. The possible choices are as follows:
    - Save to **Memory**, in which case the data will be lost if you do not use the **Export Data** field which is available in the **Preview** window.
    - Save to **Disk**, in which case the data will be saved to your computer's disk using the `VideoWriter` function, in the path and under the filename that you choose in the **Disk Logging (VideoWriter)** setting.
    - Save to **Disk and memory**, in which case the data will be stored both in your computer's disk and memory.

- The **Memory logging** setting lets you define the **Memory limit** (in **MB**) for the stored data, in case you have selected it to be saved in the RAM.

- **Disk Logging (VideoWriter)** allows you to define the folder where the data will be stored, as well as the **Filename** of the video stream, or sequence of images (depending on your choice of output format). Optionally, you can also select the option **Automatically increment filename** that ensures that your consecutive video files will be saved with the same name, but different consecutive numbering (for example, name_001.avi, name_002.avi, and so on).

The Triggering tab

The **Triggering** tab allows you to change the following settings:

- **Number of triggers** should either be set to a user-specified number, or to **Infinite** (you get to decide when your video will stop, by clicking on the **Stop Acquisition** button in the **Preview** window).
- **Trigger type** should either be set to **Immediate** (you start the acquisition by clicking on the **Start Acquisition** button in the **Preview** window), or to **Manual** (it allows usage of the **Trigger** button in the **Preview** window).
- **Hardware** triggering is a setting that is visible only when your device supports it (it will not be available in our examples). This setting allows for your device to perform triggering based on parameters that can be altered, but are device-specific.

The Region of Interest tab

The **Region of Interest** tab allows you to define a region of the frame that you want to be acquired. By default, the entire frame will be saved, but you can limit the area either by clicking on the **Select or Edit** button and then defining a rectangular area of the frame shown in the **Preview** window (you must have clicked on **Start Preview** first), or by setting the **X-offset** and the **Y-offset** as shown in the following screenshot:

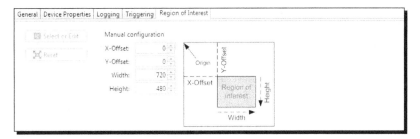

The Session Log window

The **Session Log** window is similar to the **Command History** window of the MATLAB environment, which was presented in the first chapter. It is a very useful part of the Image Acquisition Tool, since it dynamically presents the equivalent command line actions for every choice you make in the GUI. It can be used to teach you some of the core functions used for image acquisition, so that later on you can use them in your own MATLAB code.

Time for action – capturing a video using a firewire connection

Now it is time to tackle our first video acquisition assignment. We will use the most common settings to save a video in our disk, explaining every step of the process. The camera used for this example, will be a 10-year old DV camera, with a firewire (IEEE 1394) port. The connection to the PC will be via the firewire port on our motherboard. Other viable solutions can be used, for example, USB web cams, frame grabbers, and so on. A list of supported hardware per manufacturer and per operating system can be found on `https://www.mathworks.com/products/imaq/supported/index.html`.

Now, let's start our process:

1. Our first step is to connect the camera using a firewire cable and switch it on in camera mode. Once we do it, our device should be recognizable by `imaqtool`. Since we are working on Windows, we can ensure that our camera is supported, using a free utility that can be downloaded from `https://www.mathworks.com/products/imaq/supported/detect-devices-utility.zip`. Running the 64 bit executable file `detectDevices.exe` on our 64 bit system yields to the following result:

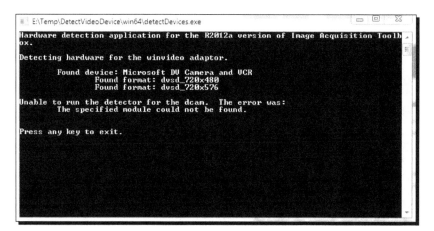

2. Since the camera is detected, we should be able to use it in the **Image Acquisition Tool** window. Let's verify it by invoking it:

```
>> imaqtool
```

The output of the previous command is as follows:

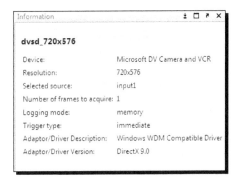

As expected, the camera was recognized and it showed up in the **Hardware Browser** window, under the name **Microsoft DV Camera and VCR (winvideo-1)**.

3. Now that the camera is recognized, we can start setting up the recording. First, let's change the resolution we will use, from the default 720 x 480, to the slightly larger 720 x 576 resolution. We do this by clicking on the second available item on the list of supported formats in the **Hardware Browser** window. Clicking on it leads to the following result in the **Information** window:

Information	± □ ⊼ ×
dvsd_720x576	
Device:	Microsoft DV Camera and VCR
Resolution:	720x576
Selected source:	input1
Number of frames to acquire:	1
Logging mode:	memory
Trigger type:	immediate
Adaptor/Driver Description:	Windows WDM Compatible Driver
Adaptor/Driver Version:	DirectX 9.0

4. The next step is to select some of the details of the acquisition process. For this first example, we will not use the triggering process. We will just make a simple video recorder that starts and stops at our command. To achieve this, we will set the **Frames per trigger** option in the **General** tab of the **Acquisition Parameters** window to **Infinite**.

5. In order to demonstrate the logging options, we will use both the RAM and the disk. To do it, we first go to the **Acquisition Parameters** window and set the **Log to** option of the **Logging** tab to **Disk and Memory**.

6. Then, we define the **Memory limit** to be 500.0 MB (you can set it lower if you don't have enough RAM).

7. Now, it is time to select the name and format of our output video file. We will click on the **Browse...** button to select the folder in which we want to store our video. The folder we will use is `E:\Videos\Acquisition\`.

8. Then, we have to define a name for the stored video in the **Filename** field (the default name filled in for you along with the full path is `bin.avi`). We will change this to **test.avi** for this example.

9. Our final setting will be to set the format and frame rate of the video we will acquire. For this example, we will leave the default values that is the **Profile** field will be **Uncompressed AVI** and the **Frame Rate** field will be 30. If you have followed all the actions above correctly, you should see the the following **Logging** tab:

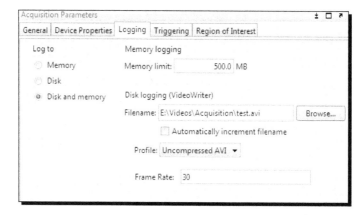

10. Now that we are finished with the settings, it is time for our final steps. The **Preview** window is where we will be working. First off, we click on the **Start Preview** button, to generate a small previewing screen that plays the role of the camera LCD screen, displaying what the camera sees in real time.

11. When we are ready to record, we click on the **Start Acquisition** button. This will start the logging process, both in the RAM and in the disk (in the file we specified in steps 7 and 8).

12. Finally, when we want to stop the recording, we click on the **Stop Acquisition** button. At this point, the `test.avi` video is safely stored in our disk and we also have a maximum of `500.0` MB of video stored in our RAM. In case we exceed the storage limit, we will get a warning message as follows:

13. After we click on the **Stop Acquisition** button, the **Preview** window will display a grid of frames from our recording. In our case, it shows 9 of the total 401 frames that were acquired (1 every 50). The test.avi video is stored in the disk at this point.

14. At this point, we can click on the **Export Data...** button to export the video that has been logged to the RAM. Since we have already saved our data to a video file, we will choose to export it also to the MATLAB **Workspace**. In the textbox defining the **Variable name**, we will type **test**. This leads to our **Workspace** window containing a four-dimensional matrix with all the acquired frames in it:

15. An optional, but useful, step for our learning purposes is to save the session log to a file, so that we get to keep and study the commands that were used in this acquisition session. To do this, we click on the disk icon in the **Session Log** window and save the commands as a MATLAB script in a folder of our choice. If we performed all the steps described above correctly, our resulting script should look something like this:

```
vid = videoinput('winvideo', 1, 'dvsd_720x576');
src = getselectedsource(vid);
vid.FramesPerTrigger = 1;
vid.FramesPerTrigger = Inf;
vid.LoggingMode = 'disk&memory';
imaqmem(500000000);
diskLogger = VideoWriter('E:\Videos\Acquisition\bin.avi',
'Uncompressed AVI');
vid.DiskLogger = diskLogger;
diskLogger = VideoWriter('E:\Videos\Acquisition\test.avi',
'Uncompressed AVI');
vid.DiskLogger = diskLogger;
preview(vid);
start(vid);
stoppreview(vid);
test = getdata(vid);
```

What just happened?

This was a rather detailed example of a simple way to work with the Image Acquisition Tool of MATLAB. The steps described the process of setting up the tool to behave as a simple video recorder, waiting for the user's command to start and stop the acquisition process. The acquisition is performed at a constant frame rate set to 30 fps and the video is saved both in the RAM and a predefined folder of the disk. A thing to beware of is that the RAM can keep a limited amount of data, defined by you. If the video exceeds the set limit, an error message like the one presented in step 12 pops up. However, you do not lose your work, since you can stop the recording and export the video logged to the RAM in any of the available ways you wish. After we saved the video both in an .avi file on the disk and in the MATLAB **Workspace** as a four-dimensional matrix, we then proceeded to save the commands generated from our process in a MATLAB script.

Have a go hero – adding a trigger to our recording

Now that you have an idea of how the Image Acquisition Tool works, it is time that you take the wheel. Let's try to make a different variation of the acquisition process by adding some functionality. You should try to set up the tool, so that it gets to do 25 manually triggered acquisitions of frames. The data should be logged only to the disk, in a folder of your choice, using the filename test2.mp4. The output file should be compressed as MPEG-4 of a quality factor of 100 and the frame rate should be 25 fps (leading to a video that is 1 second long). The choice of resolution is up to you.

If you perform the settings correctly and click on the Start Acquisition button, you will get a message with a counter that informs you what the number of your click on the **Trigger** button will be, out of a total of 25. Every time you click on the **Trigger** button, the counter will be increased by one, until it reaches 25, in which case the acquisition process will stop. This way you will produce a video file that is 1 second long, comprises 25 frames and looks like a time-lapse video, since you naturally did not click all the frames at a frequency of 1/25th of a second.

The importance of video compression

In our first example in this chapter, we saved an uncompressed AVI video. This led to a very quick appearance of the message informing us of reaching the limit of 500 MB. The number of frames captured until the appearance of the message was 401, which equals to the duration of approximately 13.37 seconds. Quite a large size for such a small video!

Let's do some math to understand how this works. As we recall from the previous chapter, the memory that an uncompressed 8-bit video consumes can be calculated by multiplying its total number of pixels, by the number of frames by three (the number of color channels). The resulting size is counted in bytes.

Checking the size of an uncompressed video

We will now try to verify that our resulting video file is as large as we expected it to be, using **Command Window**. First we will get the size of our video file:

```
>> vidInfo = dir('E:\Videos\Acquisition\test.avi'); % get file info
>> fileSize = vidInfo.bytes  % save filesize in bytes
```

The output of the previous code is as follows:

```
fileSize =
   498986856
```

Now, let's calculate our expected video file size based on its dimensions:

```
>> vidObj = VideoReader('E:\Videos\Acquisition\test.avi'); % load
  video
>> expSize = vidObj.Width * vidObj.Height * vidObj.NumberOfFrames * 3
```

The output of the previous code is as follows:

```
expSize =
   498908160
```

As you can observe, the actual video file is a little bigger than expected (approximately 58 KB). This is caused by the information overhead added by the encoder to construct the actual video file. If you want to reproduce the results in your own computer, you should, of course, change the path containing your video.

Checking the size of an MP4 video without any motion

Let's now make a compressed video like the one you created in your second exercise. For the sake of comparison, we have used a resolution of 720 x 480 and placed it in the same directory as `test.avi`. We have positioned the camera so that it looks at a window with no apparent motion for one second. The **Frames per trigger** field was set to 25, the **Trigger type** field to **Immediate**, and the **Number of triggers** field to 25. We gave the video the filename `testStill.mp4` and chose also to log it to the RAM and export it to the **Workspace** window as `testStill`. Let's see how its frames look:

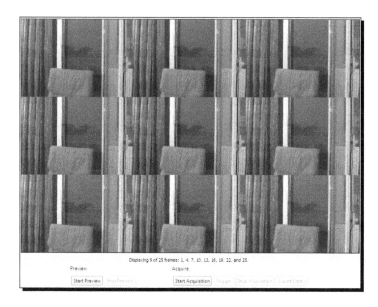

Hence, the process will be the same for getting the actual size of the file:

```
>> vidInfo = dir('E:\Videos\Acquisition\testStill.mp4'); % get file
   info
>> fileSize = vidInfo.bytes  % save filesize in bytes
```

The output is as follows:

```
fileSize =
166262
```

For the expected size of the uncompressed equivalent video, we use the number of frames, which is 25:

```
>> expSize = 720 * 576 * 25 * 3
```

The output is as follows:

```
expSize =
    31104000
```

This is the power of compression. Using MP4 compression, we have managed to limit the size of our video from an approximate expected 31 MB to approximately 166 KB. Not bad! The ratio of compression equals to:

```
>> compressionRatioStill = fileSize / expSize
```

The output is as follows:

```
compressionRatioStill =
    0.0053
```

Now, let's repeat the same thing in a scene with motion.

Checking the size of an MP4 video with high motion

For this experiment, we will start waving a pen in front of the camera for the duration of the video. This will show us if the videos with high motion have a different compression ratio than those without much motion. We'll use the same settings as in the previous section and name our video `testMotion.mp4`. We will also export the frames to a variable called `testMotion`. Let's see how the frames look:

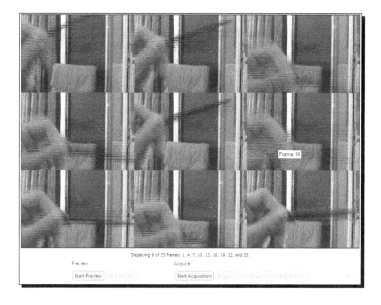

The motion included is now obvious, as is the distortion of the images caused by the fact that our video is interlaced (recall the previous chapter). The expected size of the uncompressed video remains the same. However, it is intriguing to see what happens with the actual compressed video size:

```
>> vidInfo = dir('E:\Videos\Acquisition\testMotion.mp4'); % get file
   info
>> fileSize = vidInfo.bytes  % save filesize in bytes
```

The output is as follows:

```
fileSize =
527062
```

So, it's true that the videos that include a lot of motion are bigger that is they have a larger compression ratio than the ones that include little motion. The actual ratio on this occasion is:

```
>> compressionRatioMotion = fileSize / expSize
```

The output is as follows:

```
compressionRatioMotion=
    0.0169
```

If you divide the compression ratio of the `testMotion.mp4` video to that of the `testStill.mp4` video, you will find that it is approximately 3.2 times larger. The higher the compression ratio is, the smaller the space savings derived from the compression process.

Working with uncompressed videos

A common question that you might face after reading the previous section, is why don't we work with MP4 (or other compressed formats) videos so that we do not face as many space issues? The answer is pretty simple if you stop and think about it. The advantages of compressed video files cease to exist the moment we load them in MATLAB. Once they are loaded, the frames contain all the information needed to fill all the elements of a matrix comprising all the loaded frames. Therefore, it is the same thing as loading an uncompressed video.

We can verify this by inspecting the variables `testStill` and `testMotion` created in the previous section. We will do it using MATLAB function `whos`, designed for reporting all information about a given variable. The name of the variable must be given as input, in a `string` format. Let's call this function for our two variables. The following line of code gives information for `testStill`:

```
>> whos('testStill')
```

The output of the previous code is as follows:

```
Name            Size            Bytes   Class    Attributes
testStill       4-D             25920000  uint8
```

The following line of code gives information for **testMotion**:

```
>> whos('testMotion')
```

The output of the previous code is as follows:

```
Name              Size                  Bytes  Class    Attributes
testMotion        4-D                25920000  uint8
```

As you can see, both the variables have the same size in bytes. This proves our previous speculation and leads to a new, very important question: since we can only store a very limited amount of frames in our Workspace, how can we process large videos?

The answer to this question is to design our video processing tasks so that they work with small chunks of our video (for example, 10 frames at a time) and then combine the results to form the processed video.

Working with large videos in postproduction

We will frequently need to apply some processing tasks to the frames of an already acquired video sequence. As you may have already understood, this is a very tricky problem, since we take into consideration the size of the video when it is imported to MATLAB. Let's see how we can tackle such a task.

Time for action – making an edge detection video

In this example, we will try to postprocess an already captured video file, with a size that is too big for our memory.

1. Suppose that we cannot afford 500 free MB of RAM and select the `test.avi` file we created previously. The processing task will be to convert each frame to grayscale, perform edge-detection and then save the result in a new file.

2. In order to avoid exceeding our memory limit, we will process our video in small chunks, of 10 frames each, which will be processed and added to a video file. Processing in small chunks accomplishes a trade-off between processing large videos (might lead to a memory insufficiency error) and processing videos one frame at a time (while in edge detection this approach is acceptable, it is often unfeasible, because some processing tasks require more than one frame to work). The following function will accomplish the task of edge detection:

```
functionEdgeDetectChunks(inputFn,outputFn,chunkSz)

% Function for edge detection of frames
% Inputs:
%         inputFn - Input video filename
%         outputFn- Output video filename
```

```
%            chunkSz - Size of chunks
% Output:
%          No output needed!!

vIn = VideoReader(inputFn);     % Open input file
numF = get(vIn, 'NumberOfFrames'); % Get size in frames
vOut = VideoWriter(outputFn);   % Create output file
vOut.FrameRate = vIn.FrameRate;% Equal framerates
open(vOut);                     % Open output

start = 1;       % Start frame
stop = chunkSz;  % Stop frame

while (stop <= numF) % As long as we don't exceed the frame limit
frames = read(vIn,[start stop]); % Read a chunk of frames
for i = 1:size(frames,4)     % For all frames in chunk
temp = frames(:,:,:,i); % Read a frame
temp = rgb2gray(temp);   % Convert it to grayscale
outF = edge(temp);       % Perform edge detection
outF = single(outF);     % Convert to single
writeVideo(vOut,outF);   % Write result
end
start = start + chunkSz;     % Next chunk start
stop = stop + chunkSz;       % Next chunk end
end

close(vOut); % Close output file
```

What just happened?

The function that we developed for this example may need some further explanation. First of all, the inputs were two strings, one for the input file and one for the output file, and a number that defined the number of frames to be included in our chunks. No output was needed, since our result was saved straightaway to the output video file.

The first five lines of our function opened the video input file and created an output video file with the same frame rate. Finally, the output file is opened so we can write on it.

The next couple of lines initialized the limits of our first chunk of frames. It started at the first frame and ended at the frame number that is equal to the defined size.

Next, the function entered a while loop, where all the processing will take place. The while condition (stop <= numF) told our program to keep entering the loop until the maximum limit for our chunk exceeded the total number of frames in our video. Just before each time the loop reached its end, the limits were increased by a constant chunkSz so that we moved to the next chunk of frames (see the two highlighted lines of code).

Inside the `while` loop, our function read the chunk of frames defined by our `start` and `stop` values and entered a `for` loop that processed each of the frames. The processing that took place is a conversion to grayscale, followed by edge detection. The resulting image was converted to type `single`, so that it could be used in a video. Finally, the edge detection result was saved as a new frame to our output file.

Finally, when our upper limit variable (`stop`) has exceeded the number of frames in the video, the function closed the output file and ended.

Have a go hero – getting the last chunk of frames processed

Now that you have spotted the weakness of our function, try to fix it by adding a fail-safe scenario. You should make sure that the last chunk of frames is processed no matter what. The way to verify the correctness of your code will be to compare the frame numbers of your output and input files. These two should be equal, even with a chunk size that is not a factor of the total number of frames. While you are at it, you could also experiment with other edge detection techniques, or even edge detection in all three color channels.

Pop quiz – what is the problem with our function?

Q1. Is the following statement correct?

1. The resulting output video from the function implemented above may not have an equal number of frames as our original one (used as input).

Acquiring frames for time-lapse videos

Now that you know how to acquire frames using the Image Acquisition Tool, and you have also understood the implications of enlarged uncompressed video sizes, it is time to revisit a technique covered in the previous chapter. More specifically, we will now discuss how the `imaqtool` can be used to create time-lapse videos. There are two ways we can use it:

1. By acquiring a full video and then following the process shown in the previous chapter to extract the frames that will be used to make your time-lapse video. However, this process has the obvious flaw of requiring too much disk space in cases of videos that may last a day, or more.

2. By manually triggering as many frames as you want (after having specified their number in **Number of triggers**). Of course, this way isn't ideal either, since it demands manual interaction.

This leads us to the conclusion that in order to tackle special tasks, such as time-lapse video creation, we should find alternative methods. For this reason, it is time to turn back to the powerful MATLAB command line and make use of the functions relating to image acquisition.

Detecting your acquisition hardware

The first step to acquiring videos through the command line is to detect the acquisition devices. This is a process that is performed through the use of `imaqhwinfo`:

```
>> imaqhwinfo
```

The output of the previous command is as follows:

```
ans =
InstalledAdaptors: {'gentl'  'gige'  'matrox'  'winvideo'}
MATLABVersion: '8.0 (R2012b)'
ToolboxName: 'Image Acquisition Toolbox'
ToolboxVersion: '4.4 (R2012b)'
```

This result shows us the list of installed hardware adaptors. As you may see in the example describing the session log in the beginning of the chapter, `imaqtool` has used the `winvideo` adaptor to define the video input method. Hence, this is what we will also use here. Your selection may differ, according to the hardware you have installed in your computer.

Creating a video object and acquiring a frame

Now it is time to create a video object in our **Workspace**. This is accomplished using the function `videoinput` (exactly as in the code generated by `imaqtool`):

```
>> vidObj = videoinput('winvideo', 1, 'dvsd_720x576');
```

The output of the previous code is as follows:

```
Error using videoinput (line 228)
There are no devices installed for the specified ADAPTORNAME. See
IMAQHWINFO.
```

This doesn't look right! Something went wrong here. Despite the fact that the device is switched on and it has been recognized by `imaqhwinfo`, MATLAB produces an error message. Luckily, the solution is simple. We will just reset the image acquisition objects, using `imaqreset`, and then retry using `videoinput`:

```
>> imaqreset
>> vidObj = videoinput('winvideo', 1, 'dvsd_720x576');
```

Success! This time, a video object named as `vidObj` has been created. It holds the information regarding the acquisition hardware we want to use and the resolution we will work in. The next step is to acquire a frame. Before we do, let's open a **Preview** window like the one used in `imaqtool` to get a glimpse of what our camera sees:

```
>> preview(vidObj)
```

The following screenshot is the output of the previous command:

Now, we can grab one frame at any point in time we want and save it in matrix variable snapshot, using function `getsnapshot`:

```
>> snapshot = getsnapshot(vidObj);
>> figure,imshow(snapshot)     % Take a look at what we shot
```

The following screenshot is the output of the previous command:

So, now that you know how you can capture a frame using the command line, the sky is the limit! The next step is to create a free-of-charge MATLAB-based intervalometer for our time-lapse videos. As already mentioned in the previous chapter, intervalometers are devices that take over the timing of frame capturing by our device. They also allow for more complicated adjustments, for example, the shutter speed, HDR multiple exposures, and so on. These functionalities can be also included in MATLAB, if the capturing device allows the software to manipulate them. However, the only thing that we will need for our simple example is a way to control the time intervals between sequential frame acquisitions.

The only extra function we will need is `pause`. This function pauses the execution of a program for a given number of seconds (given as input), before allowing it to continue. Let's see how this will work.

Time for action – using MATLAB as an intervalometer

Our goal here is to write MATLAB code that will create a time-lapse video. Let's suppose that we want our video to capture frames overnight that is start shooting when we want it to and then shoot 1 frame every minute, for 8 consecutive hours. This will lead to a video comprising 8 x 60 frames, which is 480 frames in total. An uncompressed video with a resolution of 720 x 576 pixels and 8-bits depth per color channel will require approximately 598 MB. Therefore, you should make sure that you have at least 598 MB of RAM available to save it.

It goes without saying, that your camera must be plugged to the power outlet so that we don't face battery problems. If you work with a laptop, it should be plugged in as well. Let's start using MATLAB as an intervalometer:

1. We first reset our hardware devices and set the video input to our preferred hardware and resolution:

   ```
   >> imaqreset
   >> vidObj = videoinput('winvideo', 1, 'dvsd_720x576');
   ```

2. It is a good idea to preallocate space for the matrix that will store our 480 frames, since this will be an early indication of whether you have enough memory. Our matrix should be of type `uint8`, so that it matches the video frames that will be acquired. To do this, type in the following command:

   ```
   >> timelapse = uint8(zeros(576,720,3,480));
   ```

3. Now, it is time to write the intervalometer code. It will be a `for` loop that executes 480 times. In the loop, we must use `getsnapshot` to acquire a frame and then pause to wait for a time interval of 1 minute (60 seconds). Printing out a message that tells us which frame has been captured will also prove useful, as will displaying the current acquired frame:

   ```
   >> for i = 1:480
   ```

```
timelapse(:,:,:,i) = getsnapshot(vidObj);  % Acquire a frame
fprintf('Just acquired frame number %d... \n',i) % Announcement
imshow(timelapse(:,:,:,i)) % Display the current frame
pause(60)  % Wait for 60 seconds
end
```

4. After 8 hours, your time-lapse video will be ready! All its frames will have been stored in matrix `timelapse`. They are ready for you to play them back, or save them to a video file. Let's first playback the video to see if we are happy with the result:

```
>> implay(timelapse)
```

5. Hopefully, our time-lapse video is what we expected to see. If we do not save it now, we will have wasted 8 hours of our lives for nothing. So, let's use VideoWriter to save it in compressed, MP4 format. First, we must create a new video file, assign an object to it, set the frame rate to 25 fps and open it:

```
>> vidObj2 = VideoWriter('AcquiredTimelapse.mp4','MPEG-4');
>> vidObj2.FrameRate = 25;
>> open(vidObj2);
```

6. Now that we have created the video object, it is time to write our 480 frames to it:

```
>>f or k = 1:size(timelapse,4)   % For all the frames
writeVideo(vidObj2,timelapse(:,:,:,k)); % Write k-th frame to
  file
end
```

7. Finally, we have to close our video object, so that we finalize our process:

```
>>close(vidObj2);
```

What just happened?

This previous example demonstrated the power of MATLAB scripting. In just a few lines of code, you managed to program a camera to shoot a time-lapse video at a frame rate of 1 frame per minute for a total of 8 hours, played back your video and then saved it to a compressed video file. Step 1 was rather common, since we used these two commands in previous sections. Step 2 is rather important when you are unsure if your memory will be enough for the video that will be acquired. It is also important in terms of processing speed, since preallocation generally helps in speeding up the execution of your code. Step 3 included all the magic, since it performed the acquisition of the video frames following the requirements set. In order to ensure that our result was what we wanted, we played back our file after 8 consecutive hours of acquisition, in Step 4. Finally, Steps 5 through 7 wrote the video in compressed MP4 format, to a file called `AcquiredTimelapse.mp4`.

Have a go hero – creating a time-lapse creation function

At this point, you have learned how to create time-lapse videos in MATLAB using various techniques and tools. For this exercise, you should try to embed some of the previous code in a custom time-lapse function that will get the number of frames to be acquired, the time delay between them and a filename string as inputs, and will save the time-lapse video created using the first two inputs to an MP4 video file with the filename given in the third input.

Real-time processing of time-lapse videos

The most advantageous in the case of time-lapse videos is the frame rate of acquisition. Since we only have to acquire frames at a very low rate, we can dedicate the rest of the video acquisition time for processing the acquired frames. For instance, when we want to acquire one frame every minute like in our previous example, the frame rate is 1/1500 of the actual PAL frame rate (in a minute we acquire 1 frame instead of 25*60 in the case of a regular PAL video).

Technically, this means that we may dedicate the remaining 1499/1500 of each minute for processing our acquired frame. This usually is enough for real-time application of all kinds of processing tasks, for example, color masking, image smoothing, and so on. Ultimately, this means that the acquired video sequence can be artistically processed to achieve very interesting visual results. To demonstrate one of these results, we will now try to blend a time-lapse acquisition process with the color isolation techniques we presented in *Chapter 4*, *Working with Color Images*.

Time for action – creating time-lapses with isolated colors

For this example, we will create a time-lapse video with the red color isolated in the scene. We will use a frame rate of 2 frames per minute and perform the acquisition for 2 hours. This will create a video consisting of 2 (frames/minute) * 2 hours * 60 (minutes / hour) = 240 frames. Between two consecutive acquisitions, the first acquired frame will be processed for color isolation:

1. The first step is to reset our hardware devices and set the video input to our preferred hardware and resolution:

```
>> imaqreset
>> vidObj = videoinput('winvideo', 1, 'dvsd_720x576');
```

2. Next, we will preallocate the space needed for the 240 frames of our video:

```
>> tl = uint8(zeros(576,720,3,240));
```

3. Next, we should write a small function to perform the color isolation. It is a simplified version of the `ROIColorIsolation.m` function developed for *Chapter 4, Working with Color Images*. It goes as follows:

```
function [output] = ColorIsolation(image,thresh)

% Function for color isolation in an image % Inputs:
%         image   - Input image
%         thresh - Thresholds matrix ([1st 2nd 3rd])
% Output:
%         output - Output image (masked)

R = image(:,:,1);   % Separate red channel
G = image(:,:,2);   % Separate green channel
B = image(:,:,3);   % Separate blue channel
grayIm = rgb2gray(image); % Keep grayscale version of image

% Create mask from three thresholds
mask = R < thresh(1) & G < thresh(2) & B < thresh(3);

% Perform masking
R(mask==0) = grayIm(mask==0);
G(mask==0) = grayIm(mask==0);
B(mask==0) = grayIm(mask==0);

% Join color channels to generate final image
output = cat(3,R,G,B);
```

4. It is now time for the core of our processing program. The essence of the `for` loop remains almost the same as before. The only thing we must do is to add a step for the color isolation. Let's isolate colors with a green value higher than `100`:

```
>> for i = 1:240
temp = getsnapshot(vidObj);  % Acquire a frame
fprintf('Processing frame number %d… \n',i) % Announcement
tl(:,:,:,i) = ColorIsolation(temp,[0 100 0]);% Perform
  isolation
subplot(1,2,1),imshow(temp ) % Display current frame
subplot(1,2,2),imshow(tl(:,:,:,i)) % Display processed frame
pause(30) % Wait for 30 seconds
end
```

5. At this point, we have a matrix called `tl`, which holds the frames of our time-lapse video. If we want to save it, we can repeat the process of the previous example:

```
>> vid = VideoWriter('TimelapseIsolation.mp4','MPEG-4');
>> vid.FrameRate = 25;
>> open(vid);
>> for k = 1:size(tl,4) % For all the frames
writeVideo(vid,tl(:,:,:,k)); % Write k-th frame to file
end
>> close(vid);
```

What just happened?

In this example, we performed a mixture of methods for color image processing and video acquisition. A core function that performs color isolation was written, creating a mask from three user-defined thresholds and using it to remove the colors from all the pixels below the thresholds (making all their colors equal to the pixel values of the grayscale image). This function was then incorporated in a `for` loop that performs frame acquisition, processing, and displaying with an interval of 30 seconds. In the fifth and final step, the created video was saved to a MP4 video file, using the process described in previous examples.

Note that the process performed does not lead to a video with frames with an exact time delay of 30 seconds. This is the natural result, caused by the delay added to our process from the commands executed between the frame acquisition and the `pause` function. A quick solution for more precise timing could be accomplished by timing the delay using `tic` and `toc`, and subtracting it from the time delay included in `pause`. The same change should be also made to previous examples using the same rationale.

Real-time processing of normal videos

As mentioned in the previous section, time-lapse videos are very advantageous for real-time processing, because of their low frame rates. When we have to perform processing on regular videos however, things start to become much more difficult. Normally, real-time processing of 25 fps or 30 fps videos is not feasible in MATLAB, except if the processing tasks are very basic and they are performed by fast hardware.

Evaluating real-time capabilities with a simple example

In the next example, we will demonstrate a basic video processing code for adjusting the contrast of the frames after they are acquired and we will time the process so that we assess the real-time capabilities of MATLAB.

Time for action – adjusting the contrast of the video

In this example, we will make a loop for continuous acquisition and per channel contrast adjustment of frames from our camera. We will time the process using the profile function of MATLAB so that we demonstrate the bottleneck of our process. This way, you can get an idea of the time issues arising when performing video processing in MATLAB. Bear in mind that the machine used for these experiments had a Q9550 Quad-Core CPU, at 2.8 GHz:

1. First off, we get our hardware ready:

```
>> imaqreset
>> vid = videoinput('winvideo', 1, 'dvsd_720x576');
```

2. Now, we preallocate space for the matrix that will hold our frames. For our experiment, 100 frames will be enough:

```
>> test = uint8(zeros(576,720,3,100));
```

3. We then start the MATLAB profiler, which will analyze the time spent on each of our functions:

```
>>profile on
```

4. Next, we write the `for` loop that will make it all happen:

```
>> for i = 1:100
temp = getsnapshot(vid);  % Acquire a frame
fprintf('Processing frame number %d... \n',i) % Announcement
test(:,:,i) = imadjust(temp); % Adjust contrast
subplot(1,2,1),imshow(temp ) % Display current frame
subplot(1,2,2),imshow(test(:,:,:,i)) % Display processed frame
end
```

Each display of the resulting frames looks like the following screenshot:

5. Now, we close the profiler and display its results:

```
>> profile off % Close profiler
>> profile viewer   % Display profiling results
```

Profile Summary
Generated 06-May-2013 17:55:30 using cpu time.

Function Name	Calls	Total Time	Self Time*	Total Time Plot (dark band = self time)
imaqdevice.getsnapshot	100	26.824 s	26.796 s	
graphics\private\clo	400	1.627 s	1.145 s	
imuitools\private\basicImageDisplay	200	1.941 s	0.930 s	
imshow	200	4.349 s	0.887 s	
imadjust>adjustWithLUT	300	0.465 s	0.305 s	
iptgetpref	600	0.330 s	0.194 s	
subplot	200	0.216 s	0.165 s	
images\private\imhistc (MEX-file)	300	0.141 s	0.141 s	
stretchlim	300	0.363 s	0.123 s	
newplot	400	1.844 s	0.122 s	

These were the profiling results. Each of the functions was analyzed with regards to the number of times it was called, the total time spent on it, and its self-time that is the time spent in the core of the functions, disregarding its child functions.

What just happened?

This example gave us an idea of the time issues hiding behind video processing tasks, even if they are very basic. The process we selected to investigate was a continuous acquisition of frames, followed by a per-channel contrast enhancement using the imadjust function (as discussed in previous chapters). The profile function provided by MATLAB was used to inspect the timing details of each step of our process. By analyzing our results, we easily concluded that getsnapshot is the bottleneck of our whole process, taking a total of 26.824 seconds of the time. Taking into account that the second most time-consuming function was imshow (4.349 seconds in total), we understood that acquiring the snapshots was unreasonably time-consuming.

Revisiting the contrast adjustment example

The results of the previous example were a huge disappointment. Needing to spend approximately 27 seconds only for the image acquisition part of our 100 frames acquisition program is prohibiting for real-time applications. It means that each acquisition takes approximately 27/100 = 0.27 seconds, leading to a frame rate of about 1/0.27 = 3.7 fps just for the acquisition. This is very far from the 25 fps goal that we need for our PAL video processing applications. It may be enough for time-lapses, but by no means does it fit the real-time video processing requirements.

In this case, the solution to our problem is surprisingly unintuitive and simple. The reason why the `getsnapshot` function takes so much time lies in the way it works. Ideally, it needs to have a **Preview** window of the acquired video open, in order to acquire the frames faster. If it does not, then the function is delayed because it tries to generate the preview and grab the frame silently. Let's try to resolve this issue.

Time for action – adding preview in our code

This time, we will repeat the previous experiment, with a minor adjustment; we will add a `preview` command in our code. Let's try it:

1. First, we will repeat steps 1 to 3 from the previous example:

```
>> imaqreset
>> vid = videoinput('winvideo', 1, 'dvsd_720x576');
>> test = uint8(zeros(576,720,3,100));
>> profile on
```

2. Now, we will invoke the **Preview** window using the following command:

```
>>preview(vid);
```

3. And then, we will once more type in the acquisition-processing nested `for` loops:

```
>> for i = 1:100
temp = getsnapshot(vid);  % Acquire a frame
fprintf('Processing frame number %d… \n',i) % Announcement
for k = 1:3  % For all 3 color channels
test(:,:,k,i) = imadjust(temp(:,:,k)); % Adjust contrast
end
subplot(1,2,1),imshow(temp ) % Display current frame
subplot(1,2,2),imshow(test(:,:,:,i)) % Display processed frame
end
```

4. Finally, we will close and display the profiling results:

```
>> profile off % Close profiler
>> profile viewer  % Display profiling results
```

Profile Summary
Generated 06-May-2013 18:31:13 using cpu time.

Function Name	Calls	Total Time	Self Time*	Total Time Plot (dark band = self time)
imshow	200	5.010 s	1.359 s	
graphics\private\clo	400	1.638 s	1.133 s	
imuitools\private\basicImageDisplay	200	2.106 s	1.081 s	
imaqdevice.getsnapshot	100	0.353 s	0.330 s	
imadjust>adjustWithLUT	300	0.399 s	0.289 s	
iptgetpref	600	0.356 s	0.199 s	
subplot	200	0.229 s	0.184 s	
stretchlim	300	0.402 s	0.149 s	
images\private\imhistc (MEX-file)	300	0.132 s	0.132 s	
newplot	400	1.842 s	0.123 s	
imu...ls\private\isSingleImageDefaultPos	200	0.232 s	0.119 s	
findall	400	0.215 s	0.096 s	

Quite different results than what we saw before.

5. Our last step is to close the **Preview** window, since we are done with our acquisition:

```
>> stoppreview(vid)
```

What just happened?

This example showed us a general truth about MATLAB programming. The solution to our problems, especially when they are relevant to processing speed, is frequently much simpler than expected. In our case here, the solution was to open a **Preview** window that continuously displays what our camera sees. This way, the total time spent for 100 calls of our getsnapshot function fell from a huge 26.824 seconds to a very low 0.353 seconds. Our code still has not reached 25 fps, since the imshow function needs 5 seconds, hence leads to a 1/0.05 = 20 fps rate alone, but this is a smaller problem that can be handled in other ways.

Have a go hero – doubling the speed of our code

Now we have reached our most crucial point. Our code is near real-time, but still not actual real-time. You should try to make adjustments in the code, which will enable it to run at least twice as fast as the one we have created so far. As different machines will produce different processing time results, you should have a goal of doubling the performance in your machine. Therefore, you should time the process of the previous example in your own machine and then try to improve the code while checking if you have accomplished your goal (at least doubling the speed). It goes without saying that we seek a performance increase without throwing out the part of the code displaying our results.

Pop quiz – acquiring and processing videos

Q1. Which of the following are true?

1. The Image Acquisition Tool only saves uncompressed video.

2. The size of an MP4 video is related only to its resolution and duration.

3. A high motion MP4 video with the same settings as a low motion MP4 video will be larger in size.

4. The creation of time-lapse videos can be accomplished by just using a `for` loop with `getsnapshot` and `pause` inside it.

5. The real-time processing of time-lapse videos is more challenging than the real-time processing of regular frame rate videos.

6. Adding preview in our code slows down the frame acquisition process using `getsnapshot`.

Summary

In this chapter, we presented the video acquisition functionality of MATLAB. The first part was dedicated to a thorough analysis of the Image Acquisition Tool, which is a basic GUI-based framework for video acquisition. After presenting a couple of examples on the usage of `imaqtool`, we moved on to a discussion on video compression and its great importance. The difference in compression ratios between still scenes and scenes with high motion was explained, using two practical, hands-on examples. Then, a small discussion on ways to work with uncompressed videos was carried out, followed by an example of processing video frames in chunks to save space. The next part of this chapter was focused on ways to create time-lapse videos using the command line, either without, or with processing of the acquired frames. The final part of the chapter revolved around the real-time video processing capabilities of MATLAB. In these sections, we discussed ways to speed up the acquisition and processing tasks in order to approach real-time performance. More specifically, this chapter covered:

- An introduction to using MATLAB as digital video recorder software
- An explanation of the GUI of the Image Acquisition Tool
- The importance and functionality of the **Hardware Browser** window
- The importance and functionality of the **Information** window
- The importance and functionality of the **Desktop Help** window
- The importance and functionality of the **Preview** window
- The importance and functionality of the **Acquisition Parameters** window
- The importance and functionality of the **Session Log** window
- The problem of video file sizes and the importance of compression
- The role of motion in compression
- The difficulty in uncompressed video processing
- Ways to process videos in chunks
- The acquisition of time-lapse videos through the command line
- The real-time processing capabilities of MATLAB in time-lapse videography
- The real-time processing capabilities of MATLAB in regular videos

In the next chapter we will get to discuss various spatiotemporal video processing techniques. Some of them will be just extensions of what you have already learned for still images, while others will also take into account motion that has temporal differences between video frames. Interesting tasks like deinterlacing of videos, motion detection, and video stabilization will be explored, by showing practical ways to achieve them in MATLAB.

9
Spatiotemporal Video Processing

By now, you should have been familiar with video acquisition and the basic processing of frames in MATLAB. In this chapter, we will discuss video processing in a little more depth, starting with basic frame manipulations based on the techniques already discussed for still images. Then, we will proceed with describing techniques for intra-frame and inter-frame processing. In this direction, we will demonstrate and analyze some basic methods for video deinterlacing and spatiotemporal filtering. These techniques will be implemented in MATLAB and evaluated with real-life examples. Extra hands-on exercises will be presented so that you can better comprehend the usage of the methods.

In this chapter, we will cover:

- How to perform some basic video processing tasks in MATLAB, for example, cropping and resizing
- How to deinterlace our videos in MATLAB using various methods
- How to apply spatiotemporal filtering to our videos

So, let's start processing!

Basic video processing with MATLAB

In the previous chapter, we were mainly concerned with ways to acquire videos and process them on the fly, using MATLAB. Furthermore, we have already discussed the basic tools and functions for loading existing videos into the MATLAB **Workspace** window in *Chapter 7, Adding Motion – From Static Images to Digital Videos.*

Now it is time to revisit the issue of processing existing video files and using MATLAB as a powerful video processing suite. We will start with basic manipulations, such as importing a video to alter its dimensions or crop it, and save it in a new file.

Cropping and resizing our video

A very common task handled efficiently by all video processing suites, is cropping and resizing of our video. Usually, the user has to define the area of the video frame that should be cropped and/or the resizing factor. The video processing software then applies the cropping and/or resizing and saves the new video file. This is a fairly simple process, which consists of loading one frame at a time, transforming it using methods from the earlier chapters of this book, and then saving it in a new video file. Let's see how in our next example.

Time for action – loading, cropping, resizing, and saving a video

This is a rather straightforward procedure that will be implemented as a MATLAB function. We will write a function that accepts the filename of an existing video file, the resizing factor, the frames to be processed, and a filename for the output file. The user will be prompted at the first processed frame to crop it to the desired size and position. The function is as follows:

```
function CropAndResize(inFnm,resF,framesP,outFnm)

% Function for loading, cropping, resizing and saving a video
% Inputs:
%         inFnm   - Input video filename
%         resF    - Resizing factor (must be positive)
%         framesP - Frames to be processed ([start end])
%         outFnm  - Output video filename
% Output:
%         No output needed!!


start = framesP(1);                    % Start frame
stop  = framesP(2);                    % End frame

% Numeric inputs validation
validateattributes(resF,{'numeric'},{'positive'},'CropAndResize','re
sF')
validateattributes(framesP,{'numeric'},{'positive'},'CropAndResize','
framesP')

% Error handling for frames
if stop > numF
```

```
        error('Exceeded maximum number of frames!')
    elseif start < 1 || stop < 1 || start > stop
        error('Something is wrong with your frame limits!')
    end

    vIn = VideoReader(inFnm);             % Open input file
    numF = get(vIn, 'NumberOfFrames');    % Get size in frames
    vOut = VideoWriter(outFnm);           % Create output file
    vOut.FrameRate = vIn.FrameRate;       % Equal framerates
    open(vOut);                           % Open output

    for i = start:stop      % See we don't exceed the frame limit
        frame = read(vIn,i);              % Read one frame
        if i == start
            disp('Please crop the image') % Prompt user for cropping
            [temp, RECT] = imcrop(frame); % Crop and keep RECT
        end
        outF = imcrop(frame,RECT);        % Perform cropping w. RECT
        outF = imresize(outF, resF);      % Perform resizing
        writeVideo(vOut,outF);            % Write result
    end
    close(vOut); % Close output file
```

Now that we have written our function, it is time for us to test it:

1. We can test the function by providing an input filename (we'll use the 2-minute long driving video from *Chapter 7, Adding Motion – From Static Images to Digital Videos*, car2min.avi), a resizing factor (we'll use 2 to double the size of the cropped image), the starting and ending frame numbers (we'll use 220 and 300), and an output filename (we'll name it testCar.avi). Using these inputs, we type in the following command:

   ```
   >> CropAndResize('car2min.avi',2,[20 100],'testCar.avi');
   ```

2. The result will be a message, prompting the user to crop the image: **Please crop the image**

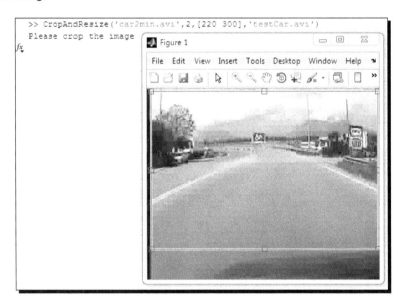

3. Now that we have cropped the image and the video file has started being filled with frames, the output video file will be visible in the **Current Folder** window.

4. We can play our new video using `implay`:

```
>> implay('testCar.avi')
```

What just happened?

In this example, we mixed some of the techniques discussed in previous chapters to write a function that handled loading, cropping, and resizing a video file, and then saved the result in a new file.

The first few lines of the function were, as usual, the comments describing the inputs and outputs expected by the function. The next two lines of code were used for assigning the start and end frame numbers provided by the user to respective variables. Then, you got an idea about ways to use defensive programming (that is foreseeing the possible user-inflicted errors). First, the two numeric inputs, `resF` and `framesP`, were checked for validity, whether they were positive numbers. This check is performed using the function `validateattributes`.

Moving on, we check whether the frame numbers were correct, by means of the two blocks of the `if` statement. The `if` clause checked for a possible error in the definition of the last frame of our video. Of course it can't exceed the maximum number of frames, hence the check `if stop > numF`. The `elseif` clause checked for other errors in the declaration of the frames to be processed, for example, the frame numbers being negative or zero, and so on. If either of the error exists, the function is aborted immediately after a proper error message is displayed in the command line. This is what the function `error` is used for.

After the validity checks, there were five lines of code we re-used in a previous function (see section: *Time for action – making an edge detection video,* from *Chapter 8, Acquiring and Processing Videos*). These lines handled the opening of the video and getting its size in frames (for error handling), then creating and opening a new video file of equal frame rate, so that we can write on it.

Then, the main block of our code followed. In this block, we acquired one frame at a time, cropped it, resized it, and wrote it in our new video file. The highlighted `if` clause will be `true` only once (for the first frame we process) and its block will prompt the user to provide the cropping area, `RECT`, which will then be used for cropping all the frames (including the first one).

When all the frames were processed and written in the new video file, the file was closed.

After the function was written, we proceeded in testing its usage in steps 1 through 4. First, we used 81 frames from a video we have used in *Chapter 7, Adding Motion – From Static Images to Digital Videos* and generated a new, cropped video with double the size of its original area.

When the process was over and we verified the existence of the new video file in our **Current Folder** window, we played back the video using `implay`. The player informed us that the frame size of the new cropped and resized video is 472 x 706. Our original video was 288 x 360. Since we cropped it before resizing, it is natural for it to be less than double the size per dimension.

Have a go hero – adding rotation and more error-checking

Now that you have a first function to use as basis, let's try to add more functionality to it. You should try to include another input to our previous function, which will be used as the angle by which to rotate our video frames, using `imrotate`. This functionality is very handy when we have used our camera in portrait orientation to shoot video. This way, our video does not show up as we would expect. Has it ever happened to you?

Another addition you can try to make to the code is an error-checking clause, for cases where the resizing factor is less than or equal to zero. This will lead to a result that is not acceptable, since the result of `imresize` with negative resizing factors is an empty matrix. No video can be constructed using empty frames, so we really should prevent this from happening.

Filtering your video frames

Now that we have discussed how we can import an existing video file and apply basic image manipulation techniques on its frames, it is time we move on to more complex filtering. You probably have already noticed that the quality of the video we have made in the previous example is not exactly optimal. It has a very intense blocking effect (neighboring rectangular blocks in the image have very visible borders), especially due to the resizing process we have used. As you may recall, in order for `imresize` to accomplish adding pixels where they don't exist, it uses the cubic interpolation method by default. This is a fast, but suboptimal method and can lead to serious blocking effects.

Instead of going back to the function we have written in the previous example and use different methods of interpolation available with `imresize` to enhance our video, we will try to accomplish it by filtering the frames. A common way to do it is to apply a smoothing filter to each of the frames, so that the blocking effect is reduced. Let's see how we can do it, using the following example.

Time for action – reducing the blocking effect

The process shown here should seem very familiar. Each of the frames in the video will be filtered using a disk filtering element and saved in a new video file, which hopefully will appear less distorted by the blocking effect:

1. Let's start by importing the video file in our **Workspace** window:

```
>> vIn = VideoReader('testCar.avi')
```

2. Now, we have to make a new video file and set its frame rate equal to the one we opened:

```
>> vOut = VideoWriter('carSmooth.avi'); % Create output file
>> vOut.FrameRate = vIn.FrameRate;      % Equal frame rates
>> open(vOut);                          % Open output
```

3. We should also get the number of total frames of the original video, so that we can use it in a `for` loop:

```
>> numF = get(vIn, 'NumberOfFrames');   % Get size in frames
```

4. Finally, we will write a `for` loop, for smoothing and writing the frames:

```
>> for i = 1:numF % For all frames in video
frame = read(vIn,i); % read i-th frame
fKernel = fspecial('disk',5); % Create filter kernel
for j = 1:3 % For all color channels
% Filter each channel using a 5 pixel radius disk element
out(:,:,j,i) =imfilter(frame(:,:,j),fKernel);
end % End inner for
end % End outer for
```

5. At this point, matrix variable `out` contains all 81 frames of the video, smoothed using a 5 pixel radius disk element. Using a disk element, reduces the blocking effect, but also leads to loss of detail (because of smoothing). We can verify this by displaying the original last frame of the video next to its smoothed version:

```
>> subplot(1,2,1), imshow(frame), title('Original Frame')
>> subplot(1,2,2), imshow(out(:,:,:,end)), title('Smoothed Frame')
```

6. An even better idea of the smoothing result can be gained by showing a smaller area of the two images. Let's use a rectangular area in the middle-left part of the image:

```
>> original = frame(250:350,10:210,:); % Crop original frame
>> filtered = out(250:350,10:210,:,end); % Crop smoothed frame
>> figure, subplot(1,2,1), imshow(original),title('Original Area')
>> subplot(1,2,2), imshow(filtered), title('Smoothed Area')
```

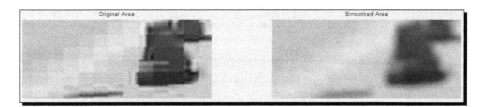

What just happened?

This example demonstrated a simple way to reduce the blocking effect that often appears in videos and images due to compression or resizing. The rationale of this process is quite simple and requires only a few basic steps, most of which you have already learned.

The first two steps handled the input and output video files, using identical functions as before. The step 3 was necessary so that we know how many frames the input video had.

The number of steps were used in the outer `for` loop of step 4, so that we processed every single one. In this loop, once we assigned a frame to a temporary variable called `frame`, we filtered each one of its three color channels using the aforementioned filter. The filter was constructed using the function `fspecial`. Each filtered frame (with index i) was assigned to a new layer of matrix `out` (also with index i), one color channel at a time.

Once the two `for` loops are terminated, we visualized our results in steps 5 and step 6. As you can easily observe, the blocking effect was reduced by the filtering process, but as a consequence there was an apparent loss of detail due to smoothing.

Deinterlacing videos in MATLAB

Now, it is time to visit a very common topic in video processing; video deinterlacing. As you might recall, videos can be split into two categories: interlaced and progressive. The former contain frames with either odd or even rows present, while the latter contain frames with all the rows present. The frame rates of videos do not let the human eye easily distinguish the difference, making interlaced videos a compelling choice when we want to save space.

However, there are cases in which interlacing is visible to the human eye. A common example is still frames from videos that include motion, which exhibit interlacing artifacts. An example of such artifacts is shown in the following example, which is a frame extracted from a driving video (shot from inside a moving vehicle). We have also cropped an area of the image where the interlacing artifacts are more intense, so that you understand the problem even better.

```
>> A = imread('interlaced.bmp');        % Load interlaced image
>> B = imcrop(A,[480 400 200 100]); % Crop detail of interlaced frame
>> subplot(1,2,1),imshow(A);title('Entire Interlaced Frame')
>> subplot(1,2,2),imshow(B);title('Cropped Area of Interlaced Frame')
```

Intra-frame filtering for deinterlacing tasks

You can now see clearly that the interlaced frame appears distorted especially on the edges of the cars. To reduce the artifacts, we will have to filter the image. Till now, we have only worked on methods for filtering a single image (or video frame), commonly known as intra-frame filtering. Therefore, we will start by using such methods for our first deinterlacing tasks.

Deinterlacing with the Computer Vision System Toolbox

For our first deinterlacing example, we will use the Computer Vision System Toolbox of MATLAB for the first time. Till here, we have not used it because most of our tasks did not demand it. Deinterlacing can also be performed without this toolbox, which we will see this later on, but we will use it anyway, to get some quick results for our examples.

Time for action – deinterlacing a video using the vision toolbox

The Computer Vision System Toolbox has an object that can handle three common methods of deinterlacing. The object is intuitively called `Deinterlacer`. Let's see its usage on our example interlaced image.

1. First, we have to load our image. If you have cleared your workspace, type the following command:

    ```
    >> A = imread('interlaced.bmp');    % Load interlaced image
    ```

2. Then, we have to initialize the `Deinterlacer` object. Let's use the default settings:

    ```
    >> deintObj = vision.Deinterlacer; % create deinterlacing
       System object
    ```

3. Now it is time to apply the deinterlacing method specified by the default settings (line repetition method) to our interlaced frame:

    ```
    >> A2 = step(deintObj, A); % Apply de-interlacing method
    ```

4. Finally, we will see the before and after images and cropped parts, side-by-side:

    ```
    >> B = imcrop(A,[480 400 200 100]); % Crop interlaced detail
    >> B2 = imcrop(B,[480 400 200 100]); % Crop deinterlaced detail
    >> subplot(2,2,1),imshow(A);title('Entire Interlaced Frame')
    >> subplot(2,2,2),imshow(A2);title('EntireDe-Interlaced Frame')
    >> subplot(2,2,3),imshow(B);title('Cropped Interlaced Area')
    >> subplot(2,2,4),imshow(B2);title('Cropped De-Interlaced
       Area')
    ```

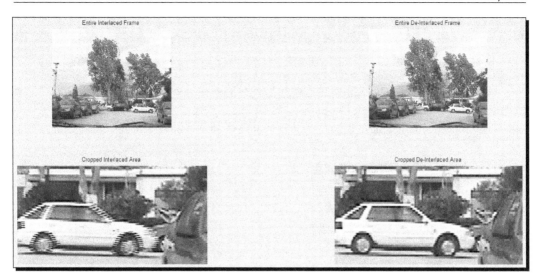

What just happened?

This example demonstrated the usage of the `Deinterlacer` object of the Computer Vision System Toolbox, with the default method setting, which is the line repetition. As the name implies, this method deinterlaces an image by repeating the odd (or even) lines to replace the even (or odd) lines, keeping the overall image size the same. The effect was obviously positive, as the jagged artifacts on the edges of the car have been significantly reduced. The repetition of lines was probably the simplest way to solve the problem. The process, as shown in the example, was quite simple; first we loaded our interlaced image, then we initialized a deinterlacing `System` object, and we called the `step` method to apply the process (deinterlacing) to our target input (the interlaced image). The final step was useful for a qualitative evaluation of the success of our method. From its results, we can see that even with the simplest method the deinterlaced result looks better than the interlaced input.

Have a go hero – comparing the deinterlacing methods

Now it is time for you to tweak the settings of the `Deinterlacer` object. You should try to initialize three different objects, one for each method (line repetition, linear interpolation, and vertical temporal median filtering). Apply all of them to the interlaced image and compare the same cropped area as before. If you implement the described process successfully, you should get an image like the one that follows:

You should also try to experiment with other areas of the image, so that you get a better idea of the pros and cons of each method depending on the content of the image.

Deinterlacing with the custom functions

As we have already mentioned, deinterlacing an image using intra-frame techniques does not necessarily have to be implemented using the Computer Vision System Toolbox. Instead, we can apply certain techniques covered in earlier chapters to implement the methods included in the `Deinterlacer` object. In fact, two of them are quite easy to implement. Let's start from the default method, line repetition.

Time for action – deinterlacing with line repetition

The first method we will implement will be deinterlacing with line repetition. This method is based on repeating the odd (or even) rows of the image to fill the blank even (or odd) ones, respectively. In this example, we will replace each even line in the image with the previous odd one. Let's start:

> **1.** First, we load our original, interlaced image:
> ```
> >> A = imread('interlaced.bmp');  % Load interlaced image
> ```

2. Then, we initialize with zero values a matrix of equal size to A, so that we can store the deinterlaced image, which is as follows:

```
>> B = uint8(zeros(size(A)));   % Pre-allocate space for the result
```

3. Next, we must perform the line repetition process, using a for loop for all rows of the image. The even rows of matrix B will be replaced by the previous odd row of matrix A, while the odd rows of both images will be equal:

```
>> for i = 1:size(A,1),    % For all rows in A
if mod(i,2) == 0,       % if i is even
B(i,:,:) = A(i-1,:,:);  % Replace i-th row of B with (i-1)-th
   of A
else      % if i is odd
B(i,:,:)= A(i,:,:);     % Replace i-th row of B with i-th row of A
end      % End if
end     % end for
```

4. Now, matrix B should have the deinterlaced version of image A in it. In the preallocation step we used uint8 as the type of the elements, so we will need no further processing. Let's display the cropped area result again:

```
>> A2 = imcrop(A,[480 400 200 100]); % Crop interlaced image
>> B2 = imcrop(B,[480 400 200 100]); % Crop deinterlaced frame
>> subplot(1,2,1),imshow(A2);title('Cropped Interlaced Area')
>> subplot(1,2,2),imshow(B2);title('CroppedDeinterlaced Area')
```

What just happened?

This time we wrote our own deinterlacing code, based on functions we already knew and one little trick to check if the row we are checking in the for loop is odd or even. After we loaded the image we have been using for our deinterlacing examples, we created some space for us to store the result of our process. The result was an 8-bit per channel color image, that's why we forced matrix B to be uint8. In the beginning it didn't have to include specific values (although it could be set equal to A to save some lines of code), so we set all of them to zero, using the zeros function.

Our main procedure comprised a `for` loop, that will let us visit all rows in the image. As already described, the odd lines of the result should be identical to the odd lines of the input, while the even rows of the result should be equal to the previous odd rows of the input. To accomplish this, we needed to use a trick based on discrete mathematics. The trick is to check the result of the Modulo 2 operation, which in MATLAB is calculated using the `mod` function. The first input of the function is the number we want to check and the second being the base of the operation. The function returns the remainder of the division of the first input by the second input In the case of even numbers being divided by 2, the remainder is always zero; hence this is the check we perform in the first highlighted line of code to see if `i` is even. If it is, we make the `i`-th row of matrix `B` (the result), equal to the (`i-1`)-th row of the input image `A`. In the opposite case, row `i` of matrix `B` is assigned the values of row `i` of matrix `A`.

Finally, we followed the same steps as before to compare a cropped area of the original image to the same cropped area of the resulting image. The result was as expected and should actually be equivalent to the one produced by applying the default `Deinterlacer` object to the input.

 There is an easy way to check if the result of our code and the result from the previous example using the line repetition method are equal. To do it, you should subtract them and check if the result of the subtraction is a matrix containing only zero values, or alternatively use the function `isequal`.

Time for action – deinterlacing with the scan line interpolation

In this example, we will demonstrate an alternative method for deinterlacing, based on the averaging of the lines above and below the interlaced one. Since only a minor change will be made in step 3 of the previous process, we will show this process in a little less detail:

1. First, we will repeat steps 1 and 2 from the previous example, to load our image and preallocate space:

   ```
   >> A = imread('interlaced.bmp');  % Load interlaced image
   >> B = uint8(zeros(size(A)));  % Pre-allocate space for the
      result
   ```

2. Before we proceed, we must first convert the input to type single so that the averaging process is not confined to the range of values 0-255:

   ```
   >> A = single(A);  % Convert input to single
   ```

3. Now, we will write the exact same loop as before, with only one minor change; we will replace the line repetition with an averaging process:

```
>> for i = 1:size(A,1)-1,   % For all rows in A (except the last)
if mod(i,2) == 0,       % if i is even
% Replace i-th row of C with average of (i-1)-th and (i+1)-th
  of A
C(i,:,:) = round((A(i-1,:,:) + A(i+1,:,:)) / 2);
else     % if i is odd
C(i,:,:) = A(i,:,:);    % Replace i-th row of B with i-th row
  of A
end      % End if
end     % end for
```

4. Before demonstrating the results, we have to do two things. Make the last row of the image equal to the one above it and revert the input to its original state (type uint8):

```
>> C(end,:,:) = A(end-1,:,:);
>> A = uint8(A); % Convert A back to uint8
```

5. Once again, we demonstrate our results:

```
>> A2 = imcrop(A,[480 400 200 100]); % Crop interlaced image
>> C2 = imcrop(C,[480 400 200 100]); % Crop deinterlaced frame
>> subplot(1,2,1),imshow(A2);title('Cropped Interlaced Area')
>> subplot(1,2,2),imshow(C2);title('CroppedDe-Interlaced Area')
```

What just happened?

This time we tried something a little more complicated than a simple line replacement. The pixels in even rows of the input were substituted by the average values of the pixels in the rows above and below (in the respective column). This way, the jagged artifacts were further reduced and there were also less blurring and flickering. The differences from the previous example were not too many.

After loading our input image and preallocating space for the output, we converted the input to type `single`, because we wanted to be able to add values that could exceed the maximum `uint8` value without being clipped to 255 (for example, the `single` type result of 140 + 180 will be 320, while the `uint8` type result would be 255).

The `for` loop had only two small differences to the one in the previous example. The first one was that we do not include the last row in the loop, because the value of `i + 1` would fall off limits. The second difference was that we did not replace even rows with the ones above them, but we replaced them with the average of the ones above and below them.

To complete our process, we converted the input back to type `uint8` and also replaced the last row of the output image (which was not filled in the loop) with the row above it. Finally, we demonstrated the results in the cropped area we used in previous examples so that we saw the differences. The result should be identical to the one generated using the linear interpolation method in previous examples.

Have a go hero – comparing the deinterlacing methods

Now that you have seen how two of the three methods included in the `Deinterlacer` object can be implemented, you should try to make your own custom function that applies them to an input image. The function (let's call it `MyDeinterlacer.m`) should take two inputs: the interlaced image and the choice of method. The output should be the deinterlaced image generated by the process.

Inter-frame filtering for the deinterlacing tasks

So far, we have discussed purely spatial filtering methods for image and video frame deinterlacing. The spatial approach however does not take into account the temporal continuity of video frames that led to the idea of interlacing to begin with. A different approach that takes into account the differences and similarities between consecutive frames so that missing lines are filled, is called inter-frame filtering. Methods based on this approach rely on blending rows from consecutive frames to construct the deinterlaced version of a frame. In this section, we will discuss two alternative inter-frame methods.

Temporal deinterlacing by field merging

The first inter-frame method used for deinterlacing is field merging. This method is pretty simple and relies on substitution of the missing odd rows of a frame with the odd rows of the next one and consequent substitution of the even rows of the next frame with the even rows of its previous one.

This way, we fill the blank rows and acquire an image with no gaps, but there is a downside; having replaced the rows of an image with rows from a later or earlier frame, we have obviously messed with the temporal consistency within the frame. In simple words, we have included image information that has not happened yet (when using rows from the next frame), or has happened in the past (when using rows from a previous frame). This method is perfectly acceptable when no (or very little) motion exists in the video we are trying to deinterlace, but in scenes with high motion it introduces a new artifact, called a ghosting effect.

Time for action – deinterlacing with field merging

For this example, we are going to make a simple function implementing the field merging technique. We will assume that our video is small and given as a matrix variable input to the function, and we are also going to include a second input that will help us decide which rows to start replacing. If the input is 1, the odd rows of the first frame will be replaced by the odd rows from the second frame and the even rows of the second frame will be replaced by the even rows of the first frame. If the input is 2, the even rows of the first frame will be replaced by the even rows from the second frame, and the odd rows of the second frame will be replaced by the odd rows of the first frame. Finally, the output will be the deinterlaced video.

1. Let's write the function implementing the field merging technique:

```
function [vid] = FieldMerge(vid,order)

% Function for de-interlacing a video using Field Merging
% Inputs:
%        vid     - Input video matrix (we assume color video)
%        order   - Choice for row replacement
%    (1: odd rows from odd frames,
%     2: even rows from odd frames)
% Output:
%        vid     - Output video matrix (de-interlaced)

for fr = 1:size(vid,4)-1% For all frames (but the last)
  for row = 1:size(vid,1) % For all rows in frame
  switch order % Checking choice for the order of merging
    case 1 % Odd rows from odd frames
      if mod(fr,2) == 0% For even frames
        if mod(row,2) == 0% Replace even rows
          vid(row,:,:,fr) = vid(row,:,:,fr-1);
        end
      else % For odd frames
        if mod(row,2) ~= 0 % Replace odd rows
          vid(row,:,:,fr) = vid(row,:,:,fr+1);
```

```
                end
            end
        case 2
          if mod(fr,2) == 0 % For even frames
              if mod(row,2) ~= 0    % Replace odd rows
                vid(row,:,:,fr) = vid(row,:,:,fr-1);
              end
          else                      % For odd frames
          if mod(row,2) == 0 % Replace even rows
            vid(row,:,:,fr) = vid(row,:,:,fr+1);
          end
          end
        otherwise
          error('Unknown method.')      % Error message
      end
    end
end
```

What just happened?

The function we just wrote performs deinterlacing based on the process of field merging. It may seem a little complicated, but it really is simple. The first thing the function does is check the choice of order for the row replacement. This check is performed by the switch statement, with two possible acceptable results for case 1 and case 2 (all other inputs will result to an error message being generated by the otherwise command).

When the input is equal to 1, we have to replace the odd rows of the odd frames with the odd rows of the next available frame. Similarly, we will replace the even rows of even frames with the even rows of the previous available frame. We have already used the Modulo 2 command to differentiate odd and even rows in previous examples. We just have to also use it here to differentiate odd and even frames. This is why we used the mod function twice in the for loop; once for the frame (fr) and once for the row (row). The two highlighted lines of code actually did the replacement of even and odd rows.

The process when the input is equal to 2 is identical to the one described in the previous code. The only difference is in the if clauses checking for odd and even rows to replace. This time, odd rows are substituted in even frames and even rows in odd frames.

You may have noticed that in the previous examples we used if and else for the replacement of the rows of the image, while in this example we only used a single if. This is because this time we replaced the rows on the input matrix itself. Therefore, the rows that do not need replacement remain intact; hence skipping the else part of the code.

Note that this method skips the last frame. This can be avoided in half the cases since, for example, the last frame of an even frame scene with order = 1 can be deinterlaced, while for order = 2 cannot (it looks for the next frame and falls off the frame limits). Our previous code does not include this check and therefore always skips the last frame to be safe. This choice was made to reduce complexity in our code.

Have a go hero – evaluating the field merge method

Now it is time for you to check if our code works or not. You should find, or shoot an interlaced video, load it in MATLAB (be careful not to use a video that is too big) and then call the function FieldMerge and compare some frames from its output to the frames of the original video stream. Try to use the function in both the still scenes and motion scenes. What do you see? Is there a difference? What about changing the second input to 2 instead of 1?

Temporal deinterlacing by field averaging

The previous method we used had obvious disadvantages caused by the usage of just one row from a different point in time to replace a blank row at the present time. This method can be improved a little, if we use field averaging. This time, instead of using just the next (or previous) frame as a source for missing information, we will use both adjacent frames, which will replace the row in our current frame with the average value of the same rows in the previous and next frames. This will have a better result in terms of temporal continuity but it demands larger storage space and also cannot deinterlace the first and the last frame (instead of just the last as in the previous example). Let's see how this process is implemented.

Time for action – deinterlacing with field averaging

This example demonstrates the use of the field averaging technique. The code in our function will be based on the previous example, but this time we have to make some minor adjustments to fit our problem. Let's see the function that performs field averaging:

```
function [vid] = FieldAverage(vid,order)

% Function for de-interlacing a video using Field Average
% Inputs:
%        vid     - Input video matrix (we assume color video)
%        order   - Choice for row replacement
%    (1: odd rows from odd frames,
%     2: even rows from odd frames)
% Output:
%        vid     - Output video matrix (de-interlaced)
```

```
vid = single(vid);  % Convert matrix to single to perform
  averaging
  for fr = 2:size(vid,4)-1% For all frames (but the first &
    last)
  for row = 1:size(vid,1) % For all rows in frame
  switch order % Checking choice for the order of merging
    case 1 % Odd rows from odd frames
      if mod(fr,2) == 0 % For even frames
        if mod(row,2) == 0 % Replace even rows
          vid(row,:,:,fr) = ...
            (vid(row,:,:,fr-1) + vid(row,:,:,fr+1)) / 2 ;
        end
      else % For odd frames
        if mod(row,2) ~= 0 % Replace odd rows
          vid(row,:,:,fr) = ...
            (vid(row,:,:,fr-1) + vid(row,:,:,fr+1)) / 2 ;
        end
      end
    case 2 % Even rows from odd frames
      if mod(fr,2) == 0 % For even frames
        if mod(row,2) ~= 0   % Replace odd rows
          vid(row,:,:,fr) = ...
            (vid(row,:,:,fr-1) + vid(row,:,:,fr+1)) / 2 ;
        end
      else % For odd frames
        if mod(row,2) == 0 % Replace even rows
          vid(row,:,:,fr) = ...
            (vid(row,:,:,fr-1) + vid(row,:,:,fr+1)) / 2 ;
        end
      end
    otherwise
      error('Unknown method.')      % Error message
    end
  end
end
vid = uint8(vid);   % Convert matrix back to uint8
```

At this point, we may want to check our results on a real interlaced video scene. We have a quite challenging one provided, named `inter.avi`. It is the driving video stream we used for the still image deinterlacing examples. Let's put our function to the test:

1. First, we load our video into the **Workspace** window:

   ```
   >> obj = VideoReader('inter.avi');
   ```

2. Then, we read in all the video frames (the video is small, so it can be done):

   ```
   >> vid = read(obj);
   ```

3. This is the part where we put our function to the test. Let's use it once with the second input being 1 and once with the second input being 2:

```
>> [vid1] = FieldAverage(vid,1);
>> [vid2] = FieldAverage(vid,2);
```

4. Now, we demonstrate the results for an odd and an even frame:

```
>> subplot(2,3,1),imshow(vid(:,:,:,5)),title('Odd frame')
>> subplot(2,3,4),imshow(vid(:,:,:,6)),title('Even frame')
>> subplot(2,3,2),imshow(vid1(:,:,:,5)),title('Odd frame-1')
>> subplot(2,3,3),imshow(vid2(:,:,:,5)),title('Odd frame-2')
>> subplot(2,3,5),imshow(vid1(:,:,:,6)),title('Even frame-1')
>> subplot(2,3,6),imshow(vid2(:,:,:,6)),title('Even frame-2')
```

What just happened?

This time our function had a few tricks. At first, the input video matrix was converted to type `single`, so that averaging could be performed. We saw this conversion used earlier in the line interpolation example. When the whole process was completed, we converted the matrix back to `uint8`.

The next alteration we made to our code was to exclude the first frame from the loop. The last frame was excluded in the previous example as well, so we need not change that. Therefore, our loops went through the values of `2:size(vid,4)-1`.

Our final change in the code was the rule for replacement. Whatever row we are in, the values of its elements will be replaced by the respective average values of the previous and next frame rows. This is accomplished by the following lines of code:

```
vid(row,:,:,fr) = … (vid(row,:,:,fr-1)+vid(row,:,:,fr+1))/2;
```

The three dots are there to indicate that the next line is the continuation of the current line and is not a new command.

The steps 1 to 4 were used for assessment of the method we implemented. The results show that, because of the nature of the scene none of the methods performed very well. In some areas we had a slight improvement of the result, but in other areas we had a deterioration of the result.

Mixing intra-frame and inter-frame deinterlacing

As we saw in the previous examples, intra-frame and inter-frame deinterlacing methods come with their advantages and disadvantages. A rather intuitive conclusion would be that, if we managed to somehow combine the advantages of the two methods, we would be able to produce much better results.

Vertical and temporal interpolation for deinterlacing

Let's try to implement a method that has the advantages of both intra-frame and inter-frame methods. One way to accomplish this is to substitute each row with the average of the neighboring rows both in time and space. More specifically, if we have to substitute the row r in the frame of the video, we will do it using the average of rows $r-1$ and $r+1$ of frame f, row r from frame $f-1$, and row r from frame $f+1$. Let's see this in action.

Time for action – vertical and temporal interpolation method

Now it is time to implement the process described in the previous paragraph. The function that we will use is based on the previous two examples:

```
function [vid] = SpatioTemporalAverage(vid,order)

% Function for de-interlacing a video using spatiotemporal averaging
% Inputs:
%       vid     - Input video matrix (we assume color video)
%       order   - Choice for row replacement
% Output:
%       vid     - Output video matrix (de-interlaced)

vid = single(vid);  % Convert matrix to single to perform averaging
```

```matlab
switch order    % Checking choice for the order of merging
  case 1  % Odd rows from odd frames
     for fr = 2:size(vid,4)-1    % For all frames (but first&last)
        for row = 2:size(vid,1)-1 % For all rows (but first&last)
           if mod(fr,2) == 0   % For even frames
              if mod(row,2) == 0  % Replace even rows
                 vid(row,:,:,fr) = ...
                    ((vid(row,:,:,fr-1) + vid(row,:,:,fr+1)) ...
                       + (vid(row-1,:,:,fr) + vid(row+1,:,:,fr))) / 4;
              end
           else % For odd frames
              if mod(row,2) ~= 0  % Replace odd rows
                 vid(row,:,:,fr) = ...
                    ((vid(row,:,:,fr-1) + vid(row,:,:,fr+1)) ...
                       + (vid(row-1,:,:,fr) + vid(row+1,:,:,fr))) / 4;
              end
           end
        end
     end
  case 2  % Even rows from odd frames
     for fr = 2:size(vid,4)-1     % For all frames (but first&last)
        for row = 2:size(vid,1)-1 % For all rows (but first&last)
           if mod(fr,2) == 0    % For even frames
              if mod(row,2) ~= 0      % Replace odd rows
                 vid(row,:,:,fr) = ...
                    ((vid(row,:,:,fr-1) + vid(row,:,:,fr+1)) ...
                       + (vid(row-1,:,:,fr) + vid(row+1,:,:,fr))) / 4;
              end
           else % For odd frames
              if mod(row,2) == 0  % Replace even rows
                 vid(row,:,:,fr) = ...
                    ((vid(row,:,:,fr-1) + vid(row,:,:,fr+1)) ...
                       + (vid(row-1,:,:,fr) + vid(row+1,:,:,fr))) / 4;
              end
           end
        end
     end
  otherwise
     disp('Unknown method.')     % Error message
end
vid = uint8(vid);   % Convert matrix back to uint8
```

At this point, we can check our results to evaluate the importance of including spatiotemporal information for the deinterlacing:

1. First, we load the same video as before into the **Workspace** window and read in all of its frames:

```
>> obj = VideoReader('inter.avi');
>> vid = read(obj);
```

2. Now, we use the new function, once with the second input as 1, and once with the second input as 2:

```
>>[vid1] = SpatioTemporalAverage(vid,1);
>>[vid2] = SpatioTemporalAverage(vid,2);
```

3. Now, we demonstrate the results for an odd and an even frame:

```
>> subplot(2,3,1),imshow(vid(:,:,:,5)),title('Odd frame')
>> subplot(2,3,4),imshow(vid(:,:,:,6)),title('Even frame')
>> subplot(2,3,2),imshow(vid3(:,:,:,5)),title('Odd frame-1')
>> subplot(2,3,3),imshow(vid4(:,:,:,5)),title('Odd frame-2')
>> subplot(2,3,5),imshow(vid3(:,:,:,6)),title('Even frame-1')
>> subplot(2,3,6),imshow(vid4(:,:,:,6)),title('Even frame-2')
```

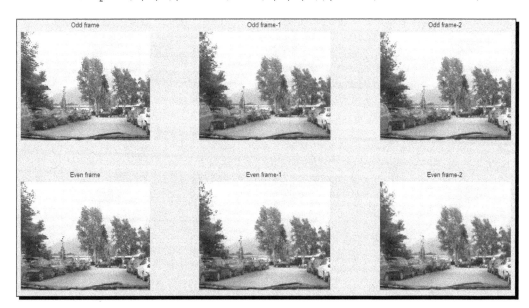

What just happened?

Once again, the function is based on previous examples, with only few alterations, highlighted in the previous code. The first alteration was the frames that were treated by the process. Instead of leaving only the last one out, here we also left the first one out. Similarly, we did not process both the first and the last rows of each frame. The last alteration was the interpolation rule, which became spatiotemporal (spatial because rows of the same frame were weighed-in, and temporal because rows from the next and previous frames were also weighed-in):

```
vid(row,:,:,fr) = ...
  ((vid(row,:,:,fr-1) + vid(row,:,:,fr+1)) ...
    + (vid(row-1,:,:,fr) + vid(row+1,:,:,fr))) / 4;
```

This way, the resulting frame carried information both from its contents and from the neighboring frames. To demonstrate our results, we loaded and processed the same video as before, using steps 1 through 3. If you compare the results generated now to those generated in the previous example, you will clearly understand the importance of the spatiotemporal technique.

Have a go hero – Comparing deinterlacing techniques

Now it is your turn to examine and evaluate the deinterlacing techniques presented so far. The goal is to apply these methods to interlaced videos of your choice and crop the frames accordingly so that you compare details of each method. Try to use both the still scene videos and high motion videos.

 As we saw in this section, scenes with a lot of motion are not handled completely effectively by the methods presented here. In these cases, to further reduce artifacts, we have to consider using more complex methods of interpolation that are motion-adaptive or motion-compensated. These methods are quite complex for the purposes of this book and require more sophisticated algorithms, with somewhat difficult mathematics.

Adding a new dimension to the filters

Till here, you should have started realizing the importance of temporal information in videos. Further using it in deinterlacing tasks, temporal information can be combined with spatial information to filter video frames. Some of the spatial filters, which we have already seen in previous chapters, as well as in this one, can easily be expanded in more dimensions, so that we include temporal information as well. In this section, we will see some of them.

Spatiotemporal averaging filter

A really straightforward to implement, spatiotemporal filter, is the averaging one. Applying it to a video is not so complicated, provided that you have understood the basics of image filtering. To demonstrate the process, we will use grayscale video streams.

The algorithmic description of the process of performing spatiotemporal averaging to a grayscale video is given by these following steps:

1. Define the neighborhood for filtering in terms of rows x columns x frames.
2. Decide what will happen in borders (if you will be padding or not).
3. Start the filtering process using three `for` loops (one for the rows, one for the columns, and one for the frames).

Let's see how we can implement this process.

Time for action – implementing a spatiotemporal averaging filter

Now that we know the steps of the process, we can write a function that performs it. The function will have some similarities to the spatiotemporal deinterlacing function implemented in the previous example. It will take as input a grayscale video in a matrix variable (if it is not grayscale it will convert each frame to grayscale) and the filtering neighborhood, and will produce as output a matrix containing the filtered video:

```
function [vid] = SpatioTemporalAveraging(vid,nhood)

% Function for de-interlacing a video using Field Merging
% Inputs:
%        vid      - Input video matrix (we assume grayscale video)
%        nhood    - Dimensions of filtering neighborhood
% Output:
%        vidOut    - Output video matrix (filtered)

vid = single(vid);  % Convert matrix to single to perform averaging
  vidOut = zeros(size(vid)); % Create a zero-valued matrix to hold
    the result
  % For all frames except the ones that fall off limits
  for frame = ceil(nhood(3)/2):size(vid,3)-ceil(nhood(3)/2)
    % For all rows except the ones that fall off limits
    for row = ceil(nhood(1)/2):size(vid,1)-ceil(nhood(1)/2)
```

```
    % For all columns except the ones tha fall off limits
    for column = ceil(nhood(2)/2):size(vid,2)-ceil(nhood(2)/2)
      % Crop the neighborhood area
      neighborhood = vid(row-
        round(nhood(1)/2)+1:row+round(nhood(1)/2),...
      column-round(nhood(2)/2)+1:column+round(nhood(2)/2),
      frame-round(nhood(3)/2)+1:frame+round(nhood(3)/2));
      % Calculate its mean and assign it to the central pixel
      vidOut(row,column,frame) = mean(neighborhood(:));
    end
  end
end
vidOut = uint8(vidOut);    % Convert matrix to type uint8
```

Now, it is time to test our function. Beware that this is a time-consuming function, because of the three nested loops. It's going to take a while for each frame, so don't use it on a very large video:

1. We'll use our driving video comprising 28 frames:

    ```
    >> obj = VideoReader('inter.avi');
    >> vid = read(obj);
    ```

2. Now, we will convert our color video matrix to grayscale, frame-by-frame, right after we initialize a new uint8 type matrix with zeros, to store our result in:

    ```
    >> grayVid = uint8(zeros(size(vid,1), size(vid,2), size(vid,4)));
    >> for i = 1:size(vid,4),
    grayVid(:,:,i) = rgb2gray(vid(:,:,:,i));
    end
    ```

3. Let's test our function now, for a cubical neighborhood of 3 rows, 3 columns, and 3 frames:

    ```
    >> filteredVid = SpatioTemporalAveraging(grayVid,[3 3 3]);
    ```

4. After a while (the time needed depends on your CPU), you will see in your workspace a variable called `filteredVid`. Let's display a frame of this matrix next to the same frame of our original matrix, to see what the results of the filtering process were:

```
>> subplot(1,2,1),imshow(grayVid(:,:,10)),title('Original
   frame')
>> subplot(1,2,2),imshow(filteredVid(:,:,10)),title('Filtered
   frame')
```

What just happened?

This example has demonstrated how you can program a spatiotemporal blurring process for grayscale video streams in MATLAB. The function began with a type conversion of the input video matrix, so that averaging was feasible followed by the initialization of a new matrix that stored the resulting video.

Then, we moved on to three nested `for` loops, by making sure to set the limits of each of the loops in a manner that ensured our process won't fall off the borders of the image. This choice resulted in an image with a small black border in all its four edges. The size of the border will depend on the size of the filtering neighborhood.

In each step of the triple `for` loop, we cropped the cubical neighborhood centered at the pixel under examination (row, column, and frame):

```
neighborhood = vid(row-round(nhood(1)/2)+1:row+round(nhood(1)/2),...
   column-round(nhood(2)/2)+1:column+round(nhood(2)/2),  ...
      frame-round(nhood(3)/2)+1:frame+round(nhood(3)/2));
```

Then, the average value of the neighborhood was calculated and used to replace the value of the central pixel of the neighborhood:

```
vidOut(row,column,frame) = mean(neighborhood(:));
```

The steps 1 through 4 evaluated the usage of the filtering process. First the video was loaded and stored to a matrix variable. Then, in step 2, the input video was converted to grayscale, frame-by-frame. Each of the frames is stored in a type `uint8` matrix initialized with zero values. The step 3 applied the filter to our grayscale video and finally, in step 4 we displayed one frame from the resulting video next to the same frame from the original video. As you can see, the result of such a spatiotemporal filtering process was adding a shaky effect to our video. The more the motion in the area of the frame was, the more intense the effect will be.

Have a go hero – creating a spatiotemporal median filter

Before we move on, you should try to alter the filtering function we made in the previous example, to give a spatiotemporal median filtering result instead of the averaging result we have programmed. The only change will be in the line where the averaging calculation was performed. If you want, you can also add a third input to the previous function to let the users choose which of the two methods they prefer to use. A third addition to the code would be to add padding, to eliminate the thin black border from the result.

Using convolution for spatiotemporal averaging

The previous implementation of the spatiotemporal averaging filter was interesting, but had a real big disadvantage; it was really slow. The alternative way to perform such a process is to take advantage of the multidimensional version of convolution. In *Chapter 5, 2-Dimensional Image Filtering*, we discussed the method of convolution and described how it can be used for image filtering. Now, it is time to expand the convolution operation to more dimensions and perform spatiotemporal (three-dimensional) filtering to our video frames.

In order to implement the process of spatiotemporal averaging by means of convolution, we have to use the function `convn` provided by MATLAB. This function is called exactly like `conv2`, with the only difference that the inputs must be n-dimensional (in our case three-dimensional). Let's see how this works.

Time for action – spatiotemporal averaging filter with the convn function

In order to see how the averaging filter is implemented, we will use the same example as before. We will follow these steps:

1. First off, we load our video and convert it to grayscale, using the first two steps of the previous example:

```
>> obj = VideoReader('inter.avi');
>> vid = read(obj);
>> grayVid = uint8(zeros(size(vid,1), size(vid,2), size(vid,4)));
>> for i = 1:size(vid,4),
grayVid(:,:,i) = rgb2gray(vid(:,:,:,i));
end
```

2. Now, we must generate a three-dimensional filter to use for the averaging process. Its dimensions can be the same as the neighborhood we used before. To perform averaging, it must have all its values equal to 1/n, where n are the number of elements in the filter. Let's create it:

```
>> avFilt = ones(3,3,3); % Make a 3x3x3 matrix full of ones
>> avFilt = avFilt/numel(avFilt); % Make all elements equal to
   1/n
```

3. All we have to do now is to apply convolution between `grayVid` and `avFilt`:

```
>> filteredVid = convn(grayVid, avFilt); % Apply convolution
>> filteredVid = uint8(filteredVid ); % Convert to uint8
```

4. Let's demonstrate one frame of the filtered stream next to the same frame from the original video:

```
>> subplot(1,2,1),imshow(grayVid(:,:,15)),title('Original
   frame')
>> subplot(1,2,2),imshow(filteredVid(:,:,15)),title('Filtered
   frame')
```

What just happened?

This was another way to implement spatiotemporal smoothing using an averaging filter. The steps were pretty simple and similar to the processes discussed in *Chapter 5, 2-Dimensional Image Filtering*. The first step was to prepare our video for the process by converting it to grayscale, frame-by-frame. Once this was over, we created the filter for the averaging process. It was a 3 x 3 x 3 filter with all its values equal to 1 / (3*3*3).

Next, we applied n-dimensional convolution for n=3. The result of the convolution was transformed to `uint8`, and then one of its frames was demonstrated next to the respective original frame for qualitative evaluation purposes.

Pop quiz – videos and filters

Q1. Which of the following are true?

1. If we filter an image or a video frame using a disk filtering element, we create the so-called blocking effect.

2. Interlaced videos take up double the space of progressive ones with the same dimensions, color depth, and number of frames.

3. Some methods for deinterlacing can lead to ghosting effects.

4. Spatiotemporal averaging leads to frame sharpening.

5. Using `convn` for averaging instead of making a triple nested `for` loop leads to faster processing speed.

Summary

This chapter was dedicated to intra-frame and inter-frame techniques for video filtering, which can be used for a variety of tasks. We discussed basic video manipulations, such as resizing, rotating, mirroring, and cropping, and proceeded to frame-by-frame spatial filtering of a video. Then, we focused extensively on a very common process in video processing, which is deinterlacing an interlaced video stream. Methods for intra-frame and inter-frame deinterlacing were discussed, as well as fusion of the two. For these processes, several advantages and disadvantages were brought to the surface and discussed. Finally, we discussed spatiotemporal filtering of videos and focused especially on spatiotemporal averaging. All these were presented and discussed with real examples and exercises. More specifically, in this chapter we discussed:

- Cropping and resizing video streams
- Rotating video streams and checking for errors
- Reducing the blocking effect using spatial filtering
- Intra-frame filtering for video deinterlacing, using the Computer Vision System Toolbox
- Intra-frame deinterlacing of videos using line repetition
- Intra-frame deinterlacing of videos using line interpolation
- Inter-frame deinterlacing using field merging
- Inter-frame deinterlacing using field averaging
- Mixing intra-frame and inter-frame de-interlacing
- Applying spatiotemporal averaging to a grayscale video
- Using `convn` to apply spatiotemporal averaging

In the next and final chapter, we will discuss various real-life video processing tasks, such as motion detection, video stabilization, feature selection, and three-dimensional image and video processing. We will use intriguing hands-on exercises to demonstrate how these tasks can be implemented in MATLAB and discuss their implications and ways to tackle them efficiently.

10

From Beginner to Expert – Handling Motion and 3-D

The methods and techniques we have presented in the previous chapters introduced you to the very basics of video processing. We did not get into the mathematical details involved in such processing and preferred to demonstrate how the theory comes into action using hands-on, practical exercises that hopefully helped you comprehend the essence of the algorithms. In this final chapter, we will try to spice things up a little, going into more complex methods that require some more mathematical insight. We will avoid going into the most difficult details, but nevertheless, this chapter may seem a little more challenging than the others, as it will demonstrate basic motion detection and estimation techniques, combine them with the notion of image registration and use them for video stabilization. Furthermore, we will indulge in the field of three-dimensional image and video processing and create our own 3-D videos.

In this chapter, we will cover:

- How we can detect motion in videos
- How motion can be estimated using optical flow
- Ways to compensate camera movement in videos using registration
- How stereoscopic videos can be easily created

So, let's dive right in!

Detecting and estimating motion in videos

So far, the only time we had to handle inter-frame processing was for the filtering methods for de-interlacing and smoothing of videos demonstrated in the previous chapter. These methods were not very sophisticated, as they did not aim at extracting useful information, for example, detecting and estimating motion from the video frame sequences.

Motion detection can be loosely defined as the process of detecting changes in the relative position of an object to its background (however, this background is defined) in the consecutive frames of a video. Intuitively, this process could be based on a simple subtraction of these consecutive frames, so that the values of the pixels that change appear brighter than those that remain constant. For various reasons, this simplistic approach is not always successful. In this chapter, we will discuss why.

On the other hand, motion estimation is a more challenging problem; it aims at estimating a set of vectors that describes the motions of pixels in consecutive frames. This means that ideally, a motion estimation process can perfectly describe the changes of all pixel positions from one frame of a video to the next. This description has several flaws, since a video captures the three-dimensional real world images and transforms them to fit the two-dimensional plane of a screen. You can understand that mapping all the pixels from one frame to all the pixels in the other frame is impossible, since real world scenes captured in video suffer from occlusions, lighting changes, camera movements, and so on.

Let's start our discussion on the issues of motion detection and estimation with some examples.

Detecting motion

The first problem in motion detection is to identify which pixels change their values in consecutive frames. Usually, this is an indication that the particular pixels represent parts of moving objects, since one of the most popular constraints used in motion estimation, as we will see later in the chapter, is the brightness constancy constraint.

Time for action – detecting a moving object in a still scene

For this first example, let's try to pinpoint the moving pixels in a video by a simple subtraction of consecutive frames. By subtracting two consecutive frames of a color video, the result we will get is a three-dimensional matrix of values near zero in pixels, which remain constant, and higher values in pixels that have a big alteration in their values.

1. First, let's load a video that does not contain a lot of motion in its entire duration. Such a video, used in a previous chapter, showed a green ball that entered a scene from the left and exited from the right after passing through a box. The video is called `singleball.avi`. Let's load it and display its montage:

```
>> vObj = VideoReader('singleball.avi');
>> video = read(vObj);  % read in all frames from video object
>> montage(video,'Size',[5 9]) % Using a 5x9 grid for 45 frames
```

2. Our next step is to subtract each frame from the previous and save the result in a new matrix. Since the video has 45 frames, the result will be a 44 frame video (the first frame does not have a previous one to use for the subtraction). For our convenience, we can use an equally-sized matrix and leave the first frame blank:

```
>> subtracted = zeros(size(video));
>> for i = 2:size(video,4), % For all frames but the first one
% Subtract each frame from its next one
subtracted(:,:,:,i) = video(:,:,:,i) - video(:,:,:,i-1);
end
```

3. Now, let's show the montage of the result. Can you predict what it will be?

```
>> montage(subtracted,'Size',[5 9]) % Show montage of
subtracted
```

4. Why don't we go one step further? Now that we have a matrix of all our frames with the detected ball standing out, we can use them to display the trajectory of the ball. How will we do it? One easy way is to add all the frames together and show them as one single image:

```
>> total = sum(subtracted,4); % Addition of all frames (4-th
dim.)
>> total = mat2gray(total); % Normalize the whole matrix to
[0,1]
```

5. Now we will display our result. Note that the image will be in color. Applying the `mat2gray` function just results in each of the channels being normalized to [0,1]:

```
>> figure,imshow(total)
```

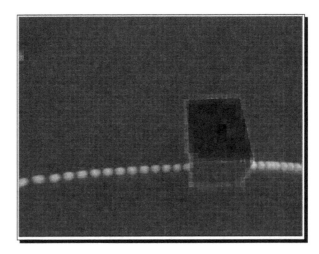

What just happened?

So, in this simple example, you made your own motion detector for a very controlled scene. As you can see from the resulting montage, the only pixels that are not dark are the pixels that belong to the moving green ball. The first step of the process consisted of a drill that you must have been very comfortable with; we read a video, loaded all its frames into the workspace, and displayed a montage of all of them (the grid we use in montage depends on the total number of frames). Next, we initialized a zero-valued matrix to store the result of the detection and proceeded to write a `for` loop that subtracted each frame from its next one. Afterwards, we displayed a montage of all the frames of the detection result. Our final step was to display the trajectory of the ball in the frames sequence. This was accomplished by adding all the frames of the detection video together, confining the result to the range [0,1] to be treated as an image by MATLAB and then displayed it using `imshow`.

Time for action – detecting motion in a complex scene

The example we saw previously is a very simple one. The background is still, there is no particular fluctuation of the brightness on the scene, and the moving object has a very distinctive color. Let's now see what happens when we have a more complex scene to handle. We will work with the driving video, presented in the previous chapter, which represents one of the most challenging scenarios; a moving camera, with a scene with moving background, and several moving objects. Let's start:

1. Our first step is, as always, to load the video we will process:

   ```
   >> obj = VideoReader('inter.avi'); % Read video file
   >> vid = read(obj); % Load all frames
   ```

2. The montage of our frames looks like this:

   ```
   >> montage(vid,'Size',[4 7]) % Using a 4x7 grid for our 28
      frames
   ```

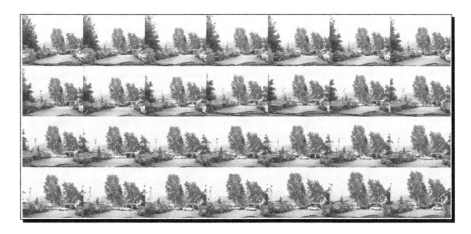

3. Now, we will subtract each frame from the next one, excluding the first. The result will be stored in a predefined matrix:

```
>> subtracted = zeros(size(vid));  % Preallocate space
>> for i = 2:size(vid,4), % For all frames but the first one
% Subtract each frame from its next one
subtracted(:,:,:,i) = vid(:,:,:,i) - vid(:,:,:,i-1);
end
```

4. Let's see the montage of all the motion detection frames:

```
>> montage(vid,'Size',[4 7]) % Using a 4x7 grid for our 28
   frames
```

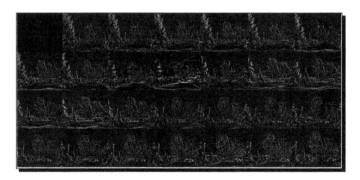

5. Now, let's add all the frames together and see what comes up. This time we will do it for both the original video and the motion detection one:

```
>> total1 = sum(vid,4); % Addition of all frames (4-th dim.)
>> total1 = mat2gray(total1); % Normalize the whole matrix
>> total2 = sum(subtracted,4); % Addition of all frames
>> total2 = mat2gray(total2); % Normalize the whole matrix
>> subplot(1,2,1),imshow(total1),title('Sum of original
   frames')
>> subplot(1,2,2),imshow(total2),title('Sum of detection
   frames')
```

What just happened?

This time around, our results are not so informative. While the subtraction results showed the moving pixels in each pair of consecutive frames, there was no real indication of which of them was moving, or were still and just have a relative motion to the moving camera. Even more vague results were produced by the addition of the frames. Both the results of adding the original frames and of adding the subtracted frames were blurry and do not give us enough information about the motion in the scene.

The only areas of the image that appear to have stayed still during the short duration of the video were the sky and a small portion of the road. However, this result is highly unintuitive, since the road surface was definitely moving relative to our camera. This, in fact, is one of the main difficulties in detecting motion in videos. Smooth objects with very little detail in them appear motionless, except for their borders (when they are colored differently to the background). When the object under examination is the road (or something of similarly large size and smoothness), a big part of it appears to be still, according to the frame subtraction result. Another difficulty in detecting motion in a video is posed by the insufficient frame rate for very quick moving objects, that is, when the objects in the video make large movements from one frame to the next, motion detection might produce a very evident **ghosting effect**.

Have a go hero – making your own surveillance system

Now that you have seen the difference in difficulties between the still scenes and complex scenes, let's go back to the easy problem. You should be able to write a piece of code that receives input from a camera, converts the frames to grayscale, and displays a warning message every time the mean difference of brightness values between the two consecutive frames exceeds a predefined level.

For a more complicated example, you could even split your frame in rectangular areas and announce in the warning message which area has been intruded (for example, by using a command, such as `disp('Area #1 appears to have high activity!')`).

All the tools you need to accomplish this task have been presented. You should revise how you can get a live video input in MATLAB, convert RGB to grayscale, and calculate mean values in two dimensions (Hint: the function `mean2` is useful). For the second task, you have to devise a way to split the image into blocks and check all of them with a `for` loop.

Estimating the motion

The task of motion detection that was presented in the previous section is a relatively easy process, especially for simple scenes. The real challenge appears when we actually have to estimate the motion between two images; that is, come up with a motion vector that gives us a way to transform the first frame to the second and vice versa.

The motion vector usually comprises two numbers (or coordinates); one showing the length of the motion in pixels, r, and one showing the direction of the motion in degrees, ϑ. This pair of coordinates is called polar. An equivalent way to portray the motion of a pixel is by defining the length of the motion in pixels, in the vertical and horizontal direction. These coordinates are called cartesian. In the example of the following figure, you can see all the coordinates needed to describe the motion of a pixel moving from point $(x1,y1) = (0,0)$ to point $(x2,y2) = (4,3)$.

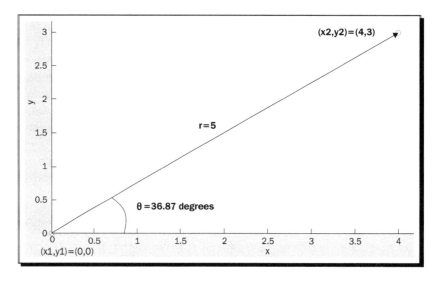

 You can use MATLAB to convert from one type of coordinates to the other. The functions that accomplish the conversions are `cart2pol` (cartesian to polar) and `pol2cart` (polar to cartesian). They need two inputs and produce two outputs.

The task of accurate motion estimation is a very complicated one and can also be deemed impossible when the video used includes a mixture of occlusions, background motion, multiple moving objects, brightness variations, shadows, camera motion, and so on. Indulging in such complex problems is beyond the scope of this book, so we will stick to easy problems with acceptable solutions.

Estimating motion using optical flow

A very popular way to estimate motion in a video is by using **optical flow algorithms**. Optical flow is a widely researched area of computer vision and several algorithms, each with their own pros and cons, have been proposed. Its ultimate goal is to use spatiotemporal information from the frame sequence of a video to estimate motion vectors between consecutive pairs of frames. The specifics of how these algorithms achieve their final goal are too technical for our purposes. Here, we will demonstrate the usage of two of them in the Computer Vision System Toolbox of MATLAB, so that you get an idea of what they can do. The optical flow algorithms that are included in the toolbox are the ones by Horn-Schunck and Lucas-Kanade.

The optical flow method by Horn and Schunck is described in: *B. K. Horn and B. G. Schunck, Determining optical flow, Artificial intelligence, vol. 17, no. 1–3, pp. 185–203, 1981.*

The method by Lucas and Kanade can be found in: *B. D. Lucas and T. Kanade, An iterative image registration technique with an application to stereo vision, in Proceedings of the 7th international joint conference on Artificial intelligence, 1981.*

Time for action – tracking people with Horn-Schunck optical flow

First, we are going to demonstrate the method described by Horn and Schunck. A good example of its usage can be found if you type `vision.OpticalFlow System object` in the search box on the top-right corner of your MATLAB window. The help page for the object includes an example based on the `viptraffic.avi` video. In this example, we will show some alternative steps for the same process, using a different video as input.

Since we will be using the Computer Vision System Toolbox for the optical flow algorithms, we might as well use another one of the videos included in its demos. The video is called `atrium.avi` and shows several people walking in an atrium in arbitrary trajectories. Our goal is to estimate their motions. Since the methods for the optical flow we will use can be applied only to grayscale videos, we will also convert our frames to grayscale of type `uint8`. Here, we will try to estimate the motion between the 89th and 90th frames.

1. First, we will load our video and get the number of its frames, using the method `VideoReader`. Before we do that, we clear our workspace:

   ```
   >> clear all;
   >> videoObj = VideoReader('atrium.avi'); % Open video
   ```

2. Then, we must create a system object for motion estimation:

```
>> opticalFlow = vision.OpticalFlow('ReferenceFrameDelay',
   1,...
'Method','Horn-Schunck',...
'OutputValue', 'Horizontal and vertical components in
   complex form');
```

3. Now, it is time to start the frame-by-frame processing of our video and estimate the motion between the pair of frames 89 and 90.

```
>> for i = 89:90 % For frames 89 and 90
frame = read(videoObj,i); % Load one frame at a time
temp = rgb2gray(frame); % Convert frame to grayscale
im(:,:,i-88) = single(temp); % Convert frame to single (for
   calculations)
of(:,:,i-88) = step(opticalFlow, im(:,:,i-88)); % Estimate
   optical flow
end
```

4. The optical flow result is in complex form. This means that the matrix holding it contains the elements of the format x+yi. The real part, *x*, is the flow in axis x and the imaginary part, *y*, is the flow in axis y. We can isolate these results by using the real and imag functions.

```
>> xMotion = real(of);
>> yMotion = imag(of);
```

5. The absolute value of the real and imaginary parts gives the magnitude of the optical flow. This measure depicts how large the motion of a pixel is, without carrying any information about its direction. It is given by:

```
>> absMotion = abs(of);
```

6. At this point, it is a good idea to display the two consecutive frames side-by-side (we have to convert them back to uint8):

```
>> subplot(2,2,1),imshow(uint8(im(:,:,1))),title('89th frame');
>> subplot(2,2,2),imshow(uint8(im(:,:,2))),title('90th frame');
```

7. And at the bottom line of the figure, we will demonstrate their difference using a color composite image and a normalized image of the absolute optical flow value:

```
>> subplot(2,2,3)
>> imshowpair(im(:,:,1),im(:,:,2), 'ColorChannels','red-cyan');
>> title('Composite Image (Red - Frame 89, Cyan - Frame 90)');
>> subplot(2,2,4)
>> imshow(mat2gray(absMotion(:,:,2)))
>> title('Normalized absolute optical flow value');
```

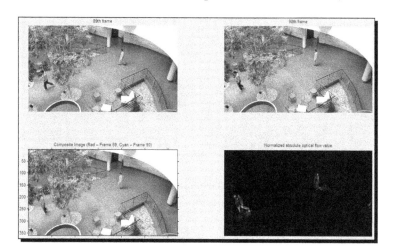

8. In order to depict the direction of the optical flow, we can use a system object that draws lines (and other shapes) on an image, called `ShapeInserter`. To use it, we have to first initialize its settings:

```
>> shapeInserter =
   vision.ShapeInserter('Shape','Lines','BorderColor','Custom',
   'CustomBorderColor', 255);
```

9. Then, we have to create a matrix containing the origin coordinates of the motion vectors we want to draw, with their magnitudes amplified by a factor of our choice (here, we will amplify them by two). For this purpose, we will use a helper function called `videooptflowlines`:

```
>> lines = videooptflowlines(of(:,:,2), 2);
```

10. Now, we can draw the motion vector map on our image, using `step` and display our result:

```
>> out =  step(shapeInserter, im(:,:,2), lines);
>> figure,imshow(uint8(out))
```

11. From the previous picture, we can observe that some vectors near or on the walking persons, appear to be unnaturally long. Also, we can see that some vectors on the background also appear longer than they should. These values are often called **outliers**. Let's fix this by setting values below or above a threshold to zero:

```
>> of(abs(of)>20)=0;
>> of(abs(of)<5)=0;
```

12. Now, let's re-draw our result:

```
>> lines = videooptflowlines(of(:,:,2), 2);
>> out =  step(shapeInserter, im(:,:,2), lines);
>> figure,imshow(uint8(out))
```

What just happened?

This example might seem to be like a little too much, a little too quickly. However, most of the steps it covers are pretty simple to follow. Let's try to explain them one by one.

In step 1, we loaded our video and in step 2, we created a system object that will be used to estimate the optical flow using the Horn-Schunck method.

Step 3 contains the core of our optical flow estimation process. It can easily be altered to estimate the optical flow for all frame pairs in the video; however, here it was used to estimate the flow only for one frame pair (frames 89 and 90).

Steps 4 and 5 demonstrated the nature of the optical flow results. We have used the `'Horizontal and vertical components in complex form'` choice, therefore the result was a matrix with complex values. These two steps showed how we can decompose it into three matrices: one with the vertical motions (xMotion), one with the horizontal motions (yMotion), and one with the absolute motions (absMotion).

In steps 6 and 7, we displayed our two frames, their composite color image, and the absolute optical flow values as a grayscale image.

Next, in steps 8 and 9 we created a shape inserter object, we made a matrix with the coordinates of the motion vector lines we wish for it to draw and then, in step 10, we drew the lines on the frame and displayed the result.

Since our resulting image contained a lot of outliers, we filtered out values that are too large (over 20 pixels absolute value) and too small (under 5 pixels absolute value) from our optical flow result in step 11. Finally, we repeated the drawing process described previously, in step 12.

From the results of steps 10 and 12, we can make the following observations:

 ◆ The motion vectors seem to be centered on the moving persons, but they also seem to be rather arbitrary. This makes it doubtful if they can be used for reconstructing the first frame using the second one and the optical flow.

 ◆ The particular optical flow estimation method does not produce entirely useful results, with many outliers that confuse the final result.

 ◆ The optical flow information seems very useful, especially in surveillance systems. As you can easily observe, it has detected the hidden person on the right of the frames.

Have a go hero – estimating optical flow using Lucas-Kanade

Now, it's your turn. Since we have covered the whole process in much detail, you can now repeat it for the Lucas-Kanade method. The only thing you have to change is the `'Method'` setting in the optical flow system object. You may also want to experiment with different frames of the atrium video or other videos. If you do that, it may be necessary also to tweak the amplification factor in step 9, or the thresholds in step 11.

Time for action – warping frames using optical flow

Now that you have seen both the methods, it is time to try and reconstruct the first frame of the pair, using the second one and the optical flow field. We will try to accomplish that by a straightforward method called interpolation. This method actually tries to estimate unknown data, given a known set of data. In our case, the known set of data comprises the pixel values in the second frame of the pair and the motion vectors. We will repeat the same procedure for both the Horn-Schunck and Lucas-Kanade methods.

1. We start by loading our video:

   ```
   >> clear all;
   >> videoObj = VideoReader('atrium.avi'); % Open video
   ```

2. Now, we'll create two system objects, one for each optical flow method:

   ```
   >> ofHS = vision.OpticalFlow('ReferenceFrameDelay', 1,...
   'Method','Horn-Schunck', 'OutputValue', 'Horizontal and vertical
   components in complex form'); % Horn Schunck method
   >> ofLK = vision.OpticalFlow('ReferenceFrameDelay', 1,...
   'Method','Lucas-Kanade', 'OutputValue', 'Horizontal and
     vertical components in complex form'); % Lucas-Kanade
     method
   ```

3. Perform the optical flow estimation with both the methods:

   ```
   >> for i = 89:90 % For frames 89 and 90
   frame = read(videoObj,i); % Load one frame at a time
   temp = rgb2gray(frame); % Convert frame to grayscale
   im(:,:,i-88) = single(temp); % Convert frame to single (for
     calculations)
   hs(:,:,i-88) = step(ofHS, im(:,:,i-88)); %Estimate HS optical
     flow
   lk(:,:,i-88) = step(ofLK, im(:,:,i-88)); %Estimate LK optical
     flow
   end
   ```

4. To make our jobs easier, we will create the x and y motion matrices from the optical flow results (the second one estimated):

```
>> xHS = real(hs(:,:,2));
>> yHS = imag(hs(:,:,2));
>> xLK = real(lk(:,:,2));
>> yLK = imag(lk(:,:,2));
```

5. We will also create the absolute motion matrices:

```
>> absHS = abs(hs(:,:,2));
>> absLK = abs(lk(:,:,2));
```

6. Now, it is time to perform the interpolation for both the results. First, we will make the grid for the coordinates of the pixels, using `meshgrid`:

```
>> [x,y]=meshgrid(1:videoObj.Width ,1:videoObj.Height);
```

7. This is the time to perform our warping, that is, the interpolation that will re-create the first frame from our pair. We will do this twice, once for every optical flow method:

```
>> warpHS=interp2(x,y,im(:,:,2),x+xHS,y+yHS); % Warped H-S
>> warpLK=interp2(x,y,im(:,:,2),x+xLK,y+yLK); % Warped L-K
```

8. Finally, we will display our results from the warping process next to the original first frame that we are trying to re-create. First, we convert every result back to type `uint8`:

```
>> im = uint8(im);
>> warpHS = uint8(warpHS);
>> warpLK = uint8(warpLK);
>> subplot(2,2,1), imshow(warpHS), title('Horn-Schunck Warp')
>> subplot(2,2,3), imshow(im(:,:,2)), title('Original frame')
>> subplot(2,2,2), imshow(warpLK), title('Lucas-Kanade Warp')
```

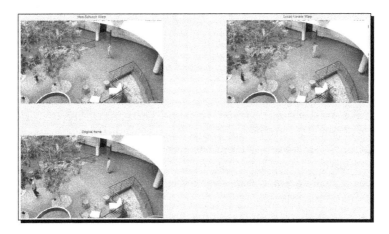

9. It is worth displaying the result in the areas around the two moving persons, so that we get a better idea of the power of each algorithm:

```
>> figure,subplot(2,3,1), imshow(warpHS(181:274,40:114)),
   title('Horn-Schunck Warp')
>> subplot(2,3,2), imshow(im(181:274,40:114,2)),
   title('Original frame')
>> subplot(2,3,3), imshow(warpLK(181:274,40:114)),
   title('Lucas-Kanade Warp')
>> subplot(2,3,4), imshow(warpHS(91:170,383:424)), title('Horn-
   Schunck Warp')
>> subplot(2,3,5), imshow(im(91:170,383:424,2)),
   title('Original frame')
>> subplot(2,3,6), imshow(warpLK(91:170,383:424)),
   title('Lucas-Kanade Warp')
```

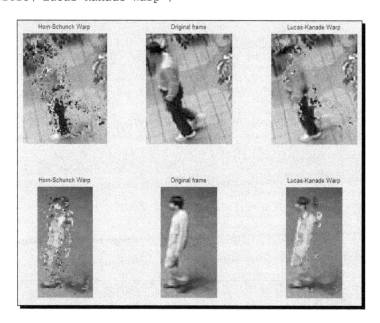

What just happened?

This example has demonstrated the quality of the two optical flow algorithms included in MATLAB, in terms of frame reconstruction. This time, we repeated the process presented in the previous example, for both the methods. After acquiring the results and isolating the vertical, horizontal, and absolute motion values, we performed warping, using two-dimensional interpolation. The results were then demonstrated, proving the superiority of the Lucas-Kanade optical flow algorithm over the Horn-Schunck one, at least for the example examined here and for the default settings for the optical flow implementations. However, even though the Lucas-Kanade method achieved better results, it as far from ideal. The ghosting effect as more apparent, especially in the case of the faster moving person.

Have a go hero – making your own surveillance system

It is now your turn to experiment some more. First, you should thoroughly read the help page of the vision.OpticalFlow system object, either inside MATLAB, or at `http://www.mathworks.com/help/vision/ref/vision.opticalflowclass.html`.

Next, you should try to implement different versions of the Horn-Schunck and the Lucas-Kanade algorithms by tweaking the settings. Some settings that you should pay attention to are the smoothness setting, the iteration count for the Horn-Schunck algorithm, and the temporal gradient filter for the Lucas-Kanade algorithm.

Compensating camera motion using feature tracking

The optical flow algorithms we have presented so far are very useful, but have limited use in the case of motion compensation in videos shot by a moving camera. In that case, the camera motion must be compensated using other techniques, as the optical flow-based warping does not produce seamless results.

For the camera motion to be estimated, we must focus on one or more points that remain stable, or have known motion and examine the change in their coordinates, which we must then compensate. The points that are chosen must be distinguishable in all frames, so that their appearances can be matched to each other. When we just need to find the correspondence between two small sets of characteristic points in two frames of a video, we are talking about the feature tracking. When the process has to do with finding the correspondences between all points in two frames of the same scene, it is called **image registration**.

One of the most challenging uses of feature tracking applications is in video stabilization. In its most difficult form, video stabilization must be performed in complex environments, with plenty of moving objects and also moving areas in the background. This is the case in the example that follows.

Time for action – tracking feature points for motion compensation of a shaky video

For this example, we will use the `shaky_car.avi` video file included in the Computer Vision System Toolbox of MATLAB. In the first frame, we will manually choose an area in which we will be looking for feature points. Then, we will try to track these feature points in the rest of the frames in the video. Finally, the coordinate differences between the points we track will be used for motion compensation. Let's start:

1. The first step will be, as always, to load our video:

```
>> videoObj = VideoReader('shaky_car.avi');
```

2. Now, we will read a frame:

```
>> frame = read(videoObj,1);
```

3. Next, we choose a rectangular area:

```
>> imshow(frame);
>> ROI=round(getPosition(imrect))
```

4. We can also show our selected area of interest (we will use the preceding car):

```
>> im = insertShape(frame, 'Rectangle', ROI, 'Color', 'red');
>> figure; imshow(im);
```

5. It is the time to detect and show the feature points in the area we chose. We will use the FAST corner detector:

```
>> points = detectFASTFeatures(rgb2gray(frame), 'ROI', ROI);
>> im = insertMarker(im, points.Location, '+', 'Color',
   'white');
>> figure, imshow(im);
```

6. This is the point where we initialize the `tracker` function for the feature points and the `MarkerInserter` function for drawing the points we track:

```
>> tracker = vision.PointTracker('MaxBidirectionalError', 1);
>> initialize(tracker, points.Location, frame);
>> markerInserter =
   vision.MarkerInserter('Shape','Plus','BorderColor','White');
```

7. Finally, we must loop through all the frames in our video and track the features inside our region of interest (`ROI`). The result will be saved in a new matrix, initialized right before the `for` loop:

```
>> vOut =
   zeros(videoObj.Height,videoObj.Width,3,videoObj.
   NumberOfFrames);
>> for i = 1:videoObj.NumberOfFrames    % For all frames
frame = read(videoObj,i); % Load a frame
[points, validity] = step(tracker, frame); % Track points
out = insertMarker(frame, points(validity, :), '+'); % Draw
   points
end
>> vOut = uint8(vOut);    % Convert vOut to uint8 for displaying
```

8. Let's see if our method proved to be robust by displaying a montage of the first 18 frames:

```
>> montage(uint8(vOut(:,:,:,1:18)),'Size',[3 6])
```

9. Since we are sure that our feature tracking is successful and robust, we can use the coordinates of the feature points to stabilize the video. All we have to do is to shift the horizontal and vertical dimensions of the second frame of each pair, by the mean amount of pixels our features have moved to each direction (relative to the first frame):

```
>> stab =
   zeros(videoObj.Height,videoObj.Width,3,videoObj.
   NumberOfFrames);
>> for i = 1:videoObj.NumberOfFrames % For all frames
frame = read(videoObj,i); % Load a frame
if i == 1
[points, validity] = step(tracker, frame); % Track points
pFirst = points(validity,:);      % Save coordinates
stab(:,:,:,i) = frame;            % Store 1st frame
else
[points, validity] = step(tracker, frame); % Track points
% Calculate shifting values
sh = round(mean(points(validity,:)-pFirst));
stab(:,:,:,i) = circshift(frame,[sh(1) sh(2) 0 0]);
end
>> stab = uint8(stab);    % Convert stab to uint8 for displaying
```

10. At this point, we can check to see if the result is acceptable, by playing back the video matrix `stab`:

```
>> implay(stab)
```

Our results are only a little bit better. This is because our method of shifting by the mean value is very simplistic and does not really ensure the stabilization of the video. A more sophisticated, yet beyond the scope of this book, way to accomplish this is included in MATLAB demos and can also be found at `http://www.mathworks.com/help/vision/ug/feature-detection-extraction-and-matching.html#btj3w6s`.

What just happened?

You have just been introduced to basic methods of feature point tracking and a first attempt of its usage in video stabilization. The first two steps involved the usual opening of a video file. In steps 3 and 4, we chose and displayed a region of interest for our feature tracking process. Step 5 detected the features residing in the ROI in the first frame and then we use step 6 to initialize a tracker object. In step 7, a loop through all the frames of the video, performed tracking of the feature points and drew them in each frame. All the annotated frames are saved in a new matrix called `vOut`. The first 18 frames of this matrix are displayed in a montage in step 8. Finally, in step 9, we attempted a very simplistic stabilization method by shifting the dimensions of each frame, by the mean number of pixels our feature points have moved towards each direction compared to their positions in the first frame. The result of this method was displayed in step 10, to come to a realization that the simplicity of the method had a very negative effect on its efficiency.

Have a go hero – tweaking the settings of the stabilization demo

As we mentioned before, MATLAB comes with a much more complicated, yet also much more efficient stabilization method. For the sake of challenging yourself, why don't you try to go to the link provided in the previous example and alter the feature detection process of the method to use alternative methods? The original demo uses the `detectFASTFeatures` function also, but on the entire image. It also introduces various complicated concepts, such as geometric transformation, but you shouldn't mess with that at this point. Your goal will be to make a function using the code you'll find in the URL, which will be able to work with other videos as well and also use the other feature detection methods (according to the choice the user provides as input):

- `detectHarrisFeatures`
- `detectMinEigenFeatures`
- `detectMSERFeatures`
- `detectSURFFeatures`

Working with stereoscopic images

The second big category of advanced image and video processing methods is dealing with stereoscopic images. Stereoscopic images are usually shot either by two normal cameras positioned in parallel and only a few centimeters apart, or by stereoscopic cameras with two lenses and separate image sensors for each one. Either way, the lenses have a distance from each other that resembles the distance between the human eyes, and allows the camera(s) to shoot images that can be fused to simulate three-dimensional vision.

The need for the two fields of view leads to a subsequent doubling of the frame rate and storage space needs. This is because instead of showing just one image, modern 3-D televisions must display two images, one for the left and one for the right eye. Similarly, to store a 3-D video, we need to have double the space compared to a normal 2-D video.

Image registration is again the most significant aspect of 3-D image and video processing. The only way to correctly display the left and right frames is to know the exact correspondence of points from one to the other. The correspondence becomes easier when the camera(s) used are placed very carefully in terms of alignment and distance from each other.

For our first example, we will demonstrate a rather old-fashioned way to make a 3-D video in MATLAB. By old-fashioned, we mean that we will be mixing both the left and right videos into one, with the red color containing the right channel information and the cyan (green and blue) carrying the left channel information. This way, our 3-D video can be watched with an ordinary pair of red-cyan 3-D glasses.

We will assume that you have done the following:

- Shot two synchronized videos (both cameras started shooting simultaneously)
- With perfect alignment (both cameras were placed perfectly parallel to each other, on the same horizontal surface) and
- With a distance not very far from each other (about 7 cm from the centre of one lens to the centre of the other will be perfect)

Time for action – creating a 3-D video from left and right videos

Assuming you have done everything right and shot your left and right video, you can follow the next steps to mix them into one that can be watched using a pair of red-cyan 3-D glasses (using the `imfuse` function we have already discussed in the previous chapter):

1. First, load the two videos:

```
>> left = VideoReader('left.avi'); % Open left video file
>> right = VideoReader('right.avi'); % Open right video file
```

2. Create and open a video file to write your results in:

```
>> vidOut = VideoWriter('Vid3D.avi'); % Open 3D video
  file
>>open(vidOut);
```

3. Now we must loop through all the frames:

```
>> for i = 1:left.NumberOfFrames  % For all frames
l = read(left,i); % Load i-th left frame
r = read(right,i); % Load i-th right frame
%Fuse the right and left channel into a red-cyan false color
  image
v3 = imfuse(r,l,'falsecolor','ColorChannels','red-cyan');
writeVideo(vidOut ,v3); % Write frame to video
end
close(vidOut);
```

What just happened?

This was pretty simple, right? The process of making a 3-D false-colored video is really a piece of cake, provided you have shot your left and right channels. The steps are very few, since the only things that have to be done are opening the input videos for the left and right camera, creating an output video for the fused 3-D frame sequence, and then reading each frame of the right and left channel and fusing them using `imfuse`. The generated image was written as a new frame in the output video. When the whole process was over, we closed the open video object used for writing, so that the video was finalized.

Time for action – creating a 3-D video from a regular one

But what happens if we do not have two cameras and we want to experiment with the 3-D video making process? Well, we can actually be creative. A left and right image from a stereoscopic video will ideally only have a horizontal shift of some pixels. This means that if we take a simple, monocular video and shift its frames towards one horizontal direction, we can create a synthetic right, or left image. More specifically, by shifting the frame to the right, we create a synthetic left frame and shifting it to the left, we create a synthetic right frame. Let's demonstrate this and adjust the previous example to work with a regular video.

1. First, we will open a regular video. We can use one of the videos included in MATLAB. Here, we will use the video file rhinos.avi distributed with the Image Processing Toolbox:

```
>> vid = VideoReader('rhinos.avi'); % Open video file
```

2. Create and open a video to write our results in:

```
>> sV = VideoWriter('Synthetic3D.avi'); % Open 3D video file
>> open(sV)
```

3. Again, we must loop through all the frames:

```
>> for i = 1:vid.NumberOfFrames  % For all frames
frame = read(vid,i); % Read i-th frame
l = circshift(frame,[0 10 0 0]); % Create synthetic left frame
r = circshift(frame,[0 -10 0 0]); % Create synthetic right
  frame
l(:,1:10,:) = 0; % Darken shifted part of left image
r(:,end-9:end,:) = 0; % Darken shifted part of right image
%Fuse the right and left channel into a red-cyan false color
  image
v3 = imfuse(r,l,'falsecolor','ColorChannels','red-cyan');
writeVideo(sV ,v3); % Write frame to video
end
close(sV);
```

4. Now, we can play back our video:

```
>> implay('Synthetic3D.avi')
```

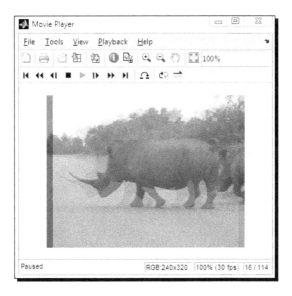

What just happened?

You just became familiar with the process of creating a synthetic red-cyan 3-D video using only a few steps, even if you don't have two cameras to shoot a real stereoscopic video. The process had only a few tweaks in comparison with the one followed in the previous example. The first two steps involved loading a regular video and also creating and opening a video file to save our synthetic 3-D frames in. Then, the `for` loop, that will load each frame of our original video, is written. In it, after loading one frame at a time, we created two synthetic right and left frames by horizontally shifting our original frame to the left and right, respectively. Then, we erased the circularly shifted areas from the right and left part of the image to avoid irregular artifacts that come from the opposite part of the image (remember that `circshift` brings the part of the image that falls off the borders into the opposite side of the image). Finally, we performed fusing of the two images into one and wrote it as a new frame in our output video file. After the `for` loop is over, we closed the output file to finalize the process.

Have a go hero – writing a function for 3-D video creation

Now that you know the process of 3-D video creation, why don't you try to turn the code given in the previous example into a function? The function should get four inputs from the user: the input video filename, the output video filename, the shifting distance in pixels, and a choice of whether the left and right parts should be darkened (as we did in the example), or cut. In the second case, the output video will not have equal dimensions to the input video.

Pop quiz –working with video frames

Q1. Which of the following are true?

1. Subtracting two frames can result in pinpointing the moving objects in a scene, when the videos are shot in confined environments.

2. Large moving objects with little detail in them can be mistaken as immobile when relying solely on information from frame subtraction.

3. We can seamlessly reconstruct a frame of a video just by knowing its next frame and the Horn-Schunck optical flow between them.

4. We can create a red-cyan stereoscopic video from a regular monocular video, just by shifting the original frames in the vertical direction.

Summary

In this chapter, we described some more complicated methods of image and video processing, focusing on explaining the rationale behind them, without using difficult mathematics. Most of the methods were presented through hands-on exercises to help you comprehend the physical meaning of the algorithms, without being too caught up in the details. More specifically, in this chapter, we discussed:

- Motion detection and its meaning
- Use of frame subtraction to detect motion in simple and complex videos
- Motion estimation and its meaning
- Estimation of motion in a video using optical flow
- To track people in video sequences using optical flow
- A simplistic method for video stabilization
- Reconstruction of video frames using optical flow information
- Feature tracking in videos using the FAST feature detector

- ◆ Some basics of image registration
- ◆ Stereo vision and its meaning
- ◆ Creation of a 3-D video from videos shot by a stereoscopic pair of cameras
- ◆ Creation of a 3-D video from a regular video by shifting its frames in both vertical directions

Pop Quiz Answers

Chapter 1, Basic Image Manupulation

Pop quiz – image processing in Matlab	
Q1	1, 3

Chapter 2, Working with Pixels in Grayscale Images

Pop quiz – contrasting enhancement methods	
Q1	1. False: It is just a warning.
	2. True
	3. True
	4. True
	5. False
	6. True
	7. True

Chapter 3, Morphological Operations and Object Analysis

Pop quiz – object analysis pros and cons

Q1	1. False
	2. True
	3. True

Chapter 4, Working with Color Images

Pop quiz – working with color

Q1	1. False: Green.
	2. True.
	3. True.
	4. False: The `imadjust` function is better at this.
	5. False: We have to take into account the region we threshold and confine it around the eyes.

Chapter 5, 2-Dimensional Image Filtering

Pop quiz – image filtering in 2-dimensions

Q1	1. False: They are 180 degrees different.
	2. True.
	3. False: Edge enhancement.
	4. False: Median.
	5. True.

Chapter 6, Mixing Images for Science or Art

Pop quiz – image mixing details

Q1.		
	1.	True.
	2.	False: It is dim and should be multiplied by two.
	3.	False: We need to dot-multiply it with a three-dimensional mask that could be made by concatenating three replicas of the original mask.
	4.	True: Using compressed, 8 bit images leads to noisy results with visible blocking effect.
	5.	False: Many more aspects must be considered, such as pairing points between images and applying geometric transformations to preserve correct image geometry.

Chapter 7, Adding Motion – From Static Images to Digital Videos

Pop quiz – image filtering in 2-dimensions

Q1.		
	1.	False: It is designed for playback of videos, or image sequences
	2.	False: It can support animations and it is widely used
	3.	False: Half the information
	4.	True
	5.	True
	6.	False: It supports only uncompressed videos
	7.	True

Chapter 8, Acquiring and Processing Videos

Pop quiz – what is the problem with our function?

Q1	True: The problem is that, if the last chunk to be processed is not exactly equal to `chunkSz`, it will be skipped because the its upper limit will exceed the total number of frames.

Pop quiz – acquiring and processing videos

Q1	1. False: It supports compressed formats, such as MP4 and Motion JPEG as well.
	2. False: It has also to do with the bit-depth of its channels, the quality of the compression, the frame rate and the amount of motion in the video.
	3. True.
	4. True: Provided that our video acquisition device is already initialized.
	5. False: The slower frame rate of time-lapse videos is beneficial for such tasks.
	6. False: It speeds it up substantially.

Chapter 9, Spatiotemporal Video Processing

Pop quiz – videos and filters

Q1	1. False: We remove the blocking effect by using disk filtering element.
	2. False: Interlaced videos take up half the size.
	3. True: Temporal and spatiotemporal filtering lead to ghosting effects.
	4. False: Spatiotemporal averaging leads to blurring of the frames.
	5. True.

Chapter 10, From Beginner to Expert – Handling Motion and 3-D

Pop quiz – working with video frames

Q1.	1. True
	2. True
	3. False - We can only partially reconstruct it
	4. False – We must shift them in the horizontal direction

Index

Symbols

A

B

C

Export Data... button 205, 211
Exposure Values (EV) 170
eye circularity
  advantages 115

F

fade in effect
  used, for creating videos 193
fade out effect
  used, for creating videos 193
false-color composite versions 163
feature tracking
  used, for compensating camera motion 281
  using, for shaky video motion compensation
    281-285
field averaging
  used, for deinterlacing 251-253
field merge method
  evaluating 251
field merging
  used, for deinterlacing 248-250
firewire connection
  used, for capturing videos 208-212
flipdim
  used, for image mirroring 22
for loops
  about 269, 289
  used, for image thresholding 41
frame
  about 180
  acquiring 220, 221
  acquiring, for time-lapse videos 219
  last chunk, getting 219
  number, calculating 182
  rates 181
  rates, selecting 182
  warping, optical flow used 278-280
frames per second (fps) 181
Frames per trigger 206
fspecial function
  used, for creating filters 131

G

gaussian filters 132
General tab, Acquisition Parameters
    window 206

geometric transformations
  applying 19
  image, cropping 24
  image mirroring, performing 21, 22
  image, resizing 23
  image rotation, performing 19, 20
  image, saving 25
getFileFormats method 188
getnhood function 71
getsnapshot function 229
ghosting effect 271
gif 199
gif file
  time-lapse videos, saving 199
Graphical User Interface. *See* GUI
graphics interchange format. *See* gif
grayscale image
  converting, to binary 62
  rectangular area, blackening 39
  rectangular area, whitening 39
GUI 204

H

Hardware Browser window 204
Hardware triggering 207
HDR images
  about 170
  composing 170, 172
  creating 170
High Dynamic Range images. *See* HDR images
histogram equalization
  performing, adapthisteq used 49, 50
histogram, of image
  calculating 45
  displaying 46
HOME tab 11
Horn-Schunck optical flow
  estimating, Lucas-Kanade used 278
  people, tracking with 273-277
HSV 102

I

illumination issues, CIE-L*a*b*
  fixing 110, 111
illumination issues, RGB color images
  fixing 108, 109

interlaced
  versus progressive 180
intervalometer
  about 197
  Matlab, using as 222, 223
intra-frame deinterlacing
  about 242
  mixing, with inter-frame deinterlacing 254
invisible spectrums
  working with 157
isolated colors
  used, for creating time-lapse videos 224-226

K

kernel 122

L

laplacian filters 132
lapse 197
lights
  brightening up 148
Linear Space Invariant (LSI) system 126
line repetition
  used, for deinterlacing 244-246
log filters 132
Logging tab, Acquisition Parameters window
  Disk Logging (VideoWriter) 207
  Log to setting 206
  Memory logging setting 206
Log to setting 206

M

makecform function 102
MarkerInserter function 283
masks 62
Matlab
  back videos, playing 188
  digital video 180
  editor 12
  frames 180
  geometric transformations, applying 19
  image, displaying 13
  image, importing 13
  implay 195
  real-time capabilities, evaluating 226

ribbon 10
time-lapse videos, creating 197
time-lapse videos, real-time processing 224
uncompressed video 216
used, for digital video recording 204
using, as intervalometer 222, 223
video compression 212
video processing 233
videos, creating from static images 190
videos inspecting, montage used 193
videos, loading 183
Matlab environment
  about 8
  default subwindows 8
medfilt2
  used, for removing salt & pepper noise 144
median filter 143
median filtering 143
Memory logging setting 206
mmreader
  videos, loading with 185, 186
montage
  used, for inspecting videos 193, 194
morphological operations
  about 62
  reference link 76
motion
  detecting 266
  estimating 271, 272
  estimating, optical flow used 273
  in complex scene, detecting 269-271
  in videos, detecting 266
  in videos, estimating 266
  moving object in still scene, detecting 267-269
motion effect
  creating 137, 138
motion filters 132
mov 192
movie 190
movie function 192
MP4 video
  size checking, with motion 215, 216
  size checking, without motion 214, 215
multiband BIL (Band Interleaved by Line)
      satellite image 156
multibandread function 153

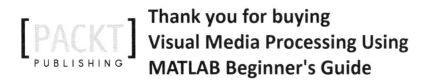

Thank you for buying
Visual Media Processing Using
MATLAB Beginner's Guide

About Packt Publishing

Packt, pronounced 'packed', published its first book "Mastering phpMyAdmin for Effective MySQL Management" in April 2004 and subsequently continued to specialize in publishing highly focused books on specific technologies and solutions.

Our books and publications share the experiences of your fellow IT professionals in adapting and customizing today's systems, applications, and frameworks. Our solution-based books give you the knowledge and power to customize the software and technologies you're using to get the job done. Packt books are more specific and less general than the IT books you have seen in the past. Our unique business model allows us to bring you more focused information, giving you more of what you need to know, and less of what you don't.

Packt is a modern, yet unique publishing company, which focuses on producing quality, cutting-edge books for communities of developers, administrators, and newbies alike. For more information, please visit our website: www.PacktPub.com.

Writing for Packt

We welcome all inquiries from people who are interested in authoring. Book proposals should be sent to author@packtpub.com. If your book idea is still at an early stage and you would like to discuss it first before writing a formal book proposal, contact us; one of our commissioning editors will get in touch with you.

We're not just looking for published authors; if you have strong technical skills but no writing experience, our experienced editors can help you develop a writing career, or simply get some additional reward for your expertise.

MATLAB Graphics and Data Visualization Cookbook

ISBN: 978-1-84969-316-5   Paperback:284 pages

Tell data stories with compelling graphics using this collection of data visualization recipes

1. Collection of data visualization recipes with functionalized versions of common tasks for easy integration into your data analysis workflow

2. Recipes cross-referenced with MATLAB product pages and MATLAB Central File Exchange resources for improved coverage

3. Includes hand created indices to find exactly what you need; such as application driven, or functionality driven solutions

OpenCV 2 Computer Vision Application Programming Cookbook

ISBN: 978-1-84951-324-1   Paperback: 304 pages

Over 50 recipes to master this library of programming functions for real-time computer vision

1. Teaches you how to program computer vision applications in C++ using the different features of the OpenCV library

2. Demonstrates the important structures and functions of OpenCV in detail with complete working examples

3. Describes fundamental concepts in computer vision and image processing

Please check **www.PacktPub.com** for information on our titles

MATLAB Graphics and Data Visualization Cookbook

ISBN: 978-1-84969-316-5   Paperback:284 pages

Tell data stories with compelling graphics using this collection of data visualization recipes

1. Collection of data visualization recipes with functionalized versions of common tasks for easy integration into your data analysis workflow

2. Recipes cross-referenced with MATLAB product pages and MATLAB Central File Exchange resources for improved coverage

3. Includes hand created indices to find exactly what you need; such as application driven, or functionality driven solutions

OpenCV 2 Computer Vision Application Programming Cookbook

ISBN: 978-1-84951-324-1   Paperback: 304 pages

Over 50 recipes to master this library of programming functions for real-time computer vision

1. Teaches you how to program computer vision applications in C++ using the different features of the OpenCV library

2. Demonstrates the important structures and functions of OpenCV in detail with complete working examples

3. Describes fundamental concepts in computer vision and image processing

Please check **www.PacktPub.com** for information on our titles

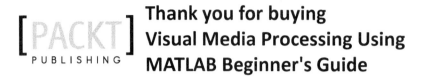

About Packt Publishing

Packt, pronounced 'packed', published its first book "Mastering phpMyAdmin for Effective MySQL Management" in April 2004 and subsequently continued to specialize in publishing highly focused books on specific technologies and solutions.

Our books and publications share the experiences of your fellow IT professionals in adapting and customizing today's systems, applications, and frameworks. Our solution-based books give you the knowledge and power to customize the software and technologies you're using to get the job done. Packt books are more specific and less general than the IT books you have seen in the past. Our unique business model allows us to bring you more focused information, giving you more of what you need to know, and less of what you don't.

Packt is a modern, yet unique publishing company, which focuses on producing quality, cutting-edge books for communities of developers, administrators, and newbies alike. For more information, please visit our website: www.PacktPub.com.

Writing for Packt

We welcome all inquiries from people who are interested in authoring. Book proposals should be sent to author@packtpub.com. If your book idea is still at an early stage and you would like to discuss it first before writing a formal book proposal, contact us; one of our commissioning editors will get in touch with you.

We're not just looking for published authors; if you have strong technical skills but no writing experience, our experienced editors can help you develop a writing career, or simply get some additional reward for your expertise.

OpenCV Computer Vision with Python

ISBN: 978-1-78216-392-3   Paperback:122 pages

Learn to capture videos, manipulate images, and track objects with Python using the OpenCV Library

1. TSet up OpenCV, its Python bindings, and optional Kinect drivers on Windows, Mac or Ubuntu

2. ICreate an application that tracks and manipulates faces

3. Identify face regions using normal color images and depth images

PHP Oracle Web Development: Data processing, Security, Caching, XML, Web Services, and Ajax

ISBN: 978-1-84719-363-6   Paperback: 440 pages

A practical guide to combining the power, performance, scalability, and reliability of the Oracle Database with the ease of use, short development time, and high performance of PHP

1. Program your own PHP/Oracle application

2. Move data processing inside the database

3. Distribute data processing between the web/PHP and Oracle database servers

4. Create reusable building blocks for PHP/Oracle solutions

Please check **www.PacktPub.com** for information on our titles

www.ingramcontent.com/pod-product-compliance
Lightning Source LLC
LaVergne TN
LVHW062306060326
832902LV00013B/2073